Library Information Systems

Library and Information Science Text Series

The Academic Library: Its Context, Its Purpose, and Its Operation. By John M. Budd.

Information Sources in Science and Technology. 3d ed. By C. D. Hurt.

The School Library Media Center. 5th ed. By Emanuel T. Prostano and Joyce S. Prostano.

The School Library Media Manager. 2d ed. By Blanche Woolls.

Introduction to Library Public Services. 6th ed. By G. Edward Evans, Anthony J. Amodeo, and Thomas L. Carter.

A Guide to the Library of Congress Classification. 5th ed. By Lois Mai Chan.

The Organization of Information. By Arlene G. Taylor.

Developing Library and Information Center Collections. 4th ed. By G. Edward Evans, with the assistance of Margaret R. Zarnosky.

The Humanities: A Selective Guide to Information Sources. 5th ed. By Ron Blazek and Elizabeth Aversa.

Wynar's Introduction to Cataloging and Classification. 9th ed. By Arlene G. Taylor.

Systems Analysis for Librarians and Information Professionals. 2d ed. By Larry N. Osborne and Margaret Nakamura.

The Economics of Information: A Guide to Economic and Cost-Benefit Analysis for Information Professionals. 2d ed. By Bruce R. Kingma.

Reference and Information Services: An Introduction. 3d ed. Richard E. Bopp and Linda C. Smith, General Editors.

The Collection Program in Schools: Concepts, Practices, and Information Sources. 3d ed. By Phyllis Van Orden and Kay Bishop, with the assistance of Patricia Pawelak-Kort.

Libraries in the Information Age: An Introduction and Career Exploration. By Denise K. Fourie and David R. Dowell.

The Social Sciences: A Cross-Disciplinary Guide to Selected Sources. 3d ed. Nancy L. Herron, General Editor.

Introduction to Technical Services. 7th ed. By G. Edward Evans, Sheila S. Intner, and Jean Weihs.

Library Information Systems: From Library Automation to Distributed Information Access Solutions. By Thomas R. Kochtanek and Joseph R. Matthews.

United States Government Information: Policies and Sources. By Peter Hernon, Harold C. Relyea, Robert E. Dugan, and Joan F. Cheverie.

Library and Information Center Management. 6th ed. By Robert D. Stueart and Barbara B. Moran.

LIBRARY INFORMATION SYSTEMS

From Library Automation to Distributed Information Access Solutions

Thomas R. Kochtanek

Joseph R. Matthews

2002

LIBRARIES UNLIMITED

A Division of Greenwood Publishing Group, Inc.

Westport, Connecticut

LIBRARIES UNLIMITED
A Division of Greenwood Publishing Group, Inc.
88 Post Road West
Westport, CT 06881
1-800-225-5800
www.lu.com

Library of Congress Cataloging-in-Publication Data
Kochtanek, Thomas R.
    Library information systems : from library automation to distributed information access solutions / Thomas R. Kochtanek,
Joseph R. Matthews.
        p. cm. --(Library and information science text series)
    Includes bibliographical references and index.
    ISBN 1-56308-966-1-- ISBN 1-59158-018-8 (pbk.)
    1. Libraries--Automation. 2. Library information networks.
3. Integrated library systems (Computer systems) 4. Information
storage and retrieval systems. 5. Information technology.
I. Matthews, Joseph R. II. Title. III. Series.
Z678.9.K59 2002
025'.00285--dc21

2002009863

This book is dedicated to the memory of the first pioneer in the mechanization and automation of library processes and the man behind the phrase "Library Information Systems," Dr. Ralph Halsted Parker. His drive for excellence in all things and his willingness to mentor a young contributor new to the profession were hallmarks of his character. I only hope that he would be proud of what has come of that influence.

I also would like to extend my thanks and appreciation to my wife, Barbara, and our sons, Jeffrey and Kyle Kochtanek, for their willingness and ability to put up with me while this book was drafted and refined. Their support has made the task all that much easier.

Thomas R. Kochtanek

To Martha, Paul, and Erin. You are the best.

Joe Matthews

Contents

Part III
MANAGEMENT ISSUES

Part IV
FUTURE CONSIDERATIONS

Part I
The Broader Context

The opening chapter of this section introduces the domain of Library Information Systems comprising two established industries (integrated library systems and online databases) and three developing industries (Web portals, eBooks, and digital libraries) associated with applications that provide end user access to information. Chapter 2 examines the marketplaces of those industries within the domain.

Chapter 1

The Evolution of LIS and Enabling Technologies

This chapter presents an overview of the evolution of technology and its impact on the application of computing systems in libraries. We begin with the origins of the phrase *library information system* (LIS) and move to consider both its historical roots and the impact of developments in related fields that have had profound influence over the development of the LIS marketplace.

ON THE ORIGINS OF LIBRARY INFORMATION SYSTEMS

The application of computing systems in libraries has been a subject of interest to professional librarians for more than 65 years. More recently, libraries have sought to implement increasingly complex solutions that involve distributed networking and access to remote information resources. The term *library information system* in its present form is defined to include a wide array of solutions that previously might have been considered separate industries with distinctly different marketplaces. This includes the integrated library system marketplace and the online database industry. As the LIS domain has developed and evolved, numerous terms have been used to describe these efforts to incorporate technological solutions that improve access to recorded knowledge.

These roots predate the actual development of the digital computer, going all the way back to the punch cards used in early circulation control systems. One might even refer to this early era as *library mechanization*, because the term *automation* was applied to processes that used the modern, digital computer.

The phrase *library automation* has been generally accepted within the profession to encompass early automation activities, yet it does not do justice to the current state of affairs, as libraries have moved well beyond the automation of internal procedures. In the 1980s, many began to refer to such applications as *integrated* li*brary systems* (ILS), *integrated online library systems*,[1] and other combinations of similar terms. Yet all these fail to grasp the essence of the rapidly developing domain of what this text refers to as library information systems, or simply LIS.

The term might be considered general enough to withstand the test of time, to move with the developments in the field. While this label may not be heavily used in the discussions among librarians at conferences, continuing education offerings, and in the open literature, the phrase does capture the basic elements of the application of computing solutions aimed at bringing the user and content together, which is the essence of service within libraries of all types and sizes.

Interestingly enough, this term was first coined around 1968 by Dr. Ralph Halsted Parker, a pioneer in library mechanization, who used computers to replicate library processes at an early stage. Dr. Parker developed a graduate level class in the masters degree program at the University of Missouri, titled "Library Information Systems." He went on to identify LIS as not only "automating" existing processes within libraries (such as circulation control procedures, cataloging, and so forth) but also including access to materials not held by the library but available in electronic form. At that time (the late 1960s), online databases were starting to be developed. For example, the National Library of Medicine was experimenting with the development of what is now MEDLINE. Parker coined the phrase "library information systems" to encompass all types of computer technology applications in the library, including those that were not yet fully developed. He selected those three words very carefully, to be able to describe both current and future applications of technology within libraries. What is perhaps remarkable is that this term is still applicable in describing a full range of technology applications available in libraries today.

What currently makes up the LIS domain? As library and information systems developers created the technologic landscape, several separate applications were established to support end user access to information. Some of these developments were about content, and some focused on dissemination. All support increased end user access to digitally recorded document surrogates or primary knowledge records. To date, these developments have included:

- ◆ Integrated Library Systems
- ◆ Online Databases
- ◆ Web-Based Resources
- ◆ Digital Library Collections
- ◆ eBooks and eJournals.

Integrated library systems (ILS) began with one-of-a-kind pioneering efforts centering on circulation control and overdue notice production,[2] moved to turnkey integrated library systems solutions (with a market of only about $50 million in 1982), and, by the turn of the century, had developed into a global industry with sales currently averaging about $500 million annually.[3] One example of an early pioneering effort was the development of a punched card circulation system at the University of Texas at Austin in the mid 1930s. Reported in the literature by Parker in 1936, many consider this to be the first known application of automation techniques to library systems. Parker later set up a more sophisticated circulation control system at the University of Missouri in 1959, based on punched cards and IBM mainframe technologies.

Typical integrated library systems include functionality in support of acquisitions, cataloging, circulation control, materials booking, serials control, and online catalogs. Initially developed as standalone solutions to a library's processing and services needs, these applications are now increasingly "welded at the seams" with other services, such as access to online databases.

The online database industry began as a separate marketplace (from the integrated library system) in the early 1970s, grew to over $1.5 billion annually,[4] and now is closely coupled with integrated library systems solutions to provide end users a "one-stop" desktop access point for materials held both locally and licensed internationally. Originally designed for professional searchers, the online database industry has grown to include users of all levels. The recent introduction of the World Wide Web has allowed database producers a clear route for disseminating their resources to a wider audience, in many instances directly to the end user (in some cases bypassing the library).

Web-based resources moved to the forefront in the mid 1990s, after libraries determined that users had begun to spend much of their time browsing the Web searching for relevant materials that could be conveniently delivered to their desktop in digital fashion. Professional librarians began to think like users in terms of "one-stop shopping" for information and, having been successful at grafting their online catalogs with electronic database resources, they next turned their attention to the numerous resources available on the Web. Using their expertise to identify, validate, and organize information content, they sought to build "portals" that offered access not only to information that was held or licensed by the library, but also to information readily available on the Web. Libraries are continuing to develop new Web portals as new resources are created and made accessible via the Internet.

The Digital Library movement, still in its early stages, has begun to evolve from its early research platform to more fully developed applications, typically in selected content areas. As funding sources continue to be identified, we are now seeing the development of specialized collections in digital format, aimed squarely at end users. The concept of the digital library is rather encompassing, and currently we are seeing only the first efforts at creating environments for storing and disseminating digital content.

The notion of eBooks includes both eJournals and eTexts. In March 2000, Stephen King released a 66-page novella, *Riding the Bullet*, as an eBook, exclusively for publication via the Web. A half million copies sold in the first 24 hours. While King was not the first to publish full text via the Internet, this event certainly identifies the potential for a new distribution medium—directly from author to the end user. Other authors and their publishing houses are rapidly developing strategies for competing in this new arena. Scholarly publishers already compete for the click of the end users' mouse, and both online full-text databases and eJournals are examples of their positioning and strategy. We will likely see more developments as creative minds begin to design new services and then market them directly to the end user via the networked desktop.

Collectively, these broad areas of interest form the basis behind LIS. To be certain, not all libraries will embrace each of these separately developing domains in the same fashion. Nor are they using the same steps towards developing a one-stop

Web site for access to all the resources identified by the library. This is what makes libraries distinct from one another, as the primary motive behind incorporating technology solutions should be to improve services to the communities served by the specific library system under consideration.

THE EVOLUTION OF
LIBRARY INFORMATION SYSTEMS

Technology applications in libraries date back to an era prior to the mass production of computers, with some of the earliest applications based on punched cards. In one of the earliest applications of technology in libraries, Ralph Halsted Parker had developed a circulation control system using 80-column "Hollerith punch cards" at the University of Texas.[5] Early technology applications focused on automating existing procedures in libraries, such as acquisitions and circulation control. Subsequent developments moved to address services to the public, including applications like online catalogs and access to remote or licensed databases.[6]

The development of library automation has been well documented. Borgman views development in this area as having three stages of evolution:[7]

1. Efficiency of Internal Operations

2. Access to Local Library Collections

3. Access to Resources Outside the Library.

This description views library automation, as it was once called, from a functional perspective, focusing on procedures and services to both librarians and end users.

The development of integrated library systems, as we are referring to it, can be chronicled by looking at four overlapping eras of development:

*   Systems Era

*   Era of Functionality

*   Focus on the End User

*   Globalization of Information Resources.

The earliest years of actual computing applications in libraries started around the late 1950s, and many applications were often centered on the technology itself. The Systems Era lasted into the 1970s and generally resulted in the development of software applications that replicated existing library procedures and processes, with heavy attention to technology on center stage. This was a period of pioneering and experimentation. The primary area of applications was circulation control, as this was a most tedious process and was done by all libraries. The primary benefit of circulation systems developed in this early era was the identification of overdue materials.

Beginning in the 1970s, library professionals moved to include additional features into existing technology, and extended functionality through purchase of software modules from "turnkey vendors." Often during this period, a library would center its decision on circulation control, then add software modules to the existing hardware base that might support cataloging, acquisitions, serials control, materials booking, and other functions. Most of these applications served to extend and modernize existing procedures common among libraries. In the early 1970s, the first so-called turnkey vendor, Computer Library Services, Incorporated (later changed to "CLSI"), offered a packaged solution of hardware and parameter-driven circulation software that addressed the general processing needs of the typical library. Ten years later, the development of the online catalog became another example of such a modular approach. The earliest editions of the online public access catalog merely mimicked previous print-based card catalogs, providing crude electronic access to collections for end users.[8] This illustrates the many disappointments and problems of information technology that arose from automating the status quo rather than rethinking, streamlining, and reconsidering work.

Today's applications of technology in libraries are more focused on information content and the end user and, as such, support the user directly in his or her quest to identify information resources, some of which are now encoded digitally. Yes, these applications still rely on technology as a tool (but not an end unto itself), and offer functional solutions to repetitive processes. Today, however, the focus is squarely on designing LIS to support end user access to recorded knowledge, whether those records exist in analog (print) or digital format and are located in the local library, other libraries, or elsewhere on the Internet. In many instances, the content being provided to the end user is drawn from global sources. The development of international networks, based on Transmission Control Protocol/Internet Protocol (TCP/IP) has allowed libraries to connect users to distributed digital resources from all over the world. Using the World Wide Web as a connecting tool, linking content with end users is but one example of such a global undertaking.

Regardless of the era, organizations, including libraries, have adopted technology at different rates. Some of the possible adoption patterns can be categorized as noted below:

Bleeding edge. Some libraries are willing to be the "guinea pigs" and experiment with technologies and software. In some cases, these organizations will have the scars and bandages testifying to their adventuresome efforts. This type of library is willing to use Release 0.5 or beta software.

Leading edge. These libraries are willing to embrace new technologies, but they are a bit more cautious than bleeding edge organizations. This type of library will adopt new technologies on a systematic and incremental basis.

In the wedge. A majority of libraries will embrace new technologies when there is ample evidence that it is stable, proven, and well tested. This type of library will install Release 2.0 or later software. To say that this type of library is risk adverse is an understatement!

Trailing edge. A small minority of libraries will be true laggards and continue to use older technologies and applications software well past the time they should have migrated to newer products. For example, some libraries persist in using character-based MS DOS products (and often complain about the lack of support).

In subsequent chapters, we will be examining selections from these four domains within LIS more closely. Besides identifying the boundaries of these applications, we will look at efforts to integrate these services and resources to improve end users' access to services. Developments in a number of areas, including the establishment of standards, ongoing developments in hardware, software design evolution, and changes in the vendor marketplace make this integration possible.

CONCURRENT DEVELOPMENTS IMPACTING LIS

Developments in the domains of hardware, software, and telecommunications all have had an impact on the evolution of LIS. The following brief overview describes the developments in each of these areas.

Hardware: From Mainframes to Minis to Personal Computers (PCs)

The first developments incorporating digital computing devices in libraries were experimental in nature, one of a kind, and often developed in an academic or research institutional setting. An example provided earlier was the circulation control system implemented by Ralph Parker in the University Library System at Missouri in 1959. The primary reasons for this type of approach were that computing resources were scarce and costly, and, in most cases, could only be afforded by larger institutions, such as research universities and larger corporations. The mainframe computing device supporting such applications was a sophisticated piece of engineering, often exceeding $1 million in price. Typically these were owned by parent institutions (e.g., a university) and shared by users within the institution. The hardware was proprietary in the sense that all components were generally sold and supported by a single Original Equipment Manufacturer (OEM), such as IBM, or the other also-ran mainframe manufacturers called the BUNCH (Burroughs, Univac, NCR, Control Data Corporation, and Honeywell).

These devices worked in a host configuration, whereby a single set of processing units were accessed in a batch processing mode using keypunch cards or in an online mode using very expensive cathode ray tubes with keyboards, often referred to as "dumb terminals." The data processing was carried out solely by the single mainframe computing device, controlled by a time-sharing operating system (see next section on software). End users did not have any local processing capabilities on their desktops, which would be supported by internal memory (RAM), or any data storage capabilities supported by magnetic drives. In a host-based or shared system, these resources were centrally maintained under the careful control of a select few.

Starting in the mid 1960s, an innovation in hardware emerged, called the minicomputer. First pioneered by Digital Equipment Corporation (DEC) and other manufacturers, these machines were not only smaller than their mainframe counterparts, but they were less costly to acquire and maintain. Individual libraries could now afford to purchase solutions based on these newer systems, choosing to develop standalone applications dedicated specifically to library procedures. As identified earlier, this led to the development of the turnkey vendor solution that emerged from the experimentation done during the pioneering era of LIS.

In the late 1970s, and early 1980s, the emergence of low-cost personal desktop devices from Apple Computer and IBM (and subsequent clones of the original IBM PC) opened up even more doors for libraries to get involved in exploring technologic solutions to procedures commonly associated with libraries. By 1984, the estimated library systems marketplace totaled more than $81 million, about $10 million of which would go to hardware and software purchases for PC-based solutions.[9] The following year this growth continued, as library-specific products that run on PCs totaled some $12 million out of a total market of about $88 million.[10] These individual PCs were even more powerful when connected together in networks, called local area networks (LANs).

Today the lines between computing devices are quite blurred, and personal desktop devices commonly seen in homes and offices around the world now perform what would once have been labeled a mainframe capability. We now see combinations of a variety of devices, ranging from very powerful host processors to personal processing devices that fit in the hand or pocket. It is this range of devices that enables the delivery of personalized information directly under control of the individual end user.

While hardware is an important component in the mix to deliver services to end users, it is software that enables the actual processing to occur. The next section outlines developments in this area.

Software: From Proprietary Designs to Use of Standard Packages

Software can be broken down into two distinct categories: *systems* software and *applications* software. Systems software includes operating systems, such as Microsoft Windows, MacOS, or Linux, and programming languages/environments (e.g., C++, Java, Assembler, MySQL). Applications software includes programs that perform specific tasks such as word processing, database management, and graphics, among others. Library applications software includes some of the functionality that we have mentioned earlier, including circulation control, shared cataloging, and online public access catalogs.

Initial software development by turnkey ILS vendors of the 1970s was primarily proprietary in nature. That is to say the Independent Software Vendor (ISV) developed or selected the programming language and the operating system that would (in their estimation) best support the applications they were developing, and subsequently wrote specific code that performed those tasks on computing devices selected to optimize performance for their intended (library) customers.

Developments in software engineering brought forward more standardized means for developing applications, specifically as it related to database management applications. Because most library procedures and services are closely linked to search and retrieve functions, these newer programming environments were chosen by those vendors seeking to develop innovative applications for sale to libraries seeking to partner with systems developers in the library systems marketplace. Thus, it was not unusual for vendors to move from proprietary databases and other processes to start using more industry-standard products such as databases from Oracle, Informix, SQL Server, and so forth.

Telecommunications Developments Affecting LIS

Developments relating to telecommunications can be viewed by examining three phases or periods of innovation in the design of several computing configurations.

+ The Host Centric Period
+ The Network Centric Period
+ The End User Centric Period

The first uses of technology within libraries depended on a computing model that was referred to as host computing. In this arrangement, a single processing unit was the basis of all computing, and users were connected to this device through dumb terminals. Thus, the network configuration generally consisted of a single powerful computer and a network of dedicated terminals that were connected directly to that central device. All information processing took place in that central computer. Dumb terminals were basically keyboards connected to cathode ray display tubes, and they had no memory or disk storage capability. The focus was most definitely on the computer as the object of attention, not the end user.

These centralized systems were generally proprietary in nature. The same manufacturer made all the equipment, including the host and all peripherals. To connect to IBM mainframes, one needed IBM terminals and printers. To connect to Hewlett Packard (HP) or DEC computers, one had to purchase HP or DEC terminals and printers. This proprietary nature not only drove the price of technology up, but stifled diversity within the technologic realm. It was considered natural to expect such proprietary designs, as this was the best means for guaranteeing that everything would work together properly. This era is often referred to as the host centric period.

As the domain of computing moved into the network centric phase, the emphasis shifted to connectivity, not on building proprietary designs. The distribution of computing devices about the network, along with a diversity of terminals and other devices that could be introduced into the networked environment, led to a more open design of architectures and computing platforms. During this network centric era, the rise of smaller, cheaper, yet powerful computing devices, known as mini-computers, was a key to bringing computing costs down to levels that could be afforded by even smaller library systems. While the mainframes of the host centric period were often complex and expensive, some exceeding $1 million, the cost of a mini-computer could be as low as $30,000. Of course, the processing capabilities were much less, but many library functions of that time did not require extensive computing capabilities.

The development of the personal microcomputer in the late 1970s and the widespread use of personal computing in the 1980s and 1990s led to the most recent era of computing, the end user centric period. In this current period, users are distributed across vast geographic distances, connected to resources stored on a number of computing devices called servers. The Internet is a prime example of a distributed networked environment that is capable of connecting both people and resources together regardless of location. The increase in the numbers of end users who have access to the Internet from one or more locations throughout the day has spurred an interest in developing resources that are capable of serving those interested in connecting to information resources regardless of time of day or location.

While efforts like standards development provide us direction in terms of recording, organizing, and searching these resources, it has been the rapid adoption of a novel software application that took the Internet by surprise that has spurred increased demand for access and dissemination of digital documents. The efforts of Tim Berners-Lee and others who collaborated in developing what we call the World Wide Web has resulted in widespread use of the Internet for connecting end users directly to content marked up in a hypertext authoring environment.

It is interesting to note that while each of these application areas has had a different gestation and development period, the Web as an access and distribution medium has served to weld these back together at the seams, so to speak. A bit like the story of Humpty Dumpty, it has proven challenging for designers and developers to put separately designed and developed pieces back together again. Some of the most successful attempts by library systems developers were in integrating access to remote online databases with the online catalog of the local library or consortium of libraries.

The Web has served as a graphical user interface that welded the seams between the two distinctly different applications. We are now seeing the same sort of weaving of services with modern library services—access to licensed databases, digital libraries, eBooks, and Web-based library portals. Certainly there will be additional amalgams of diverse print and digital resources.

The convergence of these four distinctly different LIS resources into a single desktop application is of great interest to end users. They are less likely to concern themselves with boundaries between such disparate offerings, and are more interested in accessing information from distributed locations, any time of the day, any day of the week. End users prefer one-stop, desktop solutions for accessing remote information stores. Many users tend to move around a bit during the day, so incorporating widely used access protocols like TCP/IP becomes critical. The technological pathway for integrating these resources is based on the popularity of a new distributed model for dissemination called client-server designs. Technically, client-server is a design philosophy, not a specific hardware application. It is more closely associated with software applications, as they drive the connectivity of end users working from distributed desktops to remotely distributed digitally encoded resources.

The previous design constraints of the host centric systems moved through a period of network centric developments to the current client-server environment. Most client-server applications in libraries around the world are based on the Internet protocol (TCP/IP) and generic Web-based authoring environments, allowing the end user to be located anywhere they can access the Internet and run their Web browsers (client software applications).

SUMMARY

The evolution of technology and the subsequent application of that technology to library solutions have lead to the development of several marketplaces that collectively address the information needs of the end user. These marketplaces include:

- Integrated Library Systems
- Online Databases
- Web-Based Resources
- Digital Library Collections
- eBooks and eJournals.

As we shall see in later chapters, the most established marketplaces are for the integrated library systems and the online database industries. Digital library efforts include much research and some application, but to date no easily definable marketplace exists. This will change, and the likely delivery mechanism will involve personalized Web access to information integrated from a variety of sources. The continued increase in offerings within the eBook/eJournal trade sows the seeds for developing a marketplace for that segment of the information industry. Traditional publishers seem to be most interested in these venues, extending their reach into the digital realm.

The focus in all these markets will include the end user, possibly an amateur searcher, who will be interested in connecting to information resources from a variety of locations, at any time of the day or night.

NOTES

1.   This reference is to the annual conferences held by Learned Information, formerly titled "Integrated Online Library Systems." As of 2001, this conference has been renamed "InfoToday," and it includes three core conferences: National Online, Knowledge Nets, and E-Libraries.

2.   Stephen R. Salmon. *Library Automation Systems*. New York: Marcel Dekker, 1975.

3.   Jeff Barry. "Automated Systems Marketplace 2001: Closing in on Content." *Library Journal*, 106 (6), April 1, 2001, pp. 46–58.

4.   Martha Williams. "The Online Database Industry." Delivered at the InfoToday 2001 Conference, May 15, 2001. New York, NY.

5.   Ralph H. Parker. "The Punched Card Method in Circulation Work." *Library Journal*, 1936, pp. 903–5.

6.   Reflecting this early focus on the technology itself, the professional journal dealing with libraries and automation was called *The Journal of Library Automation* or *JOLA* from its inception in March 1968 until December 1981. In early 1982, *JOLA* was renamed and became *Information Technology & Libraries*.

7.   Christine Borgman. "From Acting Locally to Thinking Globally: A Brief History of Library Automation." *The Library Quarterly*, 67, July 1997, pp. 215–49.

8.   Charles Hildreth. *Online Library Catalogues: Development and Directions*. London: Library Association, 1989.

9.   Joseph R. Matthews. "Unrelenting Change: The 1984 Automated Library System Marketplace." *Library Journal*, April 1, 1985, pp. 31–40.

10.   Joseph R. Matthews. "Growth and Consolidation: The 1985 Automated Library System Marketplace." *Library Journal*, April 1, 1986, pp. 25–35.

Chapter 2

The Library Information Systems Marketplace

In Chapter 1, we stated that library information systems (LIS) consist of five separate applications or developments:

◆ Integrated Library Systems

◆ Online Databases

◆ Web-Based Resources

◆ Digital Library Collections

◆ eBooks and eJournals.

To date, only the first two of these, integrated library systems and online databases, have active marketplaces associated with them. In this chapter, we will explore the origins of these two marketplaces, provide an overview of the current status of each, and then tie them together with the other development areas that do not yet have marketplaces in an attempt to forecast what the future LIS might be like. It is important to remember that these five separate LIS developments have their own developing or to-be-developed marketplaces, and it is likely that, at some point, these will be linked together to support a wide array of end user search and retrieval requests.

THE INTEGRATED LIBRARY SYSTEMS (ILS) MARKETPLACE

An overview of the ILS marketplace has been published in the April issues of *Library Journal* since 1982.[1] In Chapter 1, we noted that the pioneering era, the period before an ILS marketplace was established, was a time of exploration and innovation. This period ended with the beginning of the ILS marketplace, which began in 1971 when CLSI offered its first circulation control system, the LIBS 100, as a turnkey option for libraries. CLSI was soon joined by companies such as

DataPhase Systems Incorporated, Data Research Associates, and others to form the initial ILS marketplace. By 1982, this marketplace had revenues of approximately $50 million annually and was growing at a rapid pace as libraries selected from among the circulation control systems provided by the vendor market. In 1982, CLSI offered its first version of a turnkey online public access catalog, and others soon followed suit. By 1990, there were more than 30 distinct vendors participating in the marketplace, which had collective revenues of $178 million.

During the next few years, several vendors were bought, sold, and merged; and a period of vendor instability ensued. Add to that the number of changes in the top management positions within those companies, and one can see that this had become big business for these competitive vendors. Each vendor sought to claim their portion of the overall growing marketplace for integrated library systems solutions. By 2001, the overall ILS marketplace had grown to a point where annual revenues hovered around $500 million (see Figure 2-1).[2]

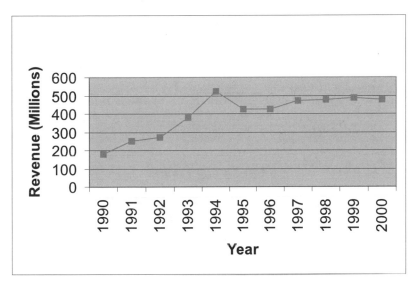

Figure 2-1. Integrated Library Systems Vendor Revenues 1990–2000

After 30 years of establishing a marketplace for integrated library systems, there appear to be some common themes. The current status of the ILS marketplace can be characterized by the following properties:[3]

- It is generally mature.
- It exhibits rich features for basic operations (e.g., cataloging, circulation control, online catalogs).
- The majority of installed systems are older "legacy systems."
- Newer installations are based on distributed network technologies and are predominantly Web-based in their approach to user-interface design.

  ♦ Serials and Acquisitions subsystems are the most complex and the last to
    be completed.

Marketplace Maturity

Marketplace maturity means that both long-standing and newly formed ILS
vendors have settled on the group of key functionalities. The industry boom in the
1970s seemed based on the move to circulation control systems and on online
public access catalogs in the 1980s. The current scene includes these solutions
but not as the "killer application" as had been the case during those earlier periods. Most of the basic functions and features regarding library operations have
been successfully identified, and procedures for implementing solutions to these
basic library operations have been coded and refined several times over.

Not that there is nothing new and exciting to look forward to! The current marketplace struggles to extend the physical library into the global, digital environment where information takes on new forms and delivery possibilities. But it is safe
to say that experimentation with existing library processes is over, and that the
focus has been for some time on new services, primarily those based on access to
remote information services such as databases and access to digital collections.
The major challenge is to provide integrated access to collections, both paper and
electronic, and to effectively link to electronic or paper copies. All of this, coupled
with the transition to a Web-based library system, means that the library community is confronting another period of serious change.

Legacy Systems

As with any established industry, there are so called legacy systems that were
developed and implemented more than a decade ago. Many of these are still operating and are supported by the ILS vendors that originally developed these solutions. They often lack connectivity or extension to the new, remote information
services mentioned above, but they do provide much of the functionality desired by
the library. And so they continue to provide access to the local collection, check out
materials, and so forth. These were often designed as centralized solutions, based
on a single computing device, with little functionality at the end user or dumb terminal side. While vendors supporting these legacy systems might have newer,
more progressive solutions, libraries might have opted to remain with the earlier
systems for a number of reasons, one of which might be replacement cost. Eventually these libraries will migrate to newer systems provided by existing vendors or
competitors. But the number of these older implementations is diminishing as the
years pass.

Serials and Acquisitions

Interestingly enough, there are some functions that vary widely from library
system to library system, and these peculiarities in processing requirements make
it challenging for ILS vendors to develop parameter-driven software that meets the
needs of the many libraries seeking to automate the procedures. These functions
include serials control and acquisitions processing. In the evolution of integrated

library systems, the attention has been on developing circulation control systems and online catalogs, while these technical service functions lagged behind. Because these procedures vary from library to library, and are more complex in variation than other functions, they are more costly to automate. Thus, the primary innovations have been in development of inventory control systems and online public access catalogs and not in serials and acquisitions subsystems.

SYSTEM ARCHITECTURES

System architectures have certainly changed over the years, as well. Mentioned earlier, many so-called legacy systems are being phased out, to be replaced by client-server solutions based on distributed networking models of operation. These legacy systems include solutions based on:

- ◆ Mainframes: NOTIS, DOBIS
- ◆ Minicomputer-based systems: DRA Classic, Sirsi
- ◆ Microcomputer-based systems: Follett, Sagebrush.

As is typically the case with legacy systems, development has ceased but support continues because revenues are still derived from continued support. In fact, some ILS vendors have acquired other vendors with legacy systems, which generate continued revenues from support and maintenance and offer possibilities for future system migration. The acquisition of INLEX by Data Research Associates (DRA) during the early 1990s, and the more recent acquisition of DRA by Sirsi, are examples of growth by acquisition.

Current System Architectures

In terms of current system architectures for integrated library systems, it appears that:

- ◆ Client/server solutions prevail.
- ◆ Non-servers include mainframes (host systems) and DOS and Windows-based systems (prevalent in the school library marketplace).
- ◆ Graphical user interfaces dominate.
- ◆ Web-based OPACs are the norm.
- ◆ Modern database technologies are being incorporated (e.g., many vendors incorporate Oracle and Microsoft's SQL Server into their systems designs).

As mentioned earlier, many ILS vendors began in an era when host computing was predominant. While they still support and possibly continue to develop those markets, many have moved forward to develop distributed computing solutions based on the client-server model. In these environments, the end user accesses the applications from any remote location (within the library or from home, office, or hotel room) using a personal computer and a connection to the Internet. The library develops its applications and stores a variety of content on one or more servers connected together, so as to support an array of end user requests. The key is that the end user is empowered with processing capabilities, can access the system around the clock from any location, and may even be able to manipulate retrieved content directly on his or her desktop devices. This results in a convenient, flexible connection to an array of digital resources secured by library for end user access.

Because the Web is a popular avenue for access by end users, this sort of client-server relationship has increasingly become the direction to proceed. The Web browser (often Internet Explorer or Netscape) acts on behalf of the user as the client software, using an interface developed for the library to interact with server side software provided by the ILS vendor. The heavy personal investment of time and talent by the end user in mastering client browsers has given lift to this means of interaction. Graphical interfaces seem to be a preferred means of interaction for end users, and while character-based solutions still exist (command- and menu-driven interfaces), development directions have focused on the more creative graphical designs. As libraries move to include richer media, including sound, motion, and video, expect to see Web-based delivery systems continually refined to support end user access.

Most of the ILS vendors now offer some version of a Web-based online catalog. Behind the scenes, within the bowels of search and retrieval, are modern database technologies supported by Oracle, Microsoft's SQL Server, and other popular and effective database authoring environments.

Some selected ILS vendors are:

- Innovative Interfaces Incorporated
- GEAC Computers, Inc.
- Endeavor Information Systems
- Epixtech
- Sirsi
- Ex Libris (USA), Inc.

Some vendors have evolved or migrated from host computing to client-server solutions. These include:[4]

- Sirsi with its Unicorn system
- Innovative Interface's Innopac has evolved into the Millenium software environment.

Some systems were created as client-server solutions:

- Endeavor's Voyager
- VTLS's Virtua
- TLC's Library Solution

- ◆ Epixtech's Horizon
- ◆ EOS International's Q Series.

As vendors gain more experience in developing these new platforms based on desktop client software connecting to server-based ILS applications, end users stand poised to take advantage of the flexibility and convenience offered by distributed computing solutions.

Operating Systems

Software choices are decisions faced by vendors when developing any new venture. Today's solutions seem to be based on two popular operating systems and several database programming environments.

When it comes to the choice of operating systems, we often see:

- ◆ UNIX for large scale implementations
- ◆ Microsoft NT for small- to medium-sized systems.

Database Environments

As for database environments:

- ◆ Oracle: Voyager, Unicorn, Virtua, Innopac, Q Series
- ◆ Microsoft SQL: Polaris.

DRA chose to go with Object Store when they began developing their TAOS system, and they subsequently moved to another object-oriented database product when performance problems were encountered. Some vendors have also developed proprietary database environments, including Innovative and Unicorn, although both vendors also offer solutions that incorporate industry-standard database products.

Choosing network protocols has been the easiest for vendors. Only TCP/IP, the so-called "Internet Protocol," is tolerated. What were once proprietary networked solutions have migrated directly to this type of network connectivity. Those offering proprietary versions of network protocols often find themselves last on the list of choices by libraries seeking to develop next-generation ILS solutions.

On the client side, MS Windows dominates. There are some Macintosh developments and some Java clients running Windows or Linux, or both (for example, Innovative Interface's Millennium). OpenText uses HTML to support their TechLib offering. Whether Java or HTML implementations, all preferred ILS client-server systems offer Web-based online public access catalogs.

THE ONLINE DATABASE INDUSTRY MARKETPLACE

As indicated in Chapter 1, the online database industry began as a separate industry in the early 1970s, and created its own marketplace. That marketplace has grown rapidly to over $1.5 billion in annual revenues with only a fraction of those revenues coming from the coffers of library organizations. Professional searchers working in corporate environments have been a primary source of searching activity in the online database industry. Currently, this market has become closely coupled with the integrated library systems marketplace to provide library end users a one-stop desktop access point for materials held both locally and licensed internationally. Originally designed for professional searchers, the online database industry has grown to include users of all levels. The recent introduction of the World Wide Web has given database producers a clear route for disseminating their resources to a wider audience, in many instances directly to the end user (bypassing the library).

The players, or components, in this industry include online search services, database producers, and the databases themselves. Often confusing to the end user and, on occasion, to the professional searcher, the lines between these three have been less than clear cut. If taken separately, it might be best to begin with the information databases presented in searchable formats.

Databases are collections of information on one or more related topics, often a "subject literature" (as opposed to a physical collection of objects) such as chemistry, medicine, psychology, and so forth. A database can be bibliographic in nature, or have full-text, numerials, images, sound, or audio. Examples include:

- Medline
- Chemical Abstracts
- Lexis-Nexis.

Database producers—agencies who identify and gather these collections and add value to them so that they may be searched by end users—create these searchable databases. Database producers are often found within government agencies (National Library of Medicine), professional associations (American Chemical Society), or for-profit companies (Reed Elsevier). Note that these producers line up with the produced databases in the previous bulleted list.

Often these producers sell or license this information to online search service providers, a sort of supermarket of online databases. These database aggregators, as some call them, add value by providing a common searching environment (hardware and software) for end users. They provide access to numerous databases, created by different database producers, directly to information professionals and end users alike.

Let us take a brief look at the historical developments of these online database service providers, as they originated from within the print publishing world. At one point in the history of the online database industry, there were the "Big Three" supermarket search services: Orbit, Dialog, and BRS. Each of these services is actually named after a piece of searching software developed by a software engineering firm in the early 1970s. For example, the National Library of Medicine (NLM) commissioned Systems Development Corporation (SDC) to write searching software for their Medical Literature and Retrieval System (MEDLARS), an offline search system that predates MEDLINE. SDC called this software "Orbit," and kept the software development rights to the code developed for NLM. In the early 1970s, SDC began to license databases produced by other secondary publishers, and subsequently opened up their business based on the Orbit searching software. Similarly, Dialog, created by Lockheed Aerospace (for the National Aeronautics and Space Administration [NASA]), also licensed various databases to add to their product offerings. In an interesting twist, Bibliographic Research Services (BRS, Inc.) was developed in the mid-1970s using the IBM STAIRS software developed for the Central Intelligence Agency (CIA). BRS licensed STAIRS from IBM to build the third supermarket of online database services. Table 2-1 depicts the "Big Three" online search services.

Table 2-1. Online Search Service Origins

Started As	Vendor	Software
NLM	SDC	Orbit
NASA	Lockheed	Dialog
CIA	BRS	BRS/Search

As can be seen from Table 2-1, these database aggregators, or supermarkets, had their origins in the U.S. contract software business of the early 1970s. The "Big Three," as they were once known, are no longer the large dominating players they once were, when they were better known by their software names (Orbit, Dialog, BRS). Fierce competition from private sources and international businesses provided more choices to the end user and the professional searcher. Each of these players was bought and sold several times in the attempt to maintain a competitive edge. As more aggregators sprung up across the globe and the industry expanded its sources and services (at one time, in the mid-1970s, there were only 100 databases, as compared to the current count of more than 100 times that number), the industry experienced mergers, acquisitions, and even company failures.

How did this marketplace initially develop? Many of the world's leading information publishers had developed computer-searchable versions of their traditional print products and made them available through various search services, generally with a licensing arrangement. These search services and database producers worked in tandem to structure and format more than 12 billion records so that they could be searched by information professionals and end users. Database producers created the secondary publications and the Online Search Services brokered access to subsets of those databases. Most services today offer online access to information in subject disciplines such as:

Medicine	Biosciences	Education
Science	Technology	Business
Politics	Social Sciences	Interdisciplinary Areas

The publishing chain begins with authors and ends with readers. Traditional connections require a series of intervening links, including:[5]

* Primary publishers
* Secondary publishers
* Database distributors
* Libraries
* Document delivery services.

Secondary publishers include those database producers we mentioned in the previous paragraphs. Initially print in nature, these producers have moved to include digital versions of their traditional resources, providing improved access for the user and new revenue streams for the secondary publisher. At each link, some agency provides a certain value-added service:

* Editing
* Indexing
* Distribution and access
* Archiving
* Delivery to end user.

In the traditional model, the role of each link is being tested against the Web model, where authors and readers can connect directly without all the intervening intermediaries.[6]

Martha Williams and Carol Tenopir, in collaboration with others, examine the database industry each year.[7] Williams presents the results of her annual survey at InfoToday's *National Online Meeting,* held each May in New York City, and a copy of the report is published in the *National Online Meeting Proceedings* each year. Since 1993, Williams has also contributed an industry analysis to the annual *Gale Directory of Databases*, published in March and September each year. Tenopir's contribution is recorded annually in the May 15 issue of *Library Journal.*[8] These sources should be examined regularly for changes in the online database marketplace. Since Williams's perspective offers a broader swath of time coverage, we present summary tables extracted from her recent publication.

Table 2-2. Growth of the Online Database Industry over Time[9]

	1975	2001
Growth of Databases	301	12,417
Producers of Databases	200	3,674
Vendors of DB Services	105	2,454
Number of records	52 million	15 billion

Databases can be thought of as being made up of classes of data. These classes can range from text-based content to multimedia content. The breakdown of these categories reveals that:[10]

- 66% are word oriented (e.g., bibliographic, full text, directory)
- 17% are number oriented
- 12% are image or picture oriented
- 3% are audio or sound oriented
- 2% are other (e.g., software)

Of the 66 percent or approximately 8,050 databases that are word oriented, more than half (5,398) claim to be full-text databases. Just 15 years ago, that percentage was 28 percent. It should be noted that those databases claiming to be "full-text" might actually contain a combination of full text and bibliographic information. Regardless, this is a significant growth area, and extremely important in terms of providing instant access to information by demanding end users.

Database Sources and Producer Status

"The digitized information world is a single universe with databases produced on all continents."[11] In fact, more than six out of ten databases are produced in the United States, while the remaining 40 percent are produced internationally. As mentioned earlier, producers can generally be categorized across three domains. Over the duration of the marketplace, the contributions to the number of databases produced has changed.

Table 2-3. Contributions to Database Productivity over Time

Category	1979	2000
Government	56%	9%
Commerce/Industry	22%	81%
Professional Society	22%	8%

From the previous statement of origin and Table 2-3, it is apparent that, while the U.S. government was an initial force in developing the online database industry, the predominant producer today has a commercial interest and is bound by profits. This may be one reason why the market fluctuates so wildly, and why databases are created for short periods of time, only to disappear if not proven to make profits in a short period of time.

Williams also classes databases by subject:

Business	30%
Science/technology/engineering	18%
General news/general	17%
Law	11%
Health/life sciences	10%
Other (humanities, multidisciplinary, social sciences)	14%

Note that the old adage of scientific, technical, and medical (STM) literatures now includes business, journalistic, and legal information as well.

The volume of search activity has grown tremendously over the past three decades as shown in Table 2-4:

Table 2-4. Search Volume (Activity over Time)

Year	Numbers of Searches	
1974	750,000	
1982	7,500,000	(Ten-fold increase)
1997	86,000,000	
1998	90,000,000	

Searches were once the province of professional searchers, some of them within libraries, others within corporate agencies conducting competitive intelligence gathering, searching patent databases, seeking research findings in medicine, identifying legal precedents, and many other database-oriented investigations. Professionals had a working knowledge of the sources, were trained in the nuances of the command-oriented search engines, and were capable of extracting end user information requirements.

During the late 1980s, database producers attempted to create more personalized versions of their databases, and many delivered them on the new CD-ROM technologies that were beginning to spread to the end user. Once end users found out about these sources that were once the domain of professional searchers, they began to demand even more content and delivery, and the marketplace grew quickly. Add the connectivity offered by personal computers and the Internet, and the online database industry literally took off in the 1990s. One means for interpreting this growth is to look at the number of hours that end users are connected and the collective revenues of database industry representatives as shown in Table 2-5.[12]

Table 2-5. Revenues and Usage

Year	Connect Hours	Revenues
1978	780,000	$ 40 million
1998	12,000,000	$ 1.5 billion

Within that usage, there are four database search services that provide some 94 percent of the activities in searching:

- Lexis-Nexis
- Westlaw
- FirstSearch
- Dialog

Usage and revenues are not evenly distributed. For example, FirstSearch is highly used, but their fees are quite low. FirstSearch is an OCLC service, but the other three (Lexis-Nexis, Westlaw, and Dialog) are all for-profit vendors, and collectively they account for 92 percent of the $1.5 billion revenues of the industry. In a marketplace where thousands of database aggregators and tens of thousands of databases thrive, we see that a small fraction of the players account for a significant proportion of both activity and revenue.

The remaining markets within LIS include those for digital libraries and eBooks, or the electronic distribution of monographs to libraries as requested by end users. The former component of LIS is still in a state of research and development, and, as such, no market has yet been established. On the other hand, the market for eBooks is a new and rapidly growing enterprise that did not exist just a few years ago. Expect the digital library marketplace to follow suit.

SUMMARY

Clearly, the integrated library system and online database markets have grown fairly rapidly over the last 20 years. Yet, as the vendors move to provide innovative new products, such as providing access to personalized content delivery using a library's online catalog, libraries will see an increasing amount of their budgets flowing to these marketplaces.

NOTES

1.   Joseph R. Matthews. "Automated Library System Marketplace 1981: Active and Heating Up." *Library Journal*, 107 (3), February 1, 1982, pp. 233–35.

2.   John Barry. "Automated System Marketplace 2001: Closing in on Content." *Library Journal*, 117 (6), April 1, 2001, pp. 46–58.

3.   Opening plenary session presented by Marshall Breeding at *11th Annual Integrated Online Library Systems Conference.* Held May 16–17, 2000, in New York City.

4.   Ibid.

5.   Carol Tenopir and Jeff Barry. "Data Dealers Forging Links." *Library Journal*, 104 (9), May 15, 1999, pp. 40–48.

6.   Ibid.

7.   Carol Tenopir, Gayle Baker, and William Robinson. "Database Marketplace 2001: Racing at Full Speed." *Library Journal*, 105, May 15, 2000, pp. 45–58.

8.   Williams's contributions began in 1976, while Tenopir's articles first appeared in 1998.

9.   Martha E. Williams. "The State of Databases Today: 2001." *Gale Directory of Databases. Volume 1: Online Databases.* Marc Faerber, ed. New York: Gale Group, 2001, Part 2.

10.   Martha E. Williams. "Highlights of the Online Database Industry and the Internet: 2000." Presented May 15, 2000, at the *21st National Online Meeting*, New York, NY.

11.   Ibid.

12.   Ibid.

Part II
The Technologies

Part II begins with a chapter focusing on the design of integrated library systems and then moves to cover open systems, an important new development.

Chapter 5 is a primer on telecommunications and networks and important considerations in these days of global communications. The section closes with a chapter on standards and standards organizations that affect these developments.

Chapter 3

Design of Integrated Library Systems

This chapter addresses the issues of database design and the construction of indexes in an ILS. The system design will determine what functional capabilities can be provided to the system's users and how those capabilities can be implemented. Next, the issue of how a library can provide access to a wide range of information resources is addressed. Identifying the issues associated with maintaining a library's database, including the issues associated with using enhanced records, and how the ILS can output records occupies the remainder of the chapter.

DATABASE DESIGN

The data in an ILS is stored in a series of databases called files. If the data is stored in a relational database management system (RDBMS), the files are called tables. Data is arrayed in the tables in a series of columns and rows. The design of these files is crucial since the presence or absence of a specific data field or fields will determine whether a particular functional capability can be provided. The fields of data can be accessed via the application software (e.g., patron data in the circulation module). In addition, each file will normally have one or more indexes that can provide access to the data.[1] As shown in Figure 3-1, understanding the inter-relationships of these files is fundamental to appreciating both the capabilities and the limitations of a particular IIS design.

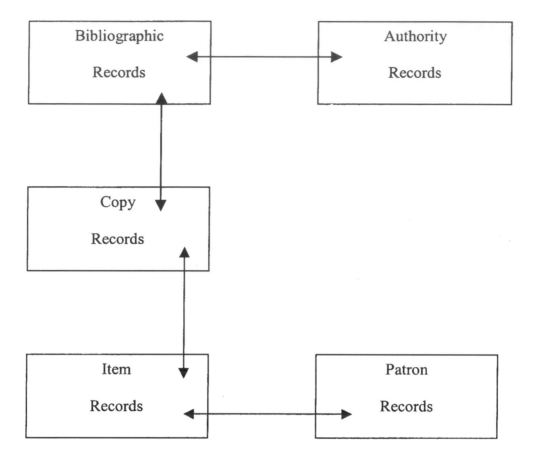

Figure 3-1. Design of Library Information System Files

Bibliographic/Copy/Item Records

The top level is where the bibliographic and authority records are stored. Only a single bibliographic record is stored, even if there are multiple copies of the title. The copy record, which typically stores information about each copy of an item (e.g., copy number, local call number, the holding location, and so forth), is linked to the bibliographic record. One bibliographic record is linked to one or more copy records, which minimizes the amount of disk space needed to store the library's bibliographic database. See Table 3-1 for a list of the data elements normally found within a copy record.

In some cases, multiple items might be received as a part of a book copy or serial publication. For example, besides the regular serial issue there might be pocket parts, supplements, indexes, a CD-ROM, a map, and so forth included. The library may wish to have each of these items tracked and uniquely identified. This is the purpose of the item record, which typically contains the item barcode number, collection name, call number, and so forth. In some cases (e.g., a book), the LIS software will allow the copy record and item record to be combined in a single record.

One copy record is linked to one or more item records. See Table 3-2 for a list of the data elements typically found within an item record.

Table 3-1. Typical Copy Level Data Elements

Field Name	Field Name
Copy	Local Call Number
Call Number Prefix	Media Type
Holding Location	Collection Type
Date Received	Previous Cost
Currency Type	Replacement Cost
Acquisition Cost	Copy Notes
Holding Summary	

Table 3-2. Typical Item Level Data Elements

Field Name	Field Name
Item ID	Local Call Number
Call Number Prefix	Media Type
Holding Location	Collection Type
Item Status	Volume Alpha
Volume Numeric	Item Title
Volume Statement	Staff Notes
Public Note	Trap Message Level
Trap Message	Security Level
Circulating	Box Number
Special Collections	Previous Cost
Currency Type	Replacement Cost
Acquisition Cost	Previous Patron
Date Received	Date Checked In
Date Checked Out	Current Patron
Due Date	Last Transaction
Usage Counter	Item Lost Flag
Renewal Counter	Data Damaged
Overdue Counter	Claimed Returned
In-house Usage	Claimed Never Out
Last Inventoried	

Some ILS have designed their systems to support this three level approach, while other systems only provide two levels (the copy and item record levels are combined). The availability of this three-level approach allows an LIS vendor to more easily provide a capability that automatically creates a detailed holding record that is in compliance with the Machine Readable Cataloging (MARC) Format for Holdings record as each issue of a serial is received. Only a few of the ILS vendors have implemented this standard completely.

Authority Records

Authority control refers to a cataloging practice that establishes "authorized" headings that will be used when creating or editing bibliographic records. Authority records are linked to a bibliographic record. The bibliographic record is likely to have multiple links to different authority records—that is, a separate authority record for each heading in the bibliographic record that is under authority control (i.e., author, uniform title, series, and subject headings). The importance of the authority file cannot be over-emphasized because this is the file that contains cross-references. Given the fact that there is a direct correlation between the number of cross-references and the success a patron experiences while searching the library's catalog, providing access to the authority file is crucial.[2]

For smaller libraries, generally there is a one-to-one correlation between the number of bibliographic records and the number of authority control records. As the size of the bibliographic database increases, the rate of addition of new authority control records will decline. Thus, a bibliographic database containing one million MARC records may be linked to about 650,000 authority control records. The size of the authority database will also vary by type of library—since public libraries have large fiction collections, there will be fewer authority records.

The Library of Congress (LC) Name Authority files contain more than 4.5 million records, while the LC Subject Heading file contains slightly less than 250,000 records. The vast majority of the Name Authority records contain no cross-references to pseudonyms (pen names) or other forms of an author's name. About 60 percent of the LC Subject Heading authority records contain *see* and *see also* cross-references. Of these, the average MARC authority record will contain about 2.45 topical *see* cross-references and 1.4 topical *see also* cross-references. There are also about 1.8 geographic *see* cross-references and 1.1 geographic *see also* cross-references.

Every library should have a program in place whereby they automatically receive updates to authority records as authorized headings are changed and cross-references added by the Library of Congress and others. The library should also be exploring other alternatives for identifying the evolving search requests being used by their patrons so that they can add cross-references to their authority file. In fact, some libraries have added cross-references to words known to be frequently misspelled in continuing attempts to improve the success rate of their OPAC users.

Circulation File

The circulation subsystem of an ILS supports the "inventory control" functions of the library, and these features are determined by the manner in which the circulation files are managed. The process is relatively straightforward: At checkout, a link is created between the patron and the unique item record. In most systems, the vendors will actually add a record to an item checkout file that contains the item barcode number; the patron barcode number; the location, date, and time the item was checked out; and the expected due date. This file is indexed with both the item barcode number and patron barcode number. The ILS software will, periodically (usually nightly), review the status of this file and identify any items that may be overdue so that the appropriate actions can be taken (preparing overdue notices, flagging the patron as overdue, flagging the item as overdue, and so forth). When a checked-out item is returned in a normal manner (not overdue and no other exception has occurred), the item checkout file is consulted and the appropriate entry can be deleted. In some systems, the location, date, and time the item was returned is added to the entry and a flag is set to "returned." At a later time, these returned items are deleted from the file.

Other important files include the vendor file, detail-level and summary-level serial holdings file, fund accounting file, order file, serial pattern file, and so forth. One of the most important implications is that if a data field or combination of several fields are not found in one of these files, then the corresponding functionality that would use that data cannot be provided. The ILS vendor must either revise the existing data structures for a field or develop a new file to provide the necessary functionality in a future release of the software.

INDEXES

Almost all ILS will provide access to basic index types—browse indexes and keyword indexes. A browse index is a character-by-character, word-for-word, left-to-right index used by those bibliographic headings that are under authority control as well as a variety of other indexes, principally numeric indexes. For example, browse indexes might include author, subject, series, record identification number, OCLC record identification number, International Standard Book Number (ISBN), International Standard Serial Number (ISSN), Superintendent of Documents identification number, Government Printing Office (GPO) number, music publishers identification number, and so forth. A browse index can also be used for fields that are not under authority control (e.g., a title index). A keyword index, by definition will, in most cases, index every word in a record or field. For example, a keyword index can be limited to a specific field, as in the case of a title keyword index or a subject keyword index.

Staff members generally have access to all indexes, while the library's patrons will only have access to a subset of the total number of available indexes. After all, not too many patrons arrive at an OPAC workstation armed with a Library of Congress Control Number (LCCN) or an OCLC record ID number.

Searches that retrieve large result sets can be limited or narrowed by using an additional set of indexes for location, year of publication, type of material, and so forth. In a similar manner, most systems allow staff and users to perform Boolean searching—combining different indexes using the Boolean operators *and, or,* and *not.* Despite the power that this tool affords an experienced searcher, it is seldom used in almost every online retrieval system. Library OPACs and Internet search engines are inconsistent in using "implied" Boolean operators. In some systems, when a user enters a phrase as a search request, the system will insert the Boolean operator AND between each word of the phrase, with the resulting retrieval set being narrowed or reduced. In other systems, the Boolean operator OR is inserted, which will expand the retrieval set.

Most vendor-provided LIS will allow the library to control what data fields and subfields will be used to construct an index. An example of the component fields and subfields that could potentially be used to construct an author index is shown in Table 3-3. To further complicate the situation, some LIS will not provide an author index, but will provide three separate name indexes (personal names, corporate names, and conference names).

Table 3-3. Fields Used to Construct an Author Index

MARC Tag	Field Name	Valid Subfields	Subfield Name
100	Author	a	Personal name
		b	Numeration
		c	Titles associated with a name
		d	Dates associated with a name
		e	Relator term
		f	Date of a work
		g	Miscellaneous information
		k	Form subheading
		l	Language of a work
		n	Number of part/section
		p	Name of part/section
		q	Fuller form of name
		t	Title of a work
		u	Affiliation
		4	Relator code
		6	Linkage

Table 3-3—Continued

MARC Tag	Field Name	Valid Subfields	Subfield Name
110	Corporate Name	a	Corporate name
		b	Subordinate unit
		c	Location of meeting
		d	Date of meeting
		f	Relator term
		g	Miscellaneous information
		k	Form subheading
		l	Language of a work
		n	Number of part/section
		p	Name of part/section
		t	Title of a work
		u	Affiliation
		4	Relator code
		6	Linkage
111	Conference/Meeting	a	Meeting or jurisdiction name
		c	Location of meeting
		d	Date of meeting
		e	Subordinate unit
		f	Date of a work
		g	Miscellaneous information
		k	Form subheading
		l	Language of a work
		n	Number of part/section
		p	Name of part/section
		q	Name of meeting following jurisdiction name
		t	Title of a work
		u	Affiliation
		4	Relator code
		6	Linkage

(Table 3-3 continues on page 36.)

Table 3-3—Continued

MARC Tag	Field Name	Valid Subfields	Subfield Name
700	Personal Name Added Entry	a	Personal name
		b	Numeration
		c	Titles associated with a name
		d	Dates associated with a name
		e	Relator term
		f	Date of a work
		g	Miscellaneous information
		h	Medium
		k	Form subheading
		l	Language of a work
		m	Medium of performance
		n	Number of part/section
		o	Arranged statement for music
		p	Name of part/section
		q	Fuller form of name
		r	Key for music
		s	Version
		t	Title of a work
		u	Affiliation
		x	ISSN
		3	Materials specified
		4	Relator code
		5	Institution to which field applies
		6	Linkage

Table 3-3—Continued

MARC Tag	Field Name	Valid Subfields	Subfield Name
710	Corporate Name Added Entry	a	Corporate name
		b	Subordinate unit
		c	Location of meeting
		d	Date of meeting
		e	Relator term
		f	Date of a work
		g	Miscellaneous information
		h	Medium
		k	Form subheading
		l	Language of a work
		m	Medium of performance
		n	Number of part/section
		o	Arranged statement for music
		p	Name of part/section
		q	Fuller form of name
		r	Key for music
		s	Version
		t	Title of a work
		u	Affiliation
		x	ISSN
		3	Materials specified
		4	Relator code
		5	Institution to which field applies
		6	Linkage

(Table 3-3 continues on page 38.)

Table 3-3—Continued

MARC Tag	Field Name	Valid Subfields	Subfield Name
711	Meeting Name Added Entry	a	Meeting or jurisdiction name
		c	Location of meeting
		d	Date of meeting
		e	Subordinate unit
		f	Date of a work
		g	Miscellaneous information
		h	Medium
		k	Form subheading
		l	Language of a work
		n	Number of part/section
		p	Name of part/section
		q	Name of meeting following jurisdiction name
		s	Version
		t	Title of a work
		u	Affiliation
		x	ISSN
		3	Materials specified
		4	Relator code
		5	Institution to which field applies
		6	Linkage

While this index construction flexibility is a wonderful characteristic of ILS, and is in response to marketplace demands by library customers, it does carry with it a significant amount of negative baggage. Some libraries will choose to include many subfields when an index is constructed, while others will only use one or two subfields. One of the implications for OPAC users is that when they are performing a Z39.50 search of another library, they are making assumptions about what they are likely to retrieve based on how their local ILS performs when they conduct an identical search. In some cases, it is likely that end users do not recognize that they are, in fact, conducting a distributed Z39.50 search (even after selecting another library to search).

When a library defines a browse title index (MARC tag 245), it may limit the index to subfields a and b (main title and subtitle), or it may add subfield c (the remainder of the title page transcription/statement of responsibility—or all the data following the first slash which contains the names of illustrators, editors, author of a foreword, and so forth). If it does the latter, then it should not be surprising when an OPAC user becomes confused about seeing the names of people in a title index (this may be a case of double indexing as the names of these individuals will likely be a part of the author index).

Another important issue for creating indexes is how punctuation, hyphens, and other symbols are treated by the system. An automated system will typically remove all punctuation and special symbols from a string of text before the index entry is created. This index construction process is called "normalization" and results in better searching because users don't need to worry about punctuation while searching. However, the normalization process will vary from system to system because normalization can either eliminate the punctuation or replace it with a space. For example, tongue-in-cheek might become "tongueincheek" in one system or "tongue in cheek" in another.

What a Difference an Index Makes!

Conducting a search of a medium-sized public library for *space shuttles* resulted in retrieving a varying number of records, depending upon the index that was searched. The results include:

Index	Records Retrieved
Browse:	
Author	0
Title	13
Subject	15
Keyword:	
Author Keyword	0
Title Keyword	20
Subject Keyword	35
Total Record Keyword	43

Clearly, the choice an OPAC user makes about what index or indexes to search will have a enormous impact on whether he or she is successful in finding items of interest in the library's collection. Depending on which fields are searched, the user could retrieve anywhere from zero to 43 records!

DIVERSITY OF INFORMATION RESOURCES

When individuals have an information need, they have a number of resources that they can turn to, as shown in Figure 3-2. Whether the information need arises from our personal lives or concerns a professional matter, the number of information resources that can be consulted remains relatively similar. The relevant information that can be retrieved from each of these resources ranges from quite modest to substantial. Historically, two inversely related measures have been used to assess an information retrieval—precision and recall. Precision measures the ratio of relevant documents located by a specific search. Recall measures the proportion of all relevant documents in the database that the search locates. As recall increases, precision often decreases.

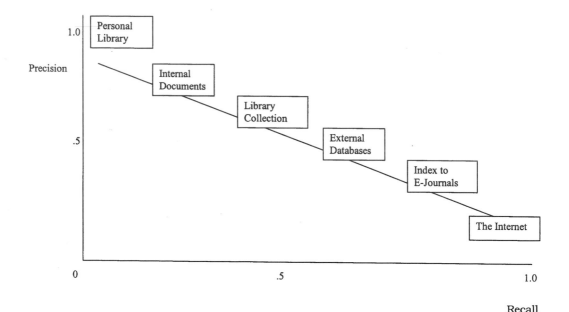

Figure 3-2. The Diversity of Information Resources

It should be noted that these measures are somewhat artificial. The measures are based on what is referred to as a "known relevant document set," and since this never occurs in real applications (if you know the known relevant set, why are you searching?), the measures only offer a glimpse of searching performance. But, to date, no better measures of information retrieval performance have been devised so they continue to be used.

Internal Documents

Most departments within an organization (e.g., sales, marketing, R&D, manufacturing, human resources, and so forth) will create a number of "documents" that others within the organization might find useful. These "internal documents" might be a word processing document, a spreadsheet, a PowerPoint presentation, or a database. Managing and providing access to these documents is a major source of difficulty in most organizations. Indeed, in an era when "born digital" is becoming the norm, this is a growing problem. As shown in Table 3-4, there are several ways in which an organization's employees might become aware of these internal documents. Several LIS vendors offer optional modules, which will provide full-text indexing of the internal documents (and the documents can be located anywhere on the LAN or the Internet).

Table 3-4. Approaches to Discovering Internal Documents

Approach	How Did You Learn of the Internal Documents?	Are the Contents of the Internal Documents Full-Text Indexed?
No organization	Chance	No
Shared LAN Directory	Check the directory periodically	No
Shared repository as a part of a Document Management System	Check the repository periodically	Generally, no. In some cases, yes.
Intranet with links to the Internal Documents	Browse the Intranet	No
Intranet with a Search Engine	Conduct a search	No
Library adds a record for each internal document	Conduct a search using the library's OPAC	No
Library adds a record for each internal document plus indexes the full-text of the document	Conduct a search using the library's OPAC	Yes

Library Catalog

The library catalog is central to providing access to the library's collection of materials whether an individual visits the library and uses an OPAC workstation or gains access to the catalog via a LAN or the Internet. The value of the library's catalog is an important asset and typically requires significant resources to keep it current.[3] The library catalog, with its associated bibliographic, authority, and copy/item records (which provide location and status information), must be kept current so it reflects the status of the library's collection on a minute-by-minute basis.

External Databases

Providing access to the plethora of online databases is a real challenge for any library. The online database industry was examined in greater detail in the previous chapter. The majority of these databases are accessible via the Internet, and the library or the individual must be licensed to be able to conduct a search. The cost of accessing one of these databases can range from free to very, very expensive.

Typically, each of these databases will have its own search interface and protocol. These determine the types of searching that is supported and how each type of search is executed. In a few cases, it is possible to use a Z39.50 interface to search an external database. Examples of external database providers include: Dialog, Lexus/Nexus, ProQuest, Information Access, Wilson Web, Questel, Ovid, the National Library of Medicine, and so forth.

Depending on the searcher's experience and his or her knowledge of the various databases, the results of the search—from an information retrieval point-of-view—will range from poor to excellent. Research has indicated that most end users are amateur searchers at best.[4] Searches by the end user are typically not as efficient or effective as when a trained librarian performs a mediated search for the end user. One of the more important services provided by special libraries is the time savings for the end user that results when the librarians perform mediated searches.

From a design perspective, the issue is simple: does the library's OPAC provide a seamless interface to these commercial database resources or does the user need to learn how to use several different user interfaces to search multiple online databases? A second and related issue is whether to provide access to these databases from the library's OPAC or its home page (or perhaps using an Intranet) or some combination.

Indexes to eJournals

Some journals are published in print only, some in electronic format only, and some are a combination of the two. If a journal is published electronically (sometimes called an eJournal), its full-text contents can be sent to one or more eJournal search engines. Some of these eJournal indexes include: OCLC First Search, EbscoHost, and Faxon's Information Quest. Typically, a library pays for a license to enable its users to access this electronic journal database. Besides being able to search the full text of several thousand eJournals, an individual using one of these services can sign up for an alert service. The user of an eJournal search engine is typically informed if the library subscribes to a print or electronic version of the journal. If the library is a subscriber, the individual can then view and/or print the journal article of interest. If the library is not a subscriber, the user has the option of paying for a copy of the article to be delivered normally via fax.

The Internet

The Internet has been described as a "constellation of communicating devices." This loose interconnection of networks provides links between a great many people (estimated to be in excess of 400 million in April 2002), organizations, and information resources. The Internet can be distinguished by its capabilities, which are primarily: Simple Mail Transport Protocol (SMTP), used to send and receive email; telnet; and File Transfer Protocol (FTP); and software that combines these basic functions. The Web is an example of software and documents that most often reside on the Internet (but is not exclusively constrained only to the Internet—witness the rise in the development of Intranets) and links users to vast amounts of "donated" or shared content.

It is this tremendous amount of connectivity that is the driving force that attracts people to the Internet and led to Metcalfe's Law: The utility or usefulness of a network equals the square of the number of users.[5] Thus, as a network grows, the value of being a part of it grows exponentially, while the cost per user remains the same or even declines. OCLC, with its large and growing customer base, provides a classic example of Metcalfe's Law within the library community.

It is often mistakenly assumed that the Internet and the World Wide Web are one and the same. The World Wide Web (and its collection of hypertext documents) is merely one of many software applications that use the Internet, although it is clearly the most visible and rapidly evolving. For millions of people, the Internet's primary use is e-mail (using SMTP), file transfer (using FTP) and instant messaging which are not part of the Web.

There are several thousand Web-based search engines, some that focus on very narrow specialty interests and others that are designed to provide the broadest possible coverage. When an individual uses one of these search engines, he or she is usually completely overwhelmed with the search results—numbering in the thousands or tens of thousands of Web sites. Clearly, from an information retrieval perspective, this is a classic example of very low precision and very high recall. Some search engines rely on a ranked-order retrieval tool to provide the sites that are most likely to meet the user's needs as expressed in his or her search request.

Recent research on actual Web searching found that most people use few search terms (60 percent of users use one or two words), few modify their search results or use advanced search options. The most frequent queries are about recreation and entertainment.[6] Most users of a Web search engine will not go beyond the results of the first page (making a judgment that one or two Web sites are "good enough," or becoming so depressed with the overwhelming number of responses that they simply leave).

While the Internet search engines provide access to breadth of Web sites, some Web sites provide access to a substantial number of records or documents (a depth of resources) that is not reflected in any search engine. BrightPlanet.com has called these content-rich Web sites the "Deep Web"—a reservoir of Internet content that is 500 times larger than the known breadth of the World Wide Web.[7] More than 100,000 deep Web sites exist, containing nearly 550 billion individual documents stored on some 7,500 terabytes of disk space. Examples of deep Web sites include NASA, the National Oceanic and Atmospheric Administration (NOAA), the High Energy Astrophysics Science Archive Research Center (HEASARC), the U.S. Patent and Trademark Office, Alexandria Digital Library, the Journal Storage Project (JSTOR; an online archive of scholarly jounals), 10K Search Wizard, the Securities and Exchange Commission's (SEC) EDGAR, the U.S. Census, CancerNet, the Library of Congress, and many more.

In addition, there have been several efforts to identify Web sites that provide access to quality information. Among these efforts are OCLC's Cooperative Online Resource Catalog (CORC), Web Scout, and Internet Public Library. In the case of OCLC's CORC Project, bibliographic records are being constructed that contain links to a uniform resourcer locator (URL). (A Web site's URL is stored in the 856 field of a MARC record.) A library can add multiple CORC records into its catalog so users will become aware of resources outside the library's collection that might have value to them.

APPROACHES TO SEARCHING

Given the plethora of information resources that someone can consult when he or she has an information need, it is not surprising that there are several approaches that can be followed. These choices include:

- **Sequential searching**. The user selects a specific information resource and, using the application user interface, conducts a search (the assumption being that the user has online access to the information resources). In some cases, for example, when searching an external database, it may be necessary to select one or more databases before the search is initiated. To the user attempting to conduct the information search, this process is both time consuming and frustrating. To be effective, the user must know not only what information is included in a particular database but he or she must also master the applicable user interface and search capabilities of each database and information resource. Furthermore, the controlled vocabulary of one database will not be the same in a different database. So, the end user could do well searching one database and be perplexed as to why they are not doing so well in another.

  In some respects, the experience is analogous to visiting a candy store—so many choices and not enough information about the ingredients in each candy bar to decide which is best. The user must also keep track of what unique records or documents have been retrieved so he or she can manually eliminate these records or documents from the results of future search efforts. To perform a fairly thorough search of these diverse information resources, the individual must search several times across several different databases or repositories.

- **Simultaneous searching of multiple information resources**. Using this approach, the user would enter a search, and the system would perform several searches simultaneously. Implicit in this approach is that the system would automatically identify databases, adjust for language, and detect and eliminate duplicate records or documents from the result set presented to the user. There are several ways in which this could be accomplished:

  Topical approach. Starting from a general-purpose search screen, the user would select a subject category (the system might display the associated databases that would be searched unless deselected by the user or the databases could remain hidden). The search is then performed in all of the target information resources and databases, and the integrated result set is presented to the user.

List approach. The user would be presented with a list of all possible information resources and databases that could be searched (in alphabetical order or grouped by subject category). The user would select one or more information resources or databases, and the system would initiate simultaneous searching for all of the user's choices. An integrated retrieval set, with duplicates eliminated, would then be presented to the user.

Recommendation approach. After the user has selected a specific database or information resource, the system could suggest other relevant resources or databases that could be of value. Depending upon the user's choice, the system could proceed with a single resource or database search or proceed with a simultaneous search. To conduct a thorough search, it may be necessary for the user to conduct several separate searches. Yet, we must not lose sight of a basic element of human nature. Zipf's "Principle of Least Effort" states, "Each individual will adopt a course of action that will involve the expenditure of the probable least average (least effort) of his work."[8] Within the library community, "least effort" has been restated as Mooers's Law: "An information retrieval system will tend not to be used whenever it is more painful and troublesome for a customer to have information than for him not to have it."[9] In other words, the amateur searcher is neither persistent nor consistent in his or her searching behavior!

Regardless of the approach taken, one of the most significant issues is to determine the extent to which the library's online catalog is, or should be, a repository of records with links to information resources outside of the library's own collection. Some ILS vendors provide an optional module that provides full-text indexing of important documents. The library can also add records to its catalog with links to quality Internet sites. So in a way, the library's OPAC begins to become a central index to a variety of information resources. But the OPAC can never be an index to the large number of external databases or an eJournal index for a number of technical, administrative, and financial reasons.

While the OPAC, with a single user interface to a plethora of resources, might be the vehicle of choice for some libraries, others have decided that a library Web "portal" can offer access to the OPAC, or local physical holdings, as well as licensed databases and Web sites, and countless other resources.

Despite the approach taken to conduct a search, the user appreciates being able to discover what records or documents that were identified during a search as being of potential value, are actually found in the library's collection. This link is created and maintained by some vendor-provided systems; in other cases, a database provider will maintain a list of the periodicals that are owned or licensed by the library.

MAINTAINING THE DATABASE

The library's bibliographic and authority databases are obviously an important asset because the records in these databases form the heart of the online public access catalog. That catalog is used by the library's patrons to perform searches that point them in the right direction to find what Arlene Taylor calls an information package[10] (the actual book, journal, image, audio or video file, or other library materials) that will meet their information needs.

A favorite, tongue-in-cheek definition of a library catalog is that "it is a place where bibliographic records get lost alphabetically." The quality of the library's database is also important because misspellings will cause records to become lost alphabetically. Jeffrey Beall has developed one quick test of the library's database. His Dirty Database Test[11] uses ten misspelled words (shown in Table 3-5). Try searching for these ten misspelled words in your library's catalog. If a search of these words retrieves more than 30 or 40 records, then the library's database probably needs to be cleaned up because records are getting lost "alphabetically."

Table 3-5. Dirty Database Test

Febuary	Grammer
Guatamala	Recieve
Mission	Wensday
Goverment	Seperate
Fransisco	Conditons

Rather than using Beall's ten words, some libraries may wish to substitute frequently misspelled words that more typically reflect their collection's subject specialization. For example, a law library might select misspelled legal terms, while a medical library would use medical terminology typos.

Initially, a library can provide a copy of their bibliographic records to a vendor, such as Library Technologies, Inc., OCLC, and others who will clean up the bibliographic records and provide a copy of all the corresponding authority records linked to the bibliographic headings. This cleaning process will typically convert abbreviations to full words, replace obsolete headings with the current authorized headings (the library has the option of keeping local headings) and automatically fixing the MARC record based on a series of consistency checks of the library's record for compliance with the MARC standard. The cost for this service is modest compared to the value derived from the linked records. The bibliographic and authority records are then returned to the library to be loaded into the ILS. Re-loading the clean bibliographic and authority records is usually called an "overlay process," and the majority of ILS vendors provide options that allow the library to control this process.

The library is then confronted with the task of maintaining the currency of the authority control files. There are two options for this task. First, the library can contract with a vendor who will receive the bibliographic records added to the library's database in the last week or month and clean them up. The vendor will return the clean bibliographic records as well as the corresponding authority records. In addition, the vendor will alert the library by forwarding a copy of all authority records that have been updated by the Library of Congress. A complementary activity that adds real value to the authority control database, although it clearly adds to the cost of cataloging, is for the library to review the logs of failed OPAC searches. These words and phrases, arranged in alphabetical form in a report, allow the cataloging and reference librarians to see what "entry vocabulary search terms" are being used by their patrons that retrieve no records. Adding some of these words and phrases as cross-references to existing authority control records will mean that the next time a patron uses the same terminology, they will be directed to relevant materials to be found in the library. The lack of authority records for names not in the Library of Congress Name Authority file is a growing problem.

Enhanced Records

Adding additional content to a bibliographic record will improve the end user's chances for success, because the number of words that can be used to retrieve a record has been increased. Pauline Atherton first articulated the concept of enhanced records in 1978. The additional content for the enhanced records might come from the table of contents, an abstract, a book jacket summary, entries from the index, or material from the Preface.[12]

While the library can create its own enhanced MARC records, it also has the option of contracting the project out to a commercial vendor. In these instances, the library sends its bibliographic records to a vendor, such as Blackwell North America, who then matches the library's records against the enhanced record database. The cost is about $1 per matched record. The enhanced bibliographic records are then returned to the library where they are overlaid on to the existing bibliographic records.

More important, the user will experience better search results, as documented in a study by Peis and Fernandez-Molina, which showed that both precision and recall will improve simultaneously when the user is searching enhanced records compared to traditional MARC-only records. (See Figure 3-4.)[13]

Record Output

A library may wish to output a subset of their bibliographic database or the complete database itself. The library may want to share its records with other libraries involved in a union catalog project or for other projects. Most ILS vendors provide a utility that will allow the library to create an export file of MARC records. In some cases, the library can include copy or item information, or both, within the MARC record itself.

Besides MARC, the library may wish to export its bibliographic records in an Extensible Markup Language (XML) format for use in Web-based access tools. Some LIS vendors provide this as an option; in other cases, the library may need to convert the records from MARC to XML using conversion software.[14] Such software will move bibliographic records from MARC to XML and from XML to MARC.

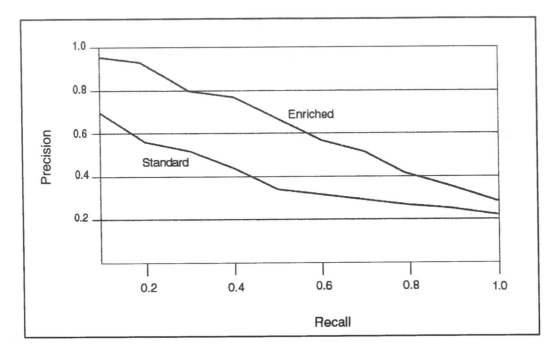

Figure 3-4. Utility of enhanced MARC Records

The library may wish to move patron data and other types of data between a campus student registration system, an accounting system, or other application. To preserve the integrity and accuracy of the data in both applications, an Application Programming Interface (API) is typically used. An API is a communication protocol that specifies that data sent to an application or received from an application adhere to a prescribed format. Either application's vendors can assume responsibility for maintaining the API, as both applications will be enhanced and will evolve over time, requiring changes to the API. Optionally, the library can assume this API maintenance responsibility if it has access to the necessary programming talent.

In some cases, the library, as a part of a data-mining project, can use the extracted data. A data-mining project increases the understanding of the relationships that exist between various databases. Thus, the library may wish to explore how its collection is being used, who is using selected portions of the collections, and so forth.

SUMMARY

As shown in this chapter, the ILS design is crucial not only to determining what flexibility a library has in controlling the software, but also in determining what functional capabilities exist as a part of the system. The wide diversity of information resources presents a unique challenge to a library in determining how much of a role it can play in assisting its users to access the desired information.

The maintenance of a library's database is central in determining how effective it is in responding to the information needs of its users.

NOTES

1. For a thorough and comprehensive review of the issues of index construction and database design, consult Michael D. Cooper's *Design of Library Automated Systems: File Structures, Data Structures, and Tools.* New York: John Wiley, 1996.

2. Carol A. Mandel and Judith Herschman. "Online Subject Access—Enhancing the Library Catalog." *The Journal of Academic Librarianship*, 9 (3), 1983, pp. 148–55.

3. Joe Matthews. "The Value of Information in Library Catalogs." *Information Outlook*, 4 (7), July 2000, pp. 18–24.

4. Christine Borgman. "Why Are Online Catalogs Still Hard to Use?" *Journal of the American Society of Information Science*, 47 (7), 1996, pp. 493–503.

5. Robert Metcalfe's Law was first published at George Gilder's technology-oriented Web site available at: www.gildertech.com/public/telecosm.html.

6. More than 1 million search queries were analyzed. See Amanda Spink, Wolfram Dietmar, Major B. J. Jansen, and Tefko Saracevic. "Searching for the Web: The Public and Their Queries." *Journal of the American Society for Information Science and Technology*, 52 (3), February 1, 2001, pp. 226–34.

7. Michael K. Bergman. *The Deep Web: Surfacing Hidden Value.* A White Paper. Sioux Falls, SD: BrightPlanet.com, July 2000.

8. G. K. Zipf. *Human Behavior and the Principle of Least Effort.* Cambridge, MA: Addison-Wesley, 1949.

9. Calvin N. Mooers. "Mooers's Law; or Why Some Retrieval Systems Are Used and Others Are Not." Editorial, *American Documentation*, 11 (3), July 1960, p. i.

10. Arlene G. Taylor. *The Organization of Information.* Englewood, CO: Libraries Unlimited, 1999.

11. Jeffrey Beall. "Dirty Data Test." *American Libraries*, 22 (3), March 1991, p. 197.

12. Pauline Atherton. *Books Are for Use: Final Report of the Subject Access Project to the Council on Library Resources.* Washington, DC: Council on Library Resources, 1978.

13. E. Peis and J. C. Fernandez-Molina. "Enrichment of Bibliographic Records of Online Catalogs Through OCR and SGML Technology." *Information Technology and Libraries*, 17 (3), March 1998, pp. 161–72.

14. MARC to XML conversion is available from OCLC and Stanford at http://xmlmarc.stanford.edu.

Chapter 4

Open Systems

COMMERCIAL SOURCES OF SOFTWARE

Third party companies, now usually referred to as independent software vendors (ISVs), started developing computer software that they could license and support. In the 1970s and 1980s, these programs were not expensive, especially when compared to the price of a mainframe computer. The ISV had to make an important decision about which hardware platforms its software would run on, as the computer equipment and operating system were proprietary. These systems were typically minicomputer-based networks of dumb terminals.

The larger and more powerful computer firms maintained their hold over customers by the proprietary nature of the computer equipment, operating systems, utilities, and programming language compilers. Information technology (IT) staff within an organization are familiar with the tools and capabilities of a particular set of hardware and software programs. Once the customer was "locked in," that is, the switching costs to move from manufacturer A to manufacture B were so high that the vast majority of customers would not switch, computer manufacturers were able to charge very high prices for system support and upgrades.

However, there were three factors affecting the marketplace:

1. The constant state of price/performance improvements, as illustrated by Moore's Law, which states that the performance of a computer chip will double every 18 months, while price remains constant.

2. Starting with the personal computer, but moving into the mainframe and minicomputer arena, as organizations migrated to client/server architecture, computer equipment became more like a commodity. And with a commodity, the customer is able to make a selection based almost solely on price.

3. Customers' increasing demands that computer hardware and software be developed that embrace and support open standards.

The net impact of these trends is that the customer is empowered with choice!

Another group of companies came into existence to help an organization integrate computer hardware, networking software, and application(s) software. These firms were known as value-added resellers (VAR). Within the library community, examples of VARs include Epixtech, Endeavor, EOS International, Innovative, and Sirsi, among others. The VARs guaranteed that their combination of hardware and software would work as advertised and meet the performance expectations in the marketplace. In fact, few individuals really appreciate the complexity and sophistication embodied in an ILS, as exemplified by the size of the programming source code.

The VAR purchases computer hardware and software wholesale, integrates it, and then sells it to the final customer at retail. The difference in prices, commonly referred to as margins, is what allowed the VAR to pay its employees and generate a profit. Yet, over time, the margins for all computer equipment declined and the prices for all kinds of software began to increase. According to the most recent article on the library automation marketplace in the annual *Library Journal*,[1] library vendors receive, on average, 12 percent of their revenue from hardware, while software license fees account for 47 percent and maintenance/service fees are 27 percent (see Figure 4-1). In the 1970s and 1980s, the hardware component could account for 40 to 50 percent of total revenues. Similarly, the importance of maintenance and service revenues has increased as the number of customers for a particular vendor also increases.

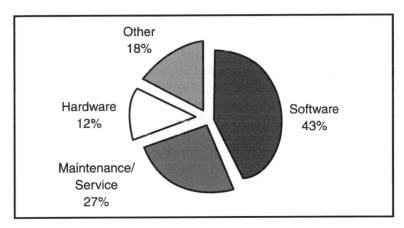

Figure 4-1. Source of Revenues for VARs

Commercial firms make an investment when developing a software product or application. The source code for this operating system, software application, or utility is considered a valuable asset. In some cases, the software may receive a patent, but in almost all cases, the software is copyrighted to protect its intellectual property. Customers purchase a license that gives them the right to use, but not own, the software. Also, customers typically purchase software support and maintenance, which entitles them to receive bug fixes and assistance from the vendor to resolve a problem or learn how to use a particular software feature. After a software product has been through a number of releases, it is not unusual for as much as 75 percent of available programming resources to be spent on maintenance.

For obvious business reasons, an ISV wants to develop software that will appeal to a large group of potential customers. For the customer, a large network means more choices and more support. This is typified by the many organizations that switched from the Macintosh to Windows-based PCs (sometimes called Wintel, a contraction of Microsoft Windows and Intel-based PCs). These people migrated because of the larger network of hardware, peripherals, software, and people who were experienced with this technology. Customers receive greater value when they are able to use a dominant technology because they are less likely to be locked in. While it's true that customers are, in fact, locked in when using a Windows-based solution, they do have more options than if they choose a competitor.

The vast majority of third-party ISVs clearly understand that they need to listen carefully to their customers so product enhancements are included in future releases and the software better meets the needs of their customers. Similarly, the ISV must also provide software that has been thoroughly tested and released with as few bugs as possible (fewer bugs means fewer support calls received by the ISV).

However, when bugs are discovered, as they invariably will be, they must be fixed and included in either a software patch (small updates to the software that fix one or more bugs) or a future release of the software. Note: increasingly, ISVs are making executable patches, as well as new versions of the software available for downloading to a customer's server using the Internet. This means that the library is able to install the new software and benefit from the bug fixes or new features provided in the latest release of the software much sooner.

Complexity of Commercial Software

The complexity of commercial software, as expressed by the number of specific functional features, set-up options, or the total lines of programming code can be considerable. For example, most library automation vendors have systems that run on minicomputers or larger servers, and the total lines of code will range from 500,000 to more than 1 million.[2] The learning curve for any new programmer to learn and understand the structure of the source code, database table structures, and the workflow associated with a given set of functional features can be considerable—in most cases, probably more than four to six months. Thus, an automation vendor needs to have a team of programmers that is able to assume the responsibility for continually enhancing the product, as well as fixing the bugs that crop up on a continuing basis.

Size of the Commercial Marketplace

The commercial ISV marketplace is large by any measure. The numbers of software packages that are available are numerous and cover a broad range of horizontal applications (e.g., accounting, human resources, and so forth that would appeal to a large number of businesses and organizations) as well as vertical-niche market applications (e.g., legal, medical, or libraries). ISVs number in the tens of thousands, from quite large (annual revenues in the billions of dollars) to quite small (a programmer working out of his home or garage). The total annual revenues for all ISVs are estimated to be tens of billions of dollars.

Size of the Commercial Library Automation Marketplace

The library automated system marketplace, with estimated annual revenues of $440 million, is very small in terms of global spending on ISV software products, but relatively large given library budgets.[3] The annual library automation marketplace article that appears in *Library Journal* typically identifies 25 to 30 vendors who are active in the market. Usually the market is segmented by type of computer: personal computers within the school library market and the client/server-based systems for academic, public, and special libraries.

OPEN SYSTEMS

An open system is a design philosophy that is antithetical to solutions designed to be proprietary. The idea is that organizations and libraries will be able to build a combination of components and deliver services that cross several vendors' offerings. For example, a library might have an integrated library system from one of the major vendors, while using another vendor's OPAC because it can be easily customized to provide the look-and-feel the library wants. Alternatively, the library may use an open source software product developed by another library or develop one or more components themselves. Clearly, such an approach requires an experienced team of talented individuals to provide the necessary integration to make this approach work well.

The issue and importance of standards will be addressed in greater detail in a subsequent chapter. However, it is important to note that industry standards can embrace standards that are vendor neutral (e.g., TCP/IP, as well as proprietary products, such as Microsoft NT, Microsoft Office, Oracle's RDBMS, and so forth). While the prospect of building open systems is attractive, in reality, an open system built on proprietary products gives some flexibility, but the library remains wedded to the vendor of a proprietary product in many ways. Aside from the seemingly yearly increases for support licenses for these products, the library system vendor or library must continually upgrade to the latest release of these open products.

For example, if the system is using an Oracle database or a licensed search engine, the library (or its vendor) must stay current with the latest release of these products because most vendors of licensed software products will only support an earlier release of its product for a short time.

As libraries move to replace their older (often character-based systems) with the next generation LIS, the need to provide a wide range of services to their patrons means that libraries will want systems that are more open. Libraries will want systems that can interface with a campus or parent organization's accounting system, purchasing system, student registration system, and so forth. Indeed, some libraries will want to be able to select one portion of a system from Vendor A and another portion from Vendor B and have the two systems "talk" to one another (be able to exchange a variety of data).

It is increasingly clear that for most organizations, and libraries, XML will be the glue that binds two or more systems together. XML, which was designed specifically for Web documents, is a smaller version of the older and more intricate Standard Generalized Markup Language (SGML). XML allows organizations to define, transmit, validate, and interpret data between applications and databases. XML's strength is that it provides structure to the data, yet it is not a language or a presentation system. XML separates the data itself from how the data is displayed or used in an application. Thus, the data itself can then be more easily organized, programmed, edited, and exchanged between Web sites, applications, and devices. XML and its associated Document Type Definition (DTD) will play an important role in exchanging information between applications of interest to libraries.

A standardized way of describing XML document structures and adding data types to XML data fields is defined using a XML Schema Definition (XSD). The XSD standard will facilitate cross-organizational document exchange and data verification. Tools for converting XML DTDs to XSD will assist the information exchange.

XML Query provides the capabilities to create queries on collections of XML files that might contain unstructured data (e.g., documents and Web pages). XML Query provides a set of searching capabilities that is comparable to those found with Structured Query Language (SQL) used when searching a RDBMS.

OPEN SOURCE SOFTWARE

After the personal computer was introduced in the early 1980s, many programmers made their programs available in one of two ways: freeware and shareware.

◆ Freeware were programs that were available without charge and could be freely distributed to friends, relatives, co-workers, and others, but not modified. The source code is *not* included with the freeware software. If a problem developed with the freeware software, it was up to the user to choose another software application to replace the freeware.

◆ Shareware was software that could also be distributed freely. However, the developer typically placed a message within the program telling users that if they liked the program and used it on a regular basis, they should send a suggested contribution to the software developer. This allowed the software developer to earn a living and, in most cases, to provide support to customers that experienced a problem. Shareware is seldom accompanied by the source code and is not free software.

The concept of open source systems is simultaneously appealing and frightening to consider. If software is open, then programmers can read, modify, and redistribute the source code for the software, and as a result the software evolves. Any number of people can fix bugs, adapt the software to better meet their needs, or improve it and then share their efforts with a larger community of interested parties. Because any number of people can be involved in making enhancements, the speed with which this open software evolves and improves can be quite astonishing. Some have suggested that open source software is similar to the peer review process used to strengthen the process of scholarly communication.

Yet, if the source code is open, then what should a library do if the software needs fixing and no one on the staff has the talent to do so? This concern illustrates the frightening aspect of open source software.

Systems built on open standards have been gaining momentum for the last 20 years, especially among those in the technical culture involved in building the Internet and the World Wide Web. Thus, everyone involved in sending emails or using the Web may likely be using open source software, as well as software based on standards. In fact, there is a plethora of open or standards-based software involved in all of the possible activities on the Internet.

The Open Source Initiative has developed a definition of open source that includes the following elements:

1. **Free Redistribution**. Open source software can be sold or given away and does not require a royalty or other fee.

2. **Source Code**. The program's source code and compiled code should be easily accessible, preferably by downloading it from the Internet. Intentionally obfuscating source code is a no-no.

3. **Derived Works**. Modifications and derived works must be allowed, and these modifications can be freely distributed.

4. **The Integrity of the Author's Source Code**. The license can require that modifications be uniquely identified and kept separate from the original base software.

5. **No Discrimination Against Persons or Groups**.

6. **No Discrimination Against Fields or Endeavor**. The type of organization or how the software would be used cannot restrict use of an open source program.

7. **Distribution of License**. Additional licensees are not required as the software is redistributed.

8. **License Must Not Be Specific to a Product**. Use of an open source program cannot be dependent on use of other software.

9. **License Must Not Contaminate Other Software**. The licensee of open source software cannot place restrictions on other software.

Some better-known open-source software products include Linux, Netscape, and Apache. A range of other open-source products and projects are shown in Table 4-1. The success of these products demonstrates that it is possible for some open source software projects to achieve "commercial quality."

Table 4-1. Open Source Software Products

Type of Software	Products
Operating Systems	Linux (GNU/Linux) Free BSD (Berkeley Standard Distribution) Open BSD NetBSD GNU/Hurd
Utilities	GNU Utilities Multi Router Traffic Grapher (MRTG) Snort Intrusion Detection System Junkbuster Majordomo Cron Sendmail
Languages	GNU C/C++ Perl Python Tel
Windowing Systems	X Window System
Desktop Environment	GNOME (GNU Network Object Model Environment) KDE (K Desktop Environment) GNUStep Xfce
Web Browser	Netscape 6 – Mozilla
Office Suites	Open Office K Office
Productivity Applications	ABI Word GNU IMAGE Manipulation Program Jabber Instant Messaging

Table 4-1—Continued

Type of Software	Products
Server-Type Software	Samba Apache PhP
Relational Database Management	MySQL PostgreSQL
Object Oriented Database	Zope
Library Applications	Free Reserves (www.lib.edu/san/freereserves) Prospero (document delivery module that complements Ariel) Jake (a journal finding aid)

Unless there is a large cadre of programmers willing to take on a large project, the utility of the source code probably declines with the size of the computer program. For the individual programmer, a computer program above a certain size will become incomprehensible.

To illustrate the potential of open source software, consider the success of Linux (pronounced "LYNN–ucks"). This operating system variant of Unix was started by Linus Torvalds while he was a student at the University of Helsinki in 1991 and, as of mid-2001, had more than 1.5 million lines of code. In a relatively short time, Linux has achieved real acceptance in the market because:

- It is trusted in mission critical environments.

- It is a best-of-breed variant of Unix that outperforms other commercial versions of Unix.

- It is the only Unix operating system to gain market share in recent years.

- New versions of Linux can appear quite quickly to respond to a particular security threat or bug.

Factors Influencing Open Source Software

There are a number of factors that have an impact on the development of open source software. Among these are:

♦ **Piracy**. Obviously, many individuals engage in the piracy of copy protected and closed source software. For some that engage in piracy, it is the price of a product that encourages them. For others (in the hacker community), it is the challenge to defeat the copy protection technology of a software program that is the thrill. Given the piracy that exists on the Internet, this fact can be leveraged by giving away software in order to capture a dominant share of the market. This is the approach that was employed by Netscape and subsequently followed by Microsoft when they distributed the Web browser for free.

According to Conner and Rumelt, if a firm chooses to protect its software, profits will fall depending upon the success of the pirates. The stigma of stealing falls as the number of pirates increase, lowering costs for all pirates.[4] Yet, the utility of the software increases as the number of paying customers and pirates increases. If there is a viable option to stealing (i.e., if there is an open source competing product), then pirates and real customers will move away from the copy protected software to the free software. Thus, Conner and Rumelt suggest making the price of the software free and consequently capturing the dominant share of the market.

With a large market comes the demand for additional complementary software and services. Marc Andreesen, one of the founders of Netscape, suggests that "If you get ubiquity, you get a lot of options . . . One of the fundamental lessons is that market share now equals revenue later. With dominant market share you can just plain win."[5]

♦ **Network Connections**. The existence of the Internet facilitates the network of programmers that can come together to work on an open source software project. And the programmers can be individuals interested in the "techie" side of things, users of the software who are willing to invest in the project, as well as selected businesses who may see their participation as leading to an economic gain. And the larger the network of participation the fewer the bugs since more eyes are examining the source code. The proponent's claim that the resulting software is best of breed since the developers and customers who are participating in the project will focus their efforts on what works well.

Thus, the Internet is used to spread an open source program, and is used to maintain and improve the base source code. To some extent, the free distribution of open source software and its continuing enhancement is similar to a "gift culture," where members of the society compete by giving things away.[6] Among the participating programmers there is both collaboration, as well as competition that works to improve the software in a relatively short period of time. Programmers who do not make a contribution are ignored by those whose efforts move the project ahead.

An examination of the contributions of programmers to Linux is revealing. The vast majority of open source developers only work on one or two computer programs, while only four developers had made more than 20 contributions.[7] Clearly the contributions of developers to Linux are quite broad-based with slightly more than one-third being European and nearly one-fourth of the developers working for a commercial firm.

For-Profit Firms Support Open Source Software

Those involved in the open source software movement have recognized that for-profit firms need to be involved, especially if the open source product is to reach a broader market. A lot of businesses and organizations want to know that they can count on a firm to provide support, training, and other implementation assistance rather than attempting to hire and retain knowledgeable programmers themselves. In reality, the open source industry is a crucial alliance between developers, for-profit firms, and the users. And as more users adopt the use of Linux, then a need for complimentary products increases fueling the continuing development of the core product, as well as the complementary ones.

Interestingly enough, the for-profit firm must be able to attract and retain knowledgeable programmers who at one level want to participate in continuing to enhance and improve the open source software, while at the same time agreeing to work for a for-profit firm. Historically, there has been considerable tension between for-profit firms and programmers who participate in open source software projects.

Reasons to Open Source

There are several reasons why open source software might be attractive to those involved with its development. Among these are:

- **Stretch a Budget**. Those involved in the development of Apache, a Web server, were programmers primarily from small independent Internet Service Providers (ISPs). By banding together and working to develop an open source product, they were able to avoid paying operating system license fees. Starting with software originally developed at the National Center Supercomputing Applications additional patches were added (thus, it was called *a patchy server* or Apache). Some industry analysts suggest that the Apache Web server is used by more than 50 percent of all Web sites in the World.

- **Loss Leader/Market Dominance**. A company might be interested in distributing open source software for free in order to capture a dominant share of the market. For example, this is the strategy that both Netscape and Microsoft employed to distribute their Web browser.

- **Supporter/Distributor**. A company such as Red Hat would invest in creating a brand name and a Web site with open source information and software resources so that it would be able to create a market for future add-on products and services. The lost software license revenue is made up with support and other service revenues.

- ◆ **Branding**. Establishing a brand name will provide to the business community and other organizations the perception that they can rely on the for-profit firm to provide services for open source software.

- ◆ **Frosting**. The company does not sell the software but does sell hardware. The open source software thus becomes an attractive lure, the "frosting on the cake," to increase the market size.

- ◆ **Content**. A company might give away the software in an attempt to sign people up for a subscription to its content. Content publishers and content aggregators use this approach with some effectiveness.

Size of Open Source Marketplace

Linux, a variant of Unix, is predominantly used for single-use application servers in the Internet infrastructure market. In addition to the Internet infrastructure; Linux is seeing significant growth in the areas of server farms, embedded systems, and thin client applications. For example, Google.com, the Internet search engine service, uses a 4,000 Linux machine cluster rather than a mainframe computer environment. As shown in Figure 4-2, most organizations running Linux servers are using it to provide Internet infrastructure database, email, file/print sharing, system management, and network management.

Linux is not much of a force as a desktop operating system given the dominance of Microsoft Office and the relatively complex user interface. Unfortunately, two competing desktop graphical user interface open source products, KDE and Gnome, make the likelihood of Linux capturing more of this marketplace difficult.

Rather than taking market share from Microsoft, Linux is actually pushing into the Unix market share of the major computer hardware manufacturers—Compaq (formerly DEC) Unix, Hewlett Packard (HP-UX), IBM (AIX), SCO (UnixWare), and Sun's Solaris. And some analysts suggest that the total Linux server market will exceed $5 billion by 2003—that's a lot of revenue from a "free" product![8]

The majority of this revenue is going to the for-profit firms that were established to provide support and service to those organizations that wish to use Linux but do not have the in-house expertise to provide for its support. Among the more prominent of these firms are Red Hat Networks, Cobalt Networks, Andover.net, and VA Linux Systems. Some have suggested that Linux will experience the fragmentation that befell Unix, although this is not likely to happen, as Linus Torvalds must approve all changes to the Linux kernel, called the Linux Standard Base. Also, any enhancements or extensions of Linux are typically released outside the Linux kernel. It is more likely that Linux will fragment according to the different devices that it runs on (i.e., servers, desktops, and embedded devices).

Interestingly, several automated library system vendors whose systems run on Unix have announced their support of Linux, as one of many variants of Unix that their system will operate with.

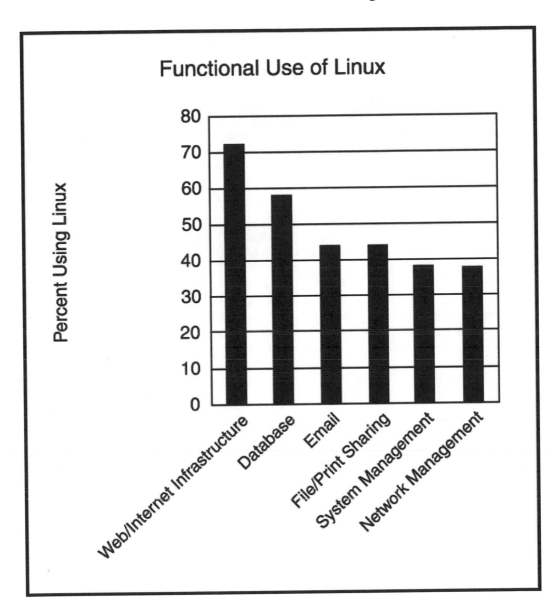

Figure 4-2. Functional Use of Linux

Open Source Library Systems

One of the earliest efforts to provide access to open source software within the library community was when several software developers, working on the Z39.50 protocol, made their software available for others to use without restrictions. Z39.50 is a communications protocol that retrieves bibliographic information from one automated system and then uses the MARC record at the local system (e.g., imports the record for cataloging purposes and displays the record at an OPAC).

An informal group of developers, called the Z39.50 Implementers Group or ZIG, came together on a regular basis to talk about the issues and problems they were encountering when implementing Z39.50. The ZIG continues to meet at various locations throughout the World on a quarterly basis.

There are several open source software projects within the library community. Some of these projects flourish and some wither on the vine. If interested in these and other related open source projects, visit http://www.oss4lib.org for the latest information. Some of the more visible projects developing an integrated library system are:

♦ **Koha**. Koha means gift in Maori. Developed in New Zealand by the Horowhenua Library Trust and Katipo Communications, Ltd., Koha provides an integrated library system with cataloging, circulation, acquisitions, and OPAC modules. The system runs on Linux, uses the MySQL database, and is written in Perl for the Web interface. The system uses Telnet to increase the speed of circulation-related transactions.

♦ **OpenBook**. OpenBook is an open-source automated library system developed by the Technology Resource Foundation, located in Seattle, Washington. The software has more than 20,000 lines of Hypertext Preprocessor (PHP) code. PHP Hypertext Preprocessor is a server-side, HTML embedded scripting language used to create dynamic Web pages. In an HTML document, PHP script (similar syntax to that of Perl or C) is enclosed within special PHP tags.

OpenBook consists of three modules: the patron search module (OPAC), the cataloging module, and the circulation module. In future releases, it may also include an acquisition module. All modules are Web-based and are multi-lingual user capable, with the initial release supporting English, Spanish, and French. OpenBook also supports MARC21 bibliographic fields for importing into its database, including basic serials support and authority control for author and subject. The cataloging client will include Z39.50 searching capabilities to allow for copy cataloging against OCLC or other larger union databases. Future releases may also support Z39.50 searches against the OpenBook database. The targeted audience is small- to medium-sized public and school libraries in the United States and throughout the world.

♦ **OCLC's Office of Research**. OCLC has several open source projects that they are working to support. These include:

1. Advanced Library Collection Management Environment (ALCME)
2. Pears, a text storage and indexing system

3. GWEN, a database search engine with an interface to Pears

4. dbutils, a set of utilities for database programming

5. SiteSearch

◆ **Freeway Library System Project (FLSP)**. The Swedish Library Company (Svenska Biblioteksbolaget) started developing an open source library system using the relational database MySQL and the free search engine PLWeb/CPL. The system runs on Windows NT. Currently, a WebOPAC and Z39.50 server (version 3) have been completed using Microsoft's Transaction Server software. Other modules (Cataloging, Circulation, Interlibrary Loan, and Booking) will be released in the future. Acquisitions and Serials modules are not being planned at this time.

◆ **Avanti**. Begun in 1998 by Peter Schlumpf, Avanti is designed to be a simple solution to automating small- and medium-sized libraries and requires minimal technical expertise to install and use. Avanti uses Java and TCP/IP (which means that the software will run on multiple hardware platforms) and will incorporate both MARC and Z39.50 standards as modules and interfaces but these standards will not be used as part of the underlying design. Avanti is being developed and a series of releases are expected to occur during 2002.

◆ **MyLibrary@NCState**. The North Carolina State University library has released the source code to its portal application called MyLibrary@NCState. This software allows the user to create a customized gateway to general and discipline-specific databases, electronic journals, current awareness features, personal bookmarks, and the library's catalog. The software runs on a Unix machine, uses the MySQL relational database, and supports both Perl and C programming languages. Note, however, that the software is not plug and play but will require some modification to be integrated into a local library setting.

Hidden Costs

Just as there is no such thing as a free lunch, there clearly are costs that will be incurred by a library attempting to implement an open source software system. Among these costs are:

◆ An appropriately sized server or multiple servers to support the operating system required by the open source application software.

◆ Support for the hardware and operating system.

◆ Support for the database.

◆ Support for the open source application software, if desired by the library and provided by a for-profit firm or coordinating organization.

◆ Consulting assistance to load the software, import bibliographic records and other installation assistance.

- One or more programmers on staff to implement the system and make changes to the software (based on library needs or to correct a software bug).

- Library staff member to assume responsibility for maintaining the automated system, including all of the organizations that will provide support.

SUMMARY

What most independent software vendors recognized long ago is that most people are users rather than builders, hackers (in the positive sense of the word), or tinkerers. People are interested in learning how to use a software product and knowing what it will do for them (i.e., make them more productive, provide a form of entertainment [game software], and so on.). Thus, it is likely that, for the foreseeable future, there will be a combination of copyright protected and open source software.

Ultimately, it will be up to each library to decide whether they have personnel with the appropriate skills, interest, and time to participate in maintaining an open source product or if the library will reply on a contractual relationship with a commercial firm to provide software for the library.

Open Source Challenge

If you answer yes to one or more of the following issues, then your library may be a candidate for implementing open source software.

- Is your library rich in computer software programming talent?

- Does staff have time to maintain and enhance the open source software?

- Do you feel managing software should be a core competency of your organization?

- Do you need to customize the functionality or look and feel of an application?

- Is the library dissatisfied with how fast new enhancements are installed or how slowly the library's commercial automation vendor makes fixes?

- Do you feel your organization cannot afford a large IT capital outlay?

- Does your library want the flexibility to switch application environments in the future?

- Does your organization have no difficulty attracting and retaining IT staff?

SUGGESTED WEB RESOURCES

Eric S. Raymond
http://www.tuxedo.org/~esr/
writings/

Freeware Library System Project
http://www.Biblioteksbolaget.se

General Open Source Sites
http://www.freshmeat.net
http://www.slashdot.org

Koha
http://www.koha.org

MyLibrary@NCState
http://my.lib.ncsu.edu

**OCLC's Open Source Software
   Projects**
http://www.oclc.org

Open Source Software for Libraries
http://www.oss4lib.org

The Open Source Initiative
http://www.opensource.org

**The Organization for the Advance-
   ment of Structured Information
   Standards (OASIS)**
http://www.xml.org

Technology Resource Foundation
http://www. trfoundation.org

World Wide Web Consortium
http://www.w3.org

XML Standards
http://www.xml.org.

Z39.50 Implementer's Group
http://lcweb.loc.gov/z3950/agency/

NOTES

1.   John Barry. "Automated System Marketplace 2001: Closing in on Content." *Library Journal*, 126 (6), April 1, 2001, pp. 46–58.

2.   Conversations with the vendors in the marketplace.

3.   Barry 2001. Op. Cit.

4.   Kathleen Conner and Richard P. Rumelt. "Software Piracy: An Analysis of Protection Strategies." *Management Science*, 37 (2), 1991, pp. 125–39.

5.   Harvard Business School Press. *The Browser Wars, 1994–1998*. Case Number 9-798-094. Boston: Harvard Business School Press, 1999.

6.   Eric S. Raymond. *The Magic Cauldron*. Available at: http://www.tuxedo.org /~esr/writings/

7.   Steven J. Vaughan-Nichols. "Who Is the Open-Source Community?" *SmartPartner*, October 29, 1999. Available at: http://www.zdnet.com/sp/stories/news/ 0,4538,2384154,00.html

8.   Barry Jaruzelski, Gerald Horkan, and Randy Lake. *Linux: Fad or Future?* White Paper. New York: Booz Allen & Hamilton, 2000. Available at: http://www.bah.com/greatideas/whitepaper.pdf

Chapter 5

Telecommunications and Networks

OVERVIEW

This chapter begins with a general discussion of networks and telecommunications. It then presents an overview of LAN and wide area network (WAN) technology. Whether a library is merely connecting to the Internet or needs to link multiple branch facilities, effectively using telecommunications is an important topic that needs to be clearly understood. We conclude by discussing the implications of infrastructure for telecommunications.

Networks have been a part of society for a long time. For our purposes, we define a network as the interconnection of points (sometimes called nodes) for the purpose of communicating information. The network is the mechanism that connects the points.

From its inception until today, the Post Offices network moves information (i.e., messages in the form of letters, catalogs, and so forth) from one location to another. As the West was settled, the Pony Express network was established to move letters about, using people riding horses between locations. The telegraph network allowed brief information messages to move about the country and then around the world.

A computer network is a mechanism that connects computers so they can exchange or communicate digital information with one another. A computer network can use a variety of media to move messages from a source location to a destination. Typically, the message moves through a number of locations or intermediate stops (sometimes called "hops") as it moves from its source to its ultimate destination.

Robert Metcalfe, originator of Ethernet (a LAN technology) and founder of 3Com, has noted that the value of a network is equal to the square of the number of users. This observation, commonly known as Metcalfe's Law, states that, as a network grows, the value of being connected to it grows exponentially. Doubling the number of participants doubles the value to *each participant*, and the total value of the *network* is increased fourfold. Thus, while a few hundred or even tens of thousands of fax machines have some limited value, a million connected fax machines provides tremendous value to users.

Telecommunications is a much broader topic, and we define it to mean an electronic means of communication including, but not limited to, radio, television, telephone, satellite, computer networks, and the Internet.

Some telecommunications technologies are unidirectional (one-directional) and some are bi-directional. "Broadcast" applies to communications that take place using a unidirectional telecommunications technology to a large audience. Broadcast television should be familiar to everyone. A television station transmits (broadcasts) a signal that everyone in a region can pick up with a television receiver. There is no ability for the person watching television to send a message back to the television station through the television. Radio is a broadcast medium. DirectTV (television broadcast from a satellite) is a broadcast medium. Broadcast technologies efficiently distribute information to large audiences using a minimal infrastructure. However, unidirectional technologies primarily empower the broadcast's source, not the end user or recipient.

The cellular phone, on the other hand, is a technology that is designed for bi-directional communications. Each end point can send and receive messages. The Internet is bi-directional. Bi-directional telecommunications technologies allow for both synchronous (messages sent at regular intervals) and asynchronous or "not synchronous" (messages can be sent at any time) interactivity. Broadcast technologies do not support these types of interactivity. Interactive technologies allow individuals to make choices and determine the information to be received. Interactive technologies (using bi-directional communication) are more challenging and more expensive to implement than broadcast technologies. However, as technologies advance and become more widespread, the cost of implementing interactive technologies will be comparable with, or even less than, broadcast technologies.

The lines between various types of telecommunications technologies are beginning to blur. Let's take radio as an example. A radio receiver picks up signals from radio stations, which are typically located within a nearby geographic locale. The signals from these radio stations carry music, talk shows, and news. With the advent of the Internet and a technology called streaming audio, it is now possible to listen to broadcasts from radio stations across the Internet. The station, rather than transmitting information via radio waves to a receiver, sends packets of digital information that contain the audio information across the Internet. Using a software application and an Internet connection, a person can gain access to hundreds of radio stations from around the world. This new streaming audio, Internet-based technology gives a radio-like experience. Is it radio? No, not exactly—it is asynchronous. But it sure feels like radio to the people who are listening. The same thing applies to broadcast video and streaming video.

The lines within the telecommunications industry are becoming blurred. Telephone companies are now cable TV providers. Cable television companies are now Internet service providers. Satellite television companies are providing Internet service. Internet service providers (ISPs) are providing long-distance telephone service. There are essentially two reasons for this: the U.S. government has deregulated the telecommunications industry, and digital technologies make it easy to blur the lines between television, phone, and Internet service. Sometimes the literature refers to this blurring of lines among service offerings as a "confluence of technology offerings."

The following sections contain a more detailed discussion on the components of LANs and WANs.

LOCAL AREA NETWORKS

When personal computers emerged in the early 1980s, they initially existed as standalone machines. When it was recognized that connecting these PCs together would allow an array of hardware and software to be shared, the LAN was born. A LAN, by its very definition, is limited geographically: an office, a floor in a building, or an entire building.

The benefits of a LAN include:

- More expensive peripheral devices, such as printers, scanners, fax machines, among others, can be shared by all users connected to LAN. The net effect is that the library will need to purchase fewer peripheral devices and is able to save money.

- Price/Performance Ratio. As personal computers became more powerful, they offered a superior price/performance ratio when compared to larger, centralized computer resources.

- Information can be shared. Data files, documents, and spreadsheets can be placed in public directories and shared with others within the library.

- Computer software programs can be shared.

- Performance Quality. Each user gets access to the resources needed, while idle time is minimized.

- Reliability. There will likely be shared resources on the network, so if one device is inoperable, other options are likely to exist.

- Users can send and receive e-mails within the organization and to the outside world.

- LANs increased the return on investment that was made when the personal computers were initially purchased.

- Telecommunication costs can be minimized, as multiple dial-out lines are not needed.

- Licensed databases can be shared by everyone within the library.

- The library need not rely on the "sneaker net"—using floppy disks to move data and/or software programs from one workstation to another.

- Incremental growth. Computer resources can be added in an incremental manner rather than having to replace a large system with an even larger system. Thus, the investment in information technology occurs in a more measured and affordable manner.

LANs can employ a variety of wiring media and this wiring can be laid out in several different ways, as we will see in the next section.

Wiring Media

Wiring a building for a LAN can be accomplished using three types of transmission media: twisted-pair copper wire, coaxial cable, and optical fiber. Data can also be transported over an "invisible wire"—the air—using wireless technology; this technology will be discussed in a later chapter. The speed with which information travels is measured in bits per second (bps) and is called the data rate. Bandwidth measures the amount of information that can be transmitted simultaneously. Bandwidth and data rates are interrelated since the greater the bandwidth, the higher the possible data rate. The bandwidth of a medium is often referred to as channel capacity. Typical transmission characteristics are shown in Table 5-1.

Table 5-1. Transmission Characteristics of Communications Media

Medium	Data Rate	Bandwidth	Repeater Spacing
Twisted-Pair Cable	10 Mbps	500 KHz	100 m
Coaxial Cable	500 Mbps	550 MHz	1-10 km
Optical Fiber	2 Gbps	2 Gbps	10-100 km

Twisted-Pair Cable

Twisted-pair cable is the most ubiquitous communications medium. Historically, it has been used for conventional analog voice communications (the telephone) and digital data transmission. To assure the highest possible quality of data transmission, one wire carries the signal, while the other wire is grounded and absorbs signal interference. Twisted-pair wire is easy to handle, splice, connect, and install.

There are two broad groups of twisted-pair wiring—unshielded and shielded. The unshielded twisted pair wiring (UTW) is sometimes called telephone wire. UTW is susceptible to interference from devices such as fluorescent lights, motors, elevators, and other electrical equipment typically found in a building. Shielded wiring incorporates a layer of insulation that blocks noise and interference from external devices.

The most popular form of shielded twisted-pair wiring is called Category 5 or Cat-5 wiring. The shielding is a layer of insulation, such as copper foil or wire braid, that protects the wires and permits data transmission without signal degradation. Cat-5 wiring consists of four twisted pairs of copper wire terminated by RJ45 connectors. Developed by the Electronics Industries Alliance and the Telecommunications Industry Association (EIA/TIA), Cat-5 is based on the EIA/TIA 568 Commercial Building Telecommunications Wiring Standard.

✐ **Tip!** Should your library have Cat-5 wiring installed, make sure the contractor tests for and certifies that the installed wiring meets the required Cat-5 standard for quality of electrical signal. It is not unusual for wiring to be damaged during installation. Thus, the need for testing and certification once the wiring has been installed is very important.

Coaxial Cable

Coaxial cable is the backbone of a LAN, both within a building and between buildings, for connecting workstations together. Coaxial cable is composed of a center wire surrounded by insulation and then a grounded shield of braided wire. Coaxial cable is less susceptible to interference or noise than a twisted-pair cable and is widely used by the cable television industry. It also provides substantially greater bandwidth than twisted-pair wiring and can typically be installed without using a conduit.

Optical Fiber

Optical fiber cables have a significant amount of bandwidth since they are made of glass or plastic fibers that transmit light pulses (digital signals). The optical fiber core is five times as wide as the wavelength of infrared light (less than 2 microns), and a single fiber has a theoretical capacity as high as 25,000 gigabits per second (roughly equivalent to transmitting the contents of 3 million books per second). Optical fiber cable is not affected by magnetic or radio frequency interference and has error rates that are 10 billion times lower than twisted-pair copper wires. Optical fiber cable is now effectively the same price as coaxial cable or twisted-pair cable, although the installation price might be slightly higher because of the need for special tools and expertise for splicing cable.

George Gilder, the technology author, has proposed "Gilder's Law," which states that available bandwidth triples every 12 months while costs decline—primarily because of fiber optics. Optical fiber is not only being used as the backbone of the Internet, but is being extended to the front doors of businesses and other organizations. Because of the huge capacity of optical fibers, over the next 10 years, available bandwidth will increase at three times the pace of Moore's Law. In addition, various existing technologies will allow for further increases in the overall capacity of optical fiber networks as shown in Table 5-2.

Table 5-2. Optical Fiber Network Speeds

Fiber Technology	Wavelength Per Fiber	Optical Carrier Speed
Single Fiber	One wavelength per fiber	10 Gigabits per second (OC-192)
Wave Division Multiplexing (WDM)	Up to four wavelengths per fiber	Up to 40 Gigabits per second
Dense Wave Division Multiplexing (DWDM)	Up to 160 wavelengths per fiber	Up to 1.6 Terabits per second

Network Interface Card (NIC)

A Network Interface Card (NIC) is a small device that allows a computer workstation, printer, fax machine, or scanner to connect to the LAN itself. Today, most NICs are designed to support one of two speeds: 10 megabits per second (Mbps) or 100 Mbps. The best choice is a NIC that can support either of those speeds, rather than one that is just limited to 10 Mbps. The cost of a 10/100 Mbps NIC is roughly equivalent to a 10 Mbps NIC.

For wireless communication capabilities, the equivalent of a NIC is a wireless modem.

Topology

There are four basic topologies or ways to configure the cabling. These include star (sometimes called hub and spoke), ring, bus, and mesh, as shown in Figure 5-1.

Star Topology

Today, almost all LANs use a star configuration, and the cables are brought together in a common wiring closet or the computer room and connected to a hub or server.

Advantages of a star topology include:

- Network maintenance. The presence of a central hub makes service or reconfiguration a straightforward exercise.

- One device, one connection. Connectors are the most common failure of a LAN. With a star configuration, only one pair of connectors needs to be repaired in the case of a failure.

- Simplified problem diagnosis. Finding faults or problems in a network is easier with a central hub.

- Simplified protocols. Because there is no contention among nodes on the network, the communication protocol is simpler.

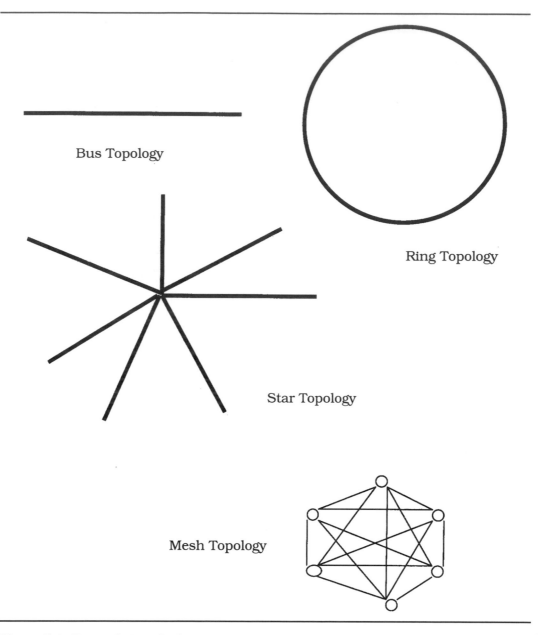

Figure 5-1. Network Topologies

Disadvantages of the star topology include:

♦ Slower data transmission rates. Because all communications traffic must pass through the central hub, the hub can prove to be a bottleneck.

♦ Amount of cabling. Because cabling is routed to each node on the network, more cable is used than with other approaches.

♦ Central node failure. If the central hub fails, the entire network fails. This is clearly the biggest risk when using the star topology.

Ring Topology

The cable for a ring topology is brought back to its starting point. All devices are connected to one another in the shape of a closed loop or ring.

The advantages of a ring topology include:

- Short cable length. Unlike the star topology, the ring configuration uses less cabling and connectors. This means increased network reliability.

- No wiring closet required.

The disadvantages with this approach include:

- Node failure = network failure. Because all data passes through each node on the ring, a failure in one node results in a total network failure.

- Difficult to diagnosis faults. Fault detection can take some time, as it may be necessary to examine and test more than one node.

- Network reconfiguration problems. The network is effectively useless while the ring network is being worked on to add nodes.

Bus Topology

A bus topology has the cable strung out, but the end of the cable does not need to be brought back to the originating point. Each device is connected to the communications media using cable taps or similar devices.

The advantages of the bus topology are:

- Short cable length. Since there is a single data path connecting all nodes, the amount of cable used is the least among the three options. The installation is simple and relatively easy to maintain—although kicking the node connectors will often render the network inoperable.

- Resilient hardware. The simplicity of the single cable approach makes network maintenance a straightforward task.

- Expandability. Additional nodes can easily be connected to an existing bus network.

Some of the disadvantages include:

- Fault diagnosis is difficult. Detection of a fault can be time consuming should a network failure occur.

- Fault isolation is difficult. Repairing a fault may require replacement of a connector, multiple connectors, or a segment of the cable itself.

- Intelligent nodes. Because there must be some method to control who has access to the network, some of this access control work must be performed by the node itself.

◆ Length of cable. The bus cable length will be somewhat limited unless re-peaters are installed so the data quality is not degraded during transmission.

Mesh Topology

In a mesh topology, devices are connected with many redundant interconnec-tions between network nodes. A robust or full mesh topology has a connection to every other node in the network and is typically used on the backbone of a net-work.

The advantages of the mesh topology include:

◆ Yields the greatest amount of redundancy so network traffic can continue in the event of a failure.

◆ A partial mesh topology only provides full redundancy to some devices while other devices, typically peripherals connected to the backbone of a network, are only connected to one or two other nodes on the network.

Some of the disadvantages include:

◆ It is the most expensive topology to implement, especially the full mesh approach.

In practice, these network topologies are often combined; a wiring specialist is the best source of information for wiring a specific building or set of buildings.

Access Methods

There are two primary schemes to allow a device to gain access to the LAN: Ethernet and Token ring. Ethernet is a statistical contention scheme that allocates resources on a first-come, first-serve basis. In technical terms, the access method is called carrier-sense multiple access with collision detection (CSMA/CD). Each device waits until the channel is idle before transmitting data and then listens to verify that no other station has also transmitted data. In the event of a collision, each device waits a random period of time before transmitting again. Because of the overhead associated with re-transmission, the effective throughput of an Ethernet-based network is about 75 percent of its theoretical bandwidth. Thus, a 10 Mbps Ethernet system will have an effective throughput of between 6 and 7 Mbps.

A Token Ring network passes a token to a device when it wants to use the net-work. Until that device has completed its required task with the network, no other workstation or device on the LAN will be able to access the network. One advantage of the Token Ring design is that contention for access is eliminated, thereby reduc-ing the chance of a packet collision to zero.

Network Design

The choice of the cabling media, access method, and topology is affected by some of the following considerations:

+ Distance. What is the maximum distance of a cabling run? In most cases, LANs are limited to a few thousand feet.

+ Number of workstations.

+ Response time requirements. What are the user expectations in terms of response times? Do response times vary by type of application or by type of transaction?

+ Throughput requirements. What is the average and peak period volume of transactions? What type of transactions will be required—audio and video file transmission, file transfer, images, and so forth? Circulation and OPAC workstations will have different requirements than will a workstation located in a manager's office. Note that the file sizes for audio, video, or images are much larger than a relatively brief circulation checkout transaction, and that the mix of these types of transactions will have a major impact on the ultimate LAN configuration.

Once the likely LAN configuration has been determined, bandwidth considerations must be addressed for three components of the LAN:

+ From the backbone to the desktop workstation

+ The LAN backbone

+ Connection to the Internet.

Wireless LANs

The Institute of Electrical and Electronics Engineers (IEEE) 802.11 standard provides for interoperability between devices that have wireless modems and a LAN. Using wireless LANs, users have immediate access to file servers, printers, and databases regardless of their location within the building. An in-building wireless LAN consists of two components: a base station that is connected to a wired LAN and a wireless modem. A wireless transmitter (base station) can support between 15 and 20 simultaneous users. Some building construction materials may block the radio signal and thus create a "dead zone." The primary advantage of wireless is the elimination of the physical "tether," or wiring, that limits mobility within the network infrastructure.

802.11A-enabled devices provide data speeds of up to 11 Mbps (and with 802.11B, 54 Mbps is possible) over distances of 400 feet, although data speeds will decline when encountering walls or metal obstructions.

One advantage of wireless technology is that an individual always has connectivity even when moving around within the building. Wireless 802.11 networks have connected two Ethernet-based LANs located in two separate buildings in lieu of a physical cable to connect the two buildings. One of the biggest potential pitfalls of a wireless LAN is security or, rather, the lack of security. It is recommended that wireless users be treated as if they were coming in over the Internet, and if they want access to a staff-only module for example, they should be authenticated.

According to a recent study, almost 90 percent of respondents indicated that their wireless implementation had been successful, and that the payback period was typically less than one year based on spending about $7,500. Using wireless applications was beneficial in that the average per-user savings were almost $16,000 per year. The payback periods were fairly consistent across all industries: retail, manufacturing, health-care, office automation, and education. James Glover provides a practical 10-step process to install a wireless LAN.[1]

Some of the advantages of using a wireless LAN include:

◆ Improved productivity using service mobility

◆ Quick and flexible installation

◆ Scalable equipment

◆ Reduced cost of ownership.

Network Requirements

The bandwidth of a network always imposes a maximum capacity for the network. The available bandwidth can be limited by the amount of network traffic, causing some messages to be delayed. In technical terms, this delay is called latency; improving the equipment and computer hardware of a network generally reduces this problem.

In most office environments, including libraries, network traffic is not constant over a period of time—there are peaks and valleys. These sporadic bursts of network traffic can have different impacts on the overall network performance (defined as the amount of waiting a user experiences) since some messages may be relatively brief and, in other cases, a user may be sending a large file to a printer. Besides LAN network traffic, Web applications are also characterized by sporadic network traffic. The user requests a Web page or a document and the server responds accordingly. Messages from the user to the Web server are usually brief, while a page or several pages may be transmitted to the user as a result of his or her request. Depending upon the available bandwidth, the time it takes to download a 5-megabyte (MB) file can vary considerably—714 seconds with 56 kilobits per second (Kbps) to four-tenths of a second with a 100-Mbps network.[2] While approximately 100 users can share a 1-Mbps (T-1 line) connection to the Internet, some users will experience delays due to the sporadic nature of the combined network traffic.

Besides this sporadic communication, in the future libraries will experience a different kind of network traffic that involves a constant demand for bandwidth: delivering audio and video services to library staff members and patrons at their workstations. There are two kinds of audio and video applications: one-way (sometimes referred to as streaming) and two-way, or interactive, communications.

Internet-based streaming applications use comprehension techniques (codes are used in lieu of transmitting repeating values, blanks, or white space) to control the amount of bandwidth required to deliver audio to the desktop. A streaming application downloads and stores a large amount of data (typically in a buffer) before it is delivered, thereby masking the latency issues in the network.

An interactive application, such as a two-way audio conversation, requires a higher performance network because the delay in speaking and hearing the voice at the other end of the network must be minimal. Obviously, an interactive application cannot buffer the conversation. An interesting new technology, called Voice over IP (VoIP) enables the Internet to be used for telephone calls.

Streaming video requires large amounts of bandwidth so delays and jitters do not affect the quality of the video images. Yet, even with unlimited bandwidth, the quality of a streaming video application (e.g., using MPEG-1 encoding) is about four to five times poorer than standard videocassettes. When an event is broadcast over the Internet, it is sometimes referred to as "Webcasting."

Interactive video or video conferencing, which provides bi-directional audio and video communications, requires a significant amount of bandwidth; experience has shown that people are willing to tolerate a poorer quality video and audio signal.

As multimedia becomes more commonplace in the home and office, the impact on the local area network will be significant. The net effect of providing either streaming or interactive audiovisual applications to staff members and library patrons at their in-library workstations is that the network will need to provide a dedicated amount of bandwidth that will not be available to support the library's other network traffic.

Practical Considerations

The library's System Manager should keep an accurate diagram of the LAN configuration along with an inventory of devices that are connected to the LAN. A list of each of the cable runs should be maintained along with the identifying number of each cable and its termination point. This list will be invaluable when attempting to troubleshoot a connectivity problem.

WIDE AREA NETWORKS (WANs)

Most libraries will want to connect themselves to the Internet via an ISP. In some cases, a library may have branch facilities that will need to be linked to the library's central computer resources. A communications capability linking two or more geographically dispersed computers is called a WAN.

There are many connection choices available to a library, and each of the options will be discussed further. As shown in Figure 5-2, switching techniques range from relatively simple to complex. Among these options are:

- Telephone Company Circuits
- Microwave
- Fiber Optics
- Frame Relay
- ATM
- Satellite

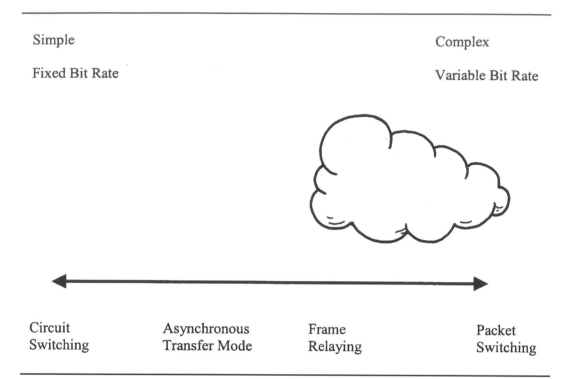

Figure 5-2. Switching Techniques

Telephone Company Circuits

The primary advantage of using the public telephone network for data transmission is its widespread availability. There are several ways in which this network can be used and each will be discussed in turn.

Dial-up Access

Using a modem (a device for converting digital signals into an analog signal used by the telephone system), the user connects to an outside computer system. Most modems in use today are designed to transmit data at 56 Kbps, but the effective throughput rate is lower depending upon the quality of the line actually used. A different telephone line is used each time a connection is made, even if the connection is made to the same number.

Because a separate modem and telephone line must be used for each computer workstation, only very small library facilities with one or two computers would consider dial-up access as a viable option.

Leased Lines

The library can lease a dedicated line from the telephone company to connect specific points. The leased line can be used 24 hours a day, 7 days a week—and requires no meter to monitor, and charge, for the actual line usage. While it is possible to lease voice-grade analog, conditioned analog, or digital lines, most libraries will only lease a digital line.

Integrated Services Digital Network (ISDN)

Integrated Services Digital Network (ISDN) allows digital transmission over ordinary telephone lines. ISDN, available in most urban areas, provides end-to-end digital connectivity between your computer and a remote computer or network by using a local telephone line for network connection. Actually, ISDN uses the standard two-wire copper phone lines. However, there is a line limit of 1,800 cable feet from the nearest switching station.

ISDN gives two 64K-bearer (B) channels for data communication (speeds of 64 Kbps to 128 Kbps) and one 16K-delta (D) channel that acts as a controller. Because the lines are digital, there is very little noise, and you're assured of getting a connection at the full speed. Thanks to the two phone lines, and two phone numbers, customers can be online and use the phone at the same time.

The local telephone company can install the ISDN line to your library. An ISDN adapter must be installed to replace the modem in both your computer and the remote access server. Note that the costs of ISDN equipment and lines may be higher than standard modems and phone lines. However, because of the higher bandwidth of another telephone-based service called the digital subscriber line (DSL), ISDN is becoming less an option for many potential customers.

In effect, ISDN merely replaces two telephone lines and, even for a small library, is not a viable data communications option.

Digital Subscriber Line (DSL)

Digital Subscriber Line (DSL) service delivers high-bandwidth information at rates up to 6 Mbps over copper telephone lines. Most DSL service is limited to a radius of three and a half miles surrounding the telephone company switch location. The attraction of DSL is financial because it still costs less than T-1 leased lines.

DSL service providers initially had to purchase the DSL service from the regional telephone companies and then, in turn, resell these services at an increased price to their customers. However, recently the telephone companies began to offer DSL services directly to the end customer, putting significant financial pressures on the DSL service providers. Early in 2001, several DSL vendors announced they were discontinuing DSL service in some areas, leaving customers just weeks to find new service providers.

T-1 Lines

A T-1 connection is designed for installations that have more than 16 Internet users or require high-capacity Internet connectivity. A T-1 line is dedicated, meaning that it is always on and there are no usage charges. With a T-1 line, you can provide Internet access to dozens of computers without modems, telephone lines, and dialup accounts for each one.

A T-1 line will provide a library with a bandwidth capacity of 1.544 Mbps for a flat fee of $500 to $600 per month. The prices for T-1 lines should continue to decline, as they have for the past decade. Libraries that have a LAN typically require this level of bandwidth as a minimum baseline. The 1.544 Mbps capacity means that 10 computers can simultaneously access the Internet and each will have 150k of bandwidth. Given that most access is not simultaneous, up to 100 computers can be easily supported with one T-1 line. Leasing a fractional T-1 line provides access to some portion of a full T-1 line.

T-3 Lines

A T-3 line is a dedicated digital communication link provided by a telephone company that offers 44.75 Mbps of bandwidth, commonly used for carrying data communications traffic to and from Internet service providers. The line actually consists of 672 individual channels, each of which supports 64 Kbps. T-3 lines are sometimes referred to as DS3 lines, and such lines are obviously much more expensive than several T-1 lines. Depending upon the distance, a T-3 line will run about $5,000 per month.

Microwave Transmission

In lieu of a physical leased line, a library may wish to consider using a microwave connection to an ISP or to its branch facilities. Using a small antenna, typically located on top of a building, the library is connected to the ISP with the same bandwidth of a T-1 leased line. However, in most cases, the microwave option is less expensive. A nice bonus of a microwave connection is being able to add incremental bandwidth as needed without having to add one or more lines (with the attendant installation charges).

While microwave transmission is wireless, it is actually a point-to-point, line-of-sight communication medium rather than a true anywhere wireless option. That is, the source and destination antennas must "see" one another to communicate. Some suggest that microwave transmission is actually an invisible wire in the sky. Microwave links are capable of connecting WANs to LANs, or any other combination of distributed and local networks.

Optical Fiber Connections

It is possible for a library to install an optical fiber link between their building and the Internet. Available bandwidth varies considerably (52 Mbps to 40 gigabits per second [Gbps]), depending on the optical fiber line option that is chosen. Typically, optical fiber cabling is installed and maintained by competitors to the local telephone company.

Packet Switching

Packet switching divides messages into packets, which are then transmitted individually and can even follow different routes to their destination. Once all packets arrive at the destination, they are reassembled into the original message. Most WANs are based on packet-switching technologies. Packet switching is more efficient and robust for data that can withstand some transmission delays, such as e-mail communications and Web page loading and linking.

Transmission Control Protocol/Internet Protocol (TCP/IP) is a suite of communications protocols used to connect computers on the Internet. Because of the Internet's tremendous impact, TCP/IP has become the de facto standard for transmitting data over networks, including LANs and wireless networks. The importance of TCP/IP is discussed in greater detail in Chapter 6. Suffice it to say that if a computer system-related device does not support TCP/IP, then its economic prospects are bleak!

Frame Relay

Frame relay is a low- to medium-speed packet-switching protocol that works well for speeds from 56 Kbps to 1.544 Mbps (T-1 speed). This is an attractive technology from a cost perspective, and many libraries use Frame Relay lines to link multiple branch locations to centralized computer resources.

Most telephone companies provide Frame Relay service to customers who want connections ranging from 56 Kbps to T-1 speeds. Pricing is based on the number of sites or locations (e.g., $200 per month per site).

Data that is transmitted across a WAN using Frame Relay uses public or semi-public space between the end points of a transmission and is often referred to as a "network cloud." Similarly, packet-switched networks are often visually represented with a network cloud since no two packets will necessarily follow the same path.

ATM

Asynchronous Transfer Mode (ATM) is a network protocol based on transferring data in cells, or packets, of a fixed length. The small (53 bytes), constant cell size allows ATM equipment to transmit video, audio, and computer data over the same network, and assures that no single type of data dominates the available bandwidth. Currently, ATM data transfer rates range from 155 Mbps to 622 Mbps. ATM creates a fixed channel or route between two points whenever data transfer begins. This differs from TCP/IP, in which messages are divided into packets and each packet can take a different route from source to destination. Proponents of ATM networks claim that ATM removes a lot of the overhead costs of packet-switched networks.

Four types of ATM service are available:

- Constant Bit Rate (CBR) specifies a fixed bit rate so data is sent in a constant stream (similar to a leased line).

- Variable Bit Rate (VBR) provides a specified throughput capacity, but data is not sent evenly (often used for audio and videoconferencing data).

- Unspecified Bit Rate (UBR) does not guarantee any throughput levels (typically used for applications that can tolerate delays, such as file transfers).

♦ Available Bit Rate (ABR) provides a guaranteed minimum throughput capacity but allows data to be sent at higher capacities when the network has unused capacity.

Metropolitan Area Network (MAN)

The term MAN is often applied to new high-speed network technologies that push the carrying capacity of the communication links into the Gbps range and are typically used over a larger area than a LAN, frequently encompassing a large city or several cities.

Satellite-Based Data Communications

Unlike satellite services for mobile voice users, emerging Internet broadband data solutions use fixed satellite services that require the desktop workstation or server to be hooked up to a satellite dish. In some cases, the uplink and downlink speeds will vary, but generally, the overall performance of the satellite data communications option is more than satisfactory. Table 5-3 presents information about a number of the satellite data communication services. For consumers, the cost is roughly equivalent to DSL service (about $60 to $70 per month). The cost for organizations such as libraries will be higher, depending upon the bandwidth requirements desired.

One interesting feature of this service is that the vendor will guarantee the minimum downlink speed (there is no cap) and the actual performance may be quite a bit higher. While it will be interesting to see whether satellite Internet access will bypass terrestrial access, initially most customers of satellite data communications are likely to be rural individuals, companies, and libraries.

Exploring Options

A library should reassess its WAN options periodically. For example, some libraries have eliminated the leased lines that linked their branch facilities to the central computer and moved to a network cloud option, typically Frame Relay. In other cases, libraries have replaced leased lines with microwave connections. The changes resulted in considerable financial savings and improved the network reliability. The effective transmission speeds of the available options are shown in Table 5-4.

Table 5-3. Satellite Data Communication Services

Type of Satellite	Name of Service	Service Area	Communication Speeds	Frequencies Used
Low Earth Orbit	Globalstar	North & South America, Europe, Australia, and some parts of Asia and Africa From: http://www .globalstar.com /pages/coverage .html	This system is capable of handling data at speeds up to 200 kbps per Globalstar frequency channel in each direction, a speed made possible by "concatenating" or combining up to 32 individual Globalstar circuits in parallel within a single frequency channel. An individual Globalstar circuit works at 9.6 kbps, so that 32 channels together could provide a theoretical speed of over 300 kbps, although the actual speed is somewhat lower since some of the bandwidth must be used for system management and other technical functions. Nevertheless, speeds of 200 kbps are assured and under certain circumstances could be even higher.	The Globalstar system uses four separate segments of the radio frequency spectrum. These four segments proposed for Globalstar MSS operations are: User links: 1610-1626.5 MHz (user-to-satellite) 2483.5-2500 MHz (satellite-to-user) Feeder links: 5091-5250 MHz (gateway-to-satellite) 6875-7055 MHz (satellite-to-gateway) From: http://www.globalstarusa.com/contact /h_01d.shtml
	Iridium	Global— including poles	The channel capacity for Iridium voice is currently only 2.4 kbps. The channel capacity for data and facsimile transmission over Iridium is 2400 baud. From: http://www2.sis.pitt.edu/~jkabara /tele-2100/iridium/iridium_final.html The "direct Internet Data" rate is 10 Kbps. (iridium.com)	Iridium uses several ranges of frequencies for communications between its transmitters, satellites, and ground stations. The service link between the phone and the satellite operates in the L-band. The L-band is between 1 and 2 GHz. The phone to satellite uplink in Iridium specifically takes place in the frequency range from 1616 MHz to 1626.5 MHz. Communication between satellites (cross links or intersatellite

(Table 5.3 continues on p. 84.)

Table 5-3—Continued

Type of Satellite	Name of Service	Service Area	Communication Speeds	Frequencies Used
				links) takes place in the Ka band of frequencies, between 23.18 GHz and 23.38 GHz. The Ka band is also used for communication between the satellites and the gateways. This link is called the feeder link, and for the Iridium system, the uplinks are in the frequency range 29.1-29.3 GHz. The downlinks, from the satellite to the gateway, are handled in the 19.4-19.6 GHz range. From: http://www2.sis.pitt.edu/~jkabara /tele-2100/iridium/iridium_final.html
	Orbcomm	Global coverage capability, but its ground equipment isn't approved for use in all areas. See link for map: http://www .satphonestore .com/servprod /orbcomm /coverage.html	The Subscriber Communicators transmit at 2400bps and receive at 4800bps. http://www.celcom.com.my/mobiles /orbcomm/technology.html	The ORBCOMM system uses 137MHz to 138MHz and 400 MHz frequencies for transmissions down to mobile or fixed data communications devices; and 148MHz to 150MHz frequencies for transmissions up to the satellites. From: http://www.celcom.com.my/mobiles /orbcomm/technology.html
	SkyBridge	Global	Downstream speeds of up to 5 Mbps and up to 0.5 Mbps on the return link per residential user; Three to five times higher bit rates will be provided to business users. http://www.skybridgesatellite.com /p21_rele/pr_12.htm	The SkyBridge System is designed to operate in the 10-18 GHz frequency bands without causing interference to either geostationary satellite operators (GSO) or terrestrial users. http://www.skybridgesatellite.com /l41_sys/index.htm

Type of Satellite	Name of Service	Service Area	Communication Speeds	Frequencies Used
Medium Earth Orbit	New ICO *	Global http://www .hughespace.com /factsheets/601 /ico/ico.html This is a really good page.	The so-called New ICO plans to be up and running commercially in 2003 with narrowband voice and two-way packet data services at data rates up to 144 kbps. From: http://www.broadbandweek.com/news /010108/010108_wireless_tele.htm	Medium-frequency Ku-band 2 to 5 GHz range
Geo-synchronous Earth Orbit	Astrolink *	Europe	The Astrolink satellites are being designed with 6.5 Gbps capacity and the ability to support downlink speeds of up to 110 Mbps and uplink speeds of 20 Mbps per channel. They will also build two satellite centers, three telemetry station and 30 to 50 Gateway Earth Stations providing interexchange, protocol conversion, and uplink to the satellites at 143 Mbps per channel. http://www.atmdigest.com/archive /v6n087.txt	Astrolink's satellites receive signals from earth at 30 GHz and transmit to earth at 20 GHz, in the Ka frequency range. http://www.spacer.com/news /astrolink-00a.html
	Hughes DirecPC	United States	400Kbps http://www.orbitsat.com/DirecPC/Index.htm	Medium-frequency Ku-band 11 to 17 GHz range
	Hughes Spaceway *	International	uplink rates between 16Kbps to 16Mbps http://www.hns.com/products/advanced _platforms/spaceway/inside_spaceway.htm	High-frequency Ka-band 20 to 30 GHz range
	Intelsat	Global	64 Kbps – 150 Mbps http://www.intelsat.com/news /mediadownload.pdf got this from the www section of their media package.	Capability for various frequencies see: http://www.intelsat.int/satellites_coverage maps.asp for a list of all sats and their various frequency options
	StarBand	United States	150 Kbps uplink 500 Kbps downlink	Medium-frequency Ku-band 11 to 17 GHz range

(Table 5.3 continues on p. 86.)

Table 5-3—Continued

Type of Satellite	Name of Service	Service Area	Communication Speeds	Frequencies Used
	Telesat Canada	Canada—in the future will be North America	**ASYNCHRONOUS** 300 bps to 19.2 kbps **SYNCHRONOUS** 4.8 kbps - 64 kbps http://www.telesat.ca/business/acc.html	Mixed frequencies
	WildBlue *	USA— interesting linkage with Telesat See: http://www .spacedaily.com /news /internet-01m .html	Up to 3.0Mbps planned http://www.wildblue.com/hot/index.htm	High-frequency Ka-band 20 to 30 GHz range

* = Planned

Table 5-4. Transmission Times, by Media

Media	Speed	Theoretical Speed to Transmit the Oxford English Dictionary (500 MB)
Dial-up modem	56 Kbps	14.9 minutes
T-1 line Microwave Frame Relay	1.544 Mbps	5.4 minutes
DSL line	6 Mbps	1.4 minutes
802.11A wireless	11 Mbps	45.5 seconds
T-3 line	44.75 Mbps	11.2 seconds
ATM	155 Mbps 622 Mbps	3.2 seconds .8 seconds
Fiber optic line	52 Mbps 40 Gbps	9.6 seconds .0125 seconds

"What we need today is a data network that can carry voice instead of what we have today, a voice network struggling to carry data."

Reed Hundt, former FCC Chairman

THE INTERNET

The Internet, the contraction of its definition "the interconnection of networks," is a global network connecting millions of computers. The Internet is decentralized by design and allows each Internet computer, called a host, to determine which Internet services to use and which local services to make available to the Internet community. There are a wide variety of optional services available on the Internet, including e-mail, file transfer, Telnet, and the World Wide Web.

These computer networks are connected using two specialized pieces of equipment called routers and switches. Typically, there are multiple connections or data lines from which a packet may be received and forwarded on. The router examines the header of the packet and, using a forwarding table, determines the best route to send the message or packet. Routers also share information about congestion that they are experiencing so delays in forwarding of messages are minimized.

A router usually does not filter or examine a packet for content. A switch is a device that filters and forwards packets between LAN segments.

INFRASTRUCTURE IMPLICATIONS

The ability for any library staff member to instantly connect to the library's LAN or the Internet, when needed, has become such a commonplace event that we no longer think about it. Yet libraries are completely reliant upon the networking and telecommunications infrastructure for their day-to-day operations, whether it be staff members cataloging materials, printing documents, or searching the Web, or patrons using the library's OPAC workstations.

Christine Borgman has suggested that any infrastructure, whether it is an electrical grid, a railroad, a highway, or a computer-based telecommunications network, has several important characteristics:[3]

1. Infrastructures are embedded in other structures, social arrangements, and technologies.

2. Infrastructures are transparent and support tasks invisibly.

3. Infrastructures are built upon standards so complementary tools and services can interconnect.

4. Infrastructures remain invisible until they fail to perform their function. Then everybody wants to know "when is the network going to be operational again!"

Planning for the sporadic types of communication transactions that occur with office applications and LIS, as well as the constant, bandwidth-intensive audio and video streaming applications likely to be found in the library's OPAC now or in the near future, means periodically reassessing the library's data communications infrastructure.

SUMMARY

This chapter has provided a primer on telecommunications and the technologies of LANs and WANs. The importance of having a stable and robust infrastructure to support the library's automation needs cannot be over-emphasized. The next chapter focuses on standards and standards organizations and the increasingly positive impacts standards are having on libraries.

Network Protocols Overview

Almost all communications protocols used today can be better understood using the Open Systems Interconnection (OSI) reference model developed by the International Organization for Standardization (ISO). The OSI reference model divides the communications process into seven categories in a layered sequence according to their relation to the user. Layers 1 through 3 pertain to data transport across the network; layers 4 through 7 deal with end-to-end communications between the message source and the message destination, usually between a client application and a server (see Figure 5-3).

- **Layer 1: Physical Layer**—Electrically encodes and physically transfers messages between adjacent nodes on the network. Examples include twisted-pair wiring, coaxial cable, SONET, fiber optic cable, and microwave transmission.

- **Layer 2: Data Link Layer**—Provides format and framing for network packets, including hardware-based data integrity facilities. On a shared-media LAN, such as Ethernet or Token Ring, it includes a Media Access Control (MAC) sublayer that defines the way the network manages contention between multiple devices that are attempting to send data simultaneously. Common Layer 2 protocols include ATM and the Point-to-Point Protocol (PPP).

- **Layer 3: Network Layer**—Routes data packets from source to destination. Network layer protocols are routed globally and can cross physical network boundaries. Network layer protocols can be characterized as either connection-oriented (all data packets in a given transmission follow the same path between source and destination) or connectionless (the route taken by each data packet is determined independently). The most common Layer 3 protocol is the IP.

- **Layer 4: Transport Layer**—Responsible for providing transparent, reliable data transfer from one end-system process on the network to another. It handles cases in which individual data packets arrive too fast, arrive out of order, or fail to arrive at all. The most common example is TCP. The transport layer and all the network layers above it are implemented only in end systems (the actual computers on a network), whereas the layers below it are implemented in both end systems and intermediate systems (bridges, routers, and other network infrastructures).

- **Layer 5: Session Layer**—Responsible for dialog control and synchronization management (i.e., determining whose turn it is to "talk") and provides checkpointing and recovery if a long transmission is interrupted.

- **Layer 6: Presentation Layer**—Converts data as necessary to ensure that data is exchanged in an understandable format. The Presentation Layer can also perform other services, such as data compression or encryption.

- **Layer 7: Applications Layer**—Provides the services that make up a particular application, such as browsing the Web, transferring files, or exchanging e-mail.

Layers 3 and 4 form the core of most network protocols and usually can be run over a variety of Layer 2 networks. In most cases, rather than being implemented as distinct software components, Layers 5 through 7 will be collapsed into a single application.

See Figure 5-3 for the OSI Reference Model.

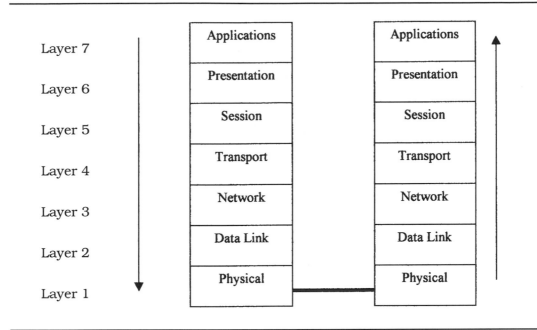

Layer 7	Applications	Applications
Layer 6	Presentation	Presentation
Layer 5	Session	Session
Layer 4	Transport	Transport
Layer 3	Network	Network
Layer 2	Data Link	Data Link
Layer 1	Physical	Physical

Figure 5-3. OSI Reference Model

SUGGESTED WEB RESOURCES

myNetWatchman

http://www.myNetWatchman.com

Performs an analysis of a firewall's log files to identify hacking.

Internet FAQ Consortium

http://www.faqs.org

Links to Usenet-based information about data communications cabling, Ethernet LAN, LAN mail protocols, and WAN protocols.

Data Comm for Business, Inc. (DCB)

http://www.dcbnet.com

Application notes and tutorials about general networking, wireless networks, LANs, WANs, connecting to the Internet, and serial connectivity.

Routing in the Internet

http://www.scit.wlv.ac.uk/~jphb/comms/iproute.html

Describes how routing works in the Internet, with specific information on physical address determination, selection of inter-network gateways, and symbolic and numeric addresses.

NOTES

1. James L. "Larry" Glover. "Look Ma, No Wires! Or the 10 Steps of Wireless Networking." *Computers in Libraries*, 21 (3), March 2001, pp. 28–33.

2. David Barber. "Networking Checklists for Library Managers." *Library Technology Reports*, 37 (3), May–June 2001, pp. 1–63.

3. Christine L. Borgman. *From Gutenberg to the Global Information Infrastructure: Access to Information in the Networked World.* Cambridge, MA: MIT Press, 2000.

Chapter 6

Standards and
Standards Organizations

This chapter addresses the role and importance of information standards, organizations that support the development and dissemination of standards, and how these measures are instituted. Library classification systems for cataloging, such as the Dewey Decimal system or the Library of Congress system, are clear examples of procedures and tools that were developed in a non-standardized fashion, but allow patrons to find the materials they are looking for with relative ease. These tools led to an interest in developing a more standardized method for representing information so an inquiring patron might locate it. In recent years, emerging library information systems have spawned the need for highly technical standards for retrieving information from remote sources in a complex networked environment. The information standards included in this chapter illustrate the useful capabilities of the more prominent library information systems, and how applying these standards might affect the direction of technology usage and vice versa.

Besides showing the present and potential advantages of integrated library systems standards, this chapter also profiles the various organizations that support the continued development of such standards. Additional organizations and selected emerging standards that are relevant to the practical implementation of online information systems standards in libraries are also discussed. The chapter closes with an argument as to why librarians must take an active role in the standards development process.

STANDARDS

Libraries have been a part of the standards process for many years. Early on, libraries developed formal standards for physical components used within the library, such as the brass pulls on the card catalog drawers. Later, as libraries began incorporating technology, the focus turned first to bibliographic standards, then to communications standards, and later to search and retrieval standards. This chapter focuses on formal library standards related to technological development. Formal standards are developed under rigorous review and validation, while industry or *de facto* standards are often developed through the dominance of a particular company or agency. There are many formal standards within librarianship that address topics such as preservation, format of print documents, and so forth that are not covered here. We also seek to identify efforts in standards developments that are occurring outside of libraries and information agencies, which have significant impact on how these collective institutions operate in the distributed networked world.

What are standards? Standards are criteria against which entries may be judged for consistency or uniformity. To standardize generally means to create or modify all entries to conform to a single pattern or format. According to the International Organization for Standardization (ISO), official "standards are documented agreements containing technical specifications or other precise criteria to be used consistently as rules, guidelines, or definitions of characteristics, to ensure that materials, products, processes, and services are fit for their purpose."[1]

Walt Crawford suggests that there are several benefits that arise through using standards.[2] Among these are:

- **A Common Language**. Terminology introduces the communication process among and between various parties (e.g., librarians, vendors, and computer programmers).

- **Stability**. Once a standard has been adopted, it provides the assurance that others can supply and support products that encompass the standard.

- **Cooperation and Competition**. Adopting a standard eases the entry for new suppliers into a marketplace. The standard also encourages existing suppliers to become more competitive and improve production efficiencies. Even vendors who are competitors will often cooperate on developing new standards or enhancing an existing standard.

- **Saves Money**. The presence of a standard means that a supplier does not need to support two potentially competing standards, which would cost more than working with a single standard.

- **Self-Regulating**. The marketplace has a wonderful positive impact on standards. Those that work are embraced, supported and, in most cases, enhanced over time. Those standards that do not work are dropped.

Why do we need standards in libraries? Imagine if all original cataloging were done in every library using locally determined structures. Each cataloger could pick and choose which fields were to be cataloged, what elements might go in each field, what the format of those fields should be, and so forth. While this might work well in that individual library, this "uniqueness" inhibits the ability to share bibliographic data, and hence, bibliographic objects, among libraries that are attempting to cooperate in programs such as interlibrary loan and collection development. If these libraries were to agree upon a standardized bibliographic structure, along with guidelines and rules for completing those bibliographic records, then cooperation across libraries would be enhanced. In fact, original cataloging could be shared as well. This is the rationale behind conforming to various bibliographic standards and to standards in general. The key point is inter-institutional cooperation.

How are standards used to design an LIS? While libraries have agreed upon a wide array of standards, not all of these are directly related to technological developments. Standards associated with LIS include bibliographic standards, communications standards, and standards that support the search and retrieve functions across libraries with disparate computing platforms, separated by geographic distances.

Not all standards are created equal. Some standards are formal, while others may be de facto, ad hoc, or industry standards. There are also government standards. The distinction is important. Formal standards are those that have been through a rigorous submission and review process by a community of volunteers who seek to establish a consensus on that particular topic. Formal standards are those "blessed" by an accredited standardizing body at the national or international level. The standards are reviewed periodically and are continually updated. The key is that these formal standards are arrived at through a process involving a consensus of practicing professionals and concerned experts. A prime example of a formal standard within libraries and information agencies is the MARC record format, formally known as the "Bibliographic Interchange Format," designated as NISO Z39.2. NISO is the National Information Standards Organization, which is part of the American National Standards Institute (ANSI), an accredited standardizing agency within the United States.

Industry standards, on the other hand, are often developed through the dominance of a particular corporation or institution. For example, the size of the cards in a card catalog is the result of an industry standard, and as such, is not a formal standard. Outside of librarianship, one example of an industry standard is Microsoft's Windows™ operating system. Industry or ad hoc standards arise out of a consensus of use and are not necessarily subject to debate or control by a formal standards accrediting agency. There are instances where industry standards have been formally adopted using a consensus process. It is not unusual for an industry standard to evolve into a formal standard. Such is the case for what is often referred to as "Ethernet," a protocol for packeting bits to be transmitted across a telecommunications system. Ethernet was developed cooperatively by corporate and research partners, but after the protocol took hold worldwide as a popular networking solution, that informal or industry standard was made formal at an international level, and eventually became an IEEE standard (IEEE 802.3).

This chapter focuses on formal standards and the processes and organizations that support their development. Industry standards can be powerful forces as well, although they are beyond the control of the rigors of consensus. Technology innovation often outpaces the slower, more carefully paced developments of formal standards. Well-developed industry standards are needed in an environment that is fast paced, as many technologic enterprises fight to remain front-runners in innovation and development.

OFFICIAL STANDARDS ORGANIZATIONS

Who decides what a standard is and how it is going to be enforced? For the most part, adopting a standard is voluntary. Representatives from both the private and public sectors, through a process involving voluntary consensus, develop formal standards. Most organizations involved with standards are nonprofit, receiving financial support from the communities they serve and intellectual support from professionals within that community.

> ✔ **Tip!** You might ask your library systems vendor to explain its participation in making standards. Some may send representatives, some may support the organization with donations, and some may even participate in the administrative aspects of an organization like NISO, which presides over standards associated with libraries and related information agencies.

ANSI serves as the administrator and coordinator of the U.S. private sector voluntary standardization system. It was founded in 1918 by five engineering societies and three government agencies, yet remains a nonprofit organization. ANSI was a founding member of the ISO and is currently the sole U.S. representative. The organization promotes U.S. standards internationally in an effort to have them adopted by other countries.

While ANSI is a rather broad-based standards agency reaching beyond libraries and information services, one of its domains is that which covers libraries, publishers, government agencies, and information-based businesses. NISO is a nonprofit association accredited as a standards developer by ANSI. NISO was originally formed in 1939 as the "American National Standards Committee Z39." In 1984, its current name was adopted. NISO is responsible for developing and maintaining standards for library and information science and related publishing practices. All NISO standards are numbered beginning with Z39.

> ✔ **Tip!** Two of the more important NISO Z39 standards are Z39.2, which formed the basis for online shared cataloging, and Z39.50, which forms the basis for shared access to remote databases.

One of the few U.S. government organizations involved with establishing standards is the National Institute of Standards and Technology (NIST). Congress formed this organization in 1901 as the "National Bureau of Standards." Over the years, NIST has been recognized worldwide for its standards development. In 1989, NIST was transferred to the U.S. Department of Commerce's Technology Administration.

These three organizations (NISO, ANSI, and NIST) are the main standards formulation entities within the United States. They rely upon the public and private sectors to adopt the standards they articulate. Because most standards are not made into law, these groups can do very little without the participation of those who will use the standards.

On a global scale, the primary standards organizations include ISO, IEEE, and CCITT. The ISO is a global federation of national standards bodies from 100 countries. It is also a non-governmental organization, first established in 1947 to help develop an international set of standards involving trade and to help promote worldwide cooperation in the sciences. The IEEE focuses primarily on standards to support electrical and computer engineering and the information and communications technologies. Founded in 1884, IEEE is a non-profit technical professional society of more than 350,000 members in more than 150 countries. One of IEEE's responsibilities is to develop and promote international standards that affect its membership.

The CCITT is an acronym for the Comité Consultatif International Téléphonique et Télégraphique, which is an organization that sets international communications standards. CCITT, now known as International Telecommunication Union (ITU—the parent organization), has defined many important standards for data communications.

The ITU is an intergovernmental organization through which public and private organizations develop telecommunications. The organization was founded in 1865 and became a United Nations agency in 1947. It is responsible for adopting international treaties, regulations, and standards governing telecommunications. A group within the ITU (CCITT) formerly performed the standardization functions, but after reorganization in 1992, the CCITT no longer exists as a separate body.

PRIMARY TECHNOLOGY-BASED STANDARDS

As mentioned earlier, it is those standards that address technology-based product development and service provision that are of interest to libraries. The ISO's standards definition stipulates that each standard contains specific criteria to be applied consistently to its respective function. These standards must also be accepted and used on a universal basis before their benefits to LIS can be realized. Standards relevant to libraries are designed "to achieve compatibility and therefore interoperability between equipment, data, practices, and procedures so information can be made easily and universally available."[3] Thus, interoperability is the key to data retrieval and these "standards make it possible to integrate hardware, software, and communications systems and to exchange information across boundaries of different systems."[4] Besides supporting interoperability, standards relating to information technology designs may be thought of as belonging to one of several categories:

- ◆ Bibliographic (including Metadata)
- ◆ Communications
- ◆ Search and Retrieve
- ◆ Markup.

Bibliographic Standards

Bibliographic standards address the means by which professional librarians create and distribute secondary information, in the form of bibliographic records, for use in modern library information systems. The most prominent bibliographic standard is the MARC format used by librarians worldwide. The NISO equivalent is referred to as Z39.2–1994, and is called the Information Interchange Format. Internationally, this standard is known as ISO 2709. The MARC format has been referred to as a communications standard, because it supports the sharing of bibliographic content across different library institutions, but here we consider it a bibliographic standard. Its usage is so pervasive that we often overlook other bibliographic standards that are important as well. There exists a set of NISO standards that also describes the bibliographic structure of the patron record (Z39.70) and the holdings statement (Z39.71), which specifies holdings statements display requirements for bibliographic items.

Metadata is "data about data." Librarians think of metadata in terms of bibliographic descriptions, where professional catalogers create secondary records and indexers identify and describe primary sources. Metadata also covers topics such as the administration, legal requirements, technical functionality, use and usage, and preservation aspects relating to those primary resources. The NISO Z39.85–2001 standard addresses the Dublin Core Metadata Element Set, and defines 15 metadata elements for resource discovery in a cross-disciplinary information environment.

Dublin Core

The Dublin Core is a set of 15 elements designed to help catalog Internet resources. In 1995, a group of 52 librarians, archivists, and scholars met at an OCLC-sponsored workshop and tried to come up with a standard descriptive record for items on the Internet. The idea was to improve public access to information. The 15 data elements include: title, author or creator, subject and keywords, description, publisher, other contributor, date, resource type, format, resource identifier, source, language, relation, coverage, and rights management.

The Dublin Core is a metadata element set that will work with MARC records. It is not expected to meet everyone's needs. OCLC began the Cooperative Online Resource Catalog (CORC) to develop a catalog of Web resources. Stuart Weibel, who first initiated the idea back in 1994, feels that libraries need "to join forces and build our gateways cooperatively."[5]

Resource Description Format (RDF)

Resource Description Framework (RDF) is a World Wide Web Consortium (W3C) initiative to support the use and exchange of metadata on the Web. RDF provides a standard means for designating metadata, creating the potential for conducting high-quality searches on the Web. Libraries will benefit from this in that they will be able to search more effectively for resources outside their own collections. Cataloging in particular may benefit from the enhanced content description and relationships of a particular Web site that RDF makes possible. As an application, RDF is coded in XML, which complements RDF as a standardized metadata structure. The basic RDF data model consists of:

- **Resources**. Anything described by RDF expressions (can be a Web page, part of a Web page, or even printed books).

♦ **Properties**. Specific characteristic, attribute, or relation used to describe a resource.

♦ **Statements**. A Resource + A Property + A Value = A Statement.

RDF allows various interest groups to use certain defined schemas. For example, libraries could use Dublin Core vocabulary by including it in the RDF tagging.[6]

As more and more software solutions incorporate metadata standards, they will be required to recognize multiple formats. To enable this, crosswalks, or similar mapping techniques, will need to be developed across various combinations of standards, such as the Dublin Core/MARC/GLIS crosswalk. A crosswalk from MARC to Dublin Core is now available from the MARC 21 Web site. This document maps MARC 21 fields to Dublin Core elements; there are separate sections for unqualified and qualified Dublin Core. The alternate mapping, Dublin Core to MARC, is being revised and will be available soon. The crosswalk can be found at: http://www.loc.gov/marc/marc2dc.html. Some international standard metadata formats are being developed, most notably ISO Metadata Standard 19115.

The trend in developing metadata standards is to design structures and formats that will support the understanding and usage of information, increase the availability and accessibility of that information, and enable interoperability among different computing systems using different formats and structures. Out of necessity, this will need to occur at the local, regional, national, and international levels.

Communications Standards

Communications standards are designed to support the interchange of information among distinctly different information systems, operated by different institutions. Having content marked up using standard bibliographic structures is a good start, but to shore up that content, one must also examine communications standards. One communications standard under development within NISO is Z39.83-200x, which is the NISO Circulation Interchange Protocol (NCIP). This is a draft standard in the making that defines the various transactions needed to support circulation activities among independent library systems.

Other communications standards have been created outside NISO that support interactions among computer systems. Many of these are technical, involving transferring packets of information within an information system that may or may not involve libraries. For example, IEEE 802.3 (Ethernet) and IEEE 802.2 (Token Passing) are common communications protocols used to support LAN development. IEEE 802.16.2–2001 is a standard currently under development that offers guidelines for linking newly developed wireless communications to existing broadband services. Entitled "Recommended Practice Local and Metropolitan Area Networks—Coexisistence of Fixed Broadband Wireless Access Systems," this standard provides developers with a blueprint for developing new services from an existing base of applications.

The most well-known communications standard is undoubtedly TCP/IP, which the Internet is based on. This standard is actually a de facto standard that underlies the Internet and supports services and applications running on the Internet.

Search and Retrieval Standards

Standards that address the search and retrieve aspects of LIS include the Common Command Language (Z39.58) and the Information Retrieval Service Definition and Protocol Specifications for Library Applications (Z39.50).

The notion of developing a common set of commands that could be used in search tools (Z39.58) arose during a period prior to client-server computing, when data stores were searched using command languages, not graphical-based clients. As database use proliferated, users were faced with memorizing an array of searching syntaxes that varied from system to system. Even inside a single database management system of the once popular dBase (from Ashton-Tate), the user was faced with a choice of verbs such as FIND, SEEK, and LOCATE, each of which had a different capability within that system. In other systems (e.g., MySQL), these verbs had totally different meanings and functionality.

A common command language identifies a common set of functions, links a certain set of verbs directly to those functions, and uses them in all applications. This was a noble idea, but became less than necessary because of several reasons. The first was the development of graphical interfaces that sheltered the end user from the specific commands within the system. Second, vendors were reluctant to implement a Common Command Language because it would eliminate an important product differentiator—unique search capabilities. Thus, it is likely that Z39.58 will die on the vine as a standard. Because each NISO standard is reviewed periodically by a designated committee for updates and continuation, standards such as the Common Command Language can and do rise and fall with use and relevance in this rapidly developing technologic age.

Certainly one of the most important standards facilitating the interoperation of information systems is Z39.50. This standard can also be categorized as a "search and retrieve" standard. Z39.50 is the designated identification number for the "Information Retrieval Service Definition and Protocol Specifications for Library Applications." Originally adopted in 1988 for sharing MARC bibliographic records, this standard was revised in 1992 and again in 1994.[7] Z39.50–1994 is presently a widely used protocol enabling communication between distributed and possibly disparate computer systems. More specifically, Z39.50 is used as a sort of translator and interpreter between a searchable database, or server, and the desktop workstation, or client, issuing the search query. In practice, the client's search query is translated into the Z39.50 standard search format and is then re-interpreted into the server's format.[8] The search results are then provided to the end user in the client's particular local format, regardless of the local system's hardware or interfaces.[9]

This search and retrieve standard has helped foster the trend in client/server computing, allowing information to be retrieved through the desktop workstation from any database utilizing it. The Z39.50 protocol guidelines provide balance between both ends of the remote search interaction process. Z39.50 is a robust protocol that facilitates:

- Restricting access to authenticated users

- Browsing indexes and thesauri

- Retrieving selected content

- ◆ Negotiating the retrieval of large search results (e.g., query refinement, limiting)
- ◆ Removing duplicates from the retrieval set
- ◆ Sorting the search results before presentation
- ◆ Searching and presenting results
- ◆ Extending services such as placing orders, updating files, saving search result sets, and exporting data (in the MARC format).[10]

> ✐ **Tip!** One of the interesting and unintended consequences of Z39.50 is that MARC records are delivered to the requesting automated library system. These records can then be imported into the requesting library's database using the Cataloging module.

Z39.50 will likely increase in importance as more integrated client/server systems rely on its communication rules for interoperability. Presently, most ILS vendors in the library community have developed a Z39.50 client module that promises access to any Z39.50-compliant database. The user can be using a Windows-based interface or a World Wide Web browser such as Netscape or Microsoft Explorer. Most vendors have also developed a Z39.50 server so a library can provide access to its collection.

A major problem associated with implementing Z39.50 is that not all vendors or libraries that develop their own software are fully compliant with the latest version of Z39.50 (currently version 3). To improve the compatibility level among different LIS, several groups have defined an acceptable functional compliance level. These definitions are called "profiles," and the more prominent of these are the Bath Profile (UK), the Union Catalogue Profile (Australia), and the Z Texas Profile (U.S.). Several other profiles have either been defined or are in the process of being defined. (See Figure 6-1.)

Markup Standards

Another model intended to promote unlimited access to digitized information is Standard Generalized Markup Language (SGML). This standard is recognized by both NISO and the ISO (ISO 8879) and is used by many commercial and governmental agencies in the online environment. The ANSI/NISO/ISO designation is 12083–1995 Electronic Manuscript Preparation and Markup, which is in complete conformance with ISO 8879 (SGML). ANSI/NISO/ISO 12083 provides a toolkit for developing customized SGML applications. Four distinct document type definitions (DTDs) are specified for books, serials, articles, and mathematics.

SGML is a digital encoding system that preserves the logical structure of the text in its entirety as it is transferred through different operating systems. In a sense, SGML can be categorized as "descriptive" for its distinction between the components in a text, such as a paragraph, and by its system of structural "tags" that define the boundaries of each part.[11]

A. Without a "Search and Retrieve" Protocol

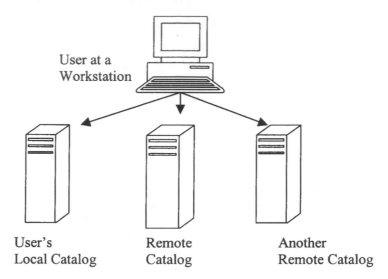

B. With a "Search and Retrieve" (Z39.50) Protocol

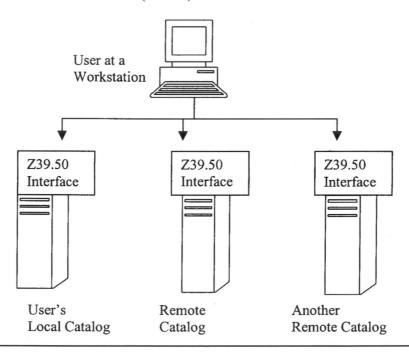

Figure 6-1. Z39.50 Searching

SGML documents consist of three layers: structure, content, and style. For structure, SGML works with an application file called the DTD. The DTD describes and provides a framework for the document's structure. The content element of an SGML document is the actual text with added tags that are defined in the SGML DTD. The third element, style, defines how the document will appear on the screen or in print.

SGML encoded text maintains its coherency for end users even as it is propelled through varying systems: "SGML allows users to manage information as data objects instead of as characters on a page. Rather than a stream of indistinguishable bits and bytes, the data are broken into discrete objects of information that carry intelligence about their meaning within the overall system. This technology enables users to store and reuse the information efficiently, share it with others, and maintain it in a database."[12]

Proponents of SGML look to its internal structural tagging system as the key to "context-sensitive search capabilities." One such conglomeration is the Text Encoding Initiative (TEI), made up of the Association for Literary and Linguistic Computing (ALLC), the Association for Computers and the Humanities (ACH), and the Association for Computational Linguistics (ACL), which promotes the retrospective encoding of educational literature into SGML.[13] The SGML format meets the first priority of the TEI, which is to allow the compatible exchange of information between systems, while avoiding the "Tower of Babel Syndrome."[14] The initiative's second reason for implementing SGML is its potential scalability that will allow it to add finer text detail as technology advances, thus retaining the text's readability even as computer systems become obsolete.[15] The TEI has promoted digital text documentation in higher education by offering standards on SGML encoding. The first edition of their "Guidelines for the Encoding and Interchange of Machine Readable Texts," was distributed to scholars in the humanities and social sciences in 1990.[16] By consulting this manual, Rutgers and Princeton University began work the following year on a model for SGML-based scholarly publishing on the Internet, known as the Center for Electronic Texts in the Humanities (CETH).[17]

For the Web, SGML has manifested itself as Hyper Text Markup Language (HTML). HTML is a DTD of SGML, an example of a use of SGML. The current version of HTML (version 4.0) is not a formal standard on its own, but rather a DTD of SGML. As such, HTML can be considered a de facto or industry standard, popularized by the rise in the use of the World Wide Web.

Hypertext Markup Language (HTML)

Simple, ASCII-based HTML documents began appearing in 1991, shortly after Tim Berners-Lee created the hypertext transfer protocol (the http:// portion of the address you used to have to enter in the Open field of a Web browser). With the release of a graphical user interface (GUI) Web browser in early 1993 (developed by Marc Andreesen and others at the National Center for Supercomputing Applications (NCSA) site at the University of Illinois and originally called "Mosaic"), the potential for Internet delivery of hypertext dawned on a host of net users. Currently HTML is the *lingua franca* for publishing hypertext on the World Wide Web. It is a non-proprietary format based upon SGML and can be created and processed by a wide range of tools, from simple plain text editors to sophisticated "what you see is what you get" (WYSIWYG) authoring tools.

The concepts of HTML were based on notions of hypertext that had been floating around in computer science and other fields for some time. In 1945, Vannevar Bush first wrote an article published in the *Atlantic Monthly* entitled "As We May Think," where, among other things, he planted the notion of retrieving knowledge records by "associative trails" and actually used the word "web" in his text. In 1965, J.C.R. Licklider wrote a book entitled *The Future of Libraries*, in which he referred to a sort of digital library of the future, based on bits, not atoms. In 1977, another pioneer, Theodor Nelson, was the first to articulate a vision for personal computers. In his book *The Home Computer Revolution*, Nelson envisioned the world's knowledge being available to all persons via desktop devices. He called his ambitious project "Xanadu." Nelson is usually credited with inventing hypertext in the 1960s. Licklider, who was the first head of the Advanced Research Projects Agency (ARPA) in 1962, is often credited with conceptualizing and seeding the development of what we now call the "Internet."

Berners-Lee created the original tags and format for HTML when he created the HTTP protocol (the Web or hypertext protocol, if you will). HTML originated as an application (a DTD) of SGML. By 1995, Berners-Lee and David Connolly had completed work on version 2.0 of HTML, and this effort became the de facto standard for Web page authoring. In January 1997, the W3C released HTML version 3.2, elevating the Web markup language from a crude functional beginning to a more effective authoring environment. Work continued on the standard, and version 4.0 (late 1997) brought the controversial "frames" tag and improved display and layout tags. Tables were also included and HTML now supported style sheets. Also included was a means to standardize the use of scripts, which brought us sound and motion and other compelling media. It also brought us those proprietary plug-ins that we generally have to download to view that mixed media.

The first W3C HTML Working Group owed its origins to discussions begun in 1995 by W3C for resolving interoperability concerns for browsers from different vendors. The group developed the W3C Recommendation for HTML 3.2 and, subsequently, for HTML 4.0. The group then disbanded.

Following the workshop on the future of HTML, held in 1998, the second HTML Working Group was chartered to reformulate HTML as a modular application of XML. The second HTML Working Group produced W3C Recommendations for HTML 4.01 (a maintenance release superseding HTML 4.0), and for XHTML 1.0 (a reformulation of HTML 4.01 in XML). The second edition of XHTML 1.0, which incorporated errata submitted since the first publication of XHTML 1.0 in January 2000, was published as a Working Draft in October 2001 to gather public feedback.[18]

eXtensible Markup Language (XML)

Approved in October 1998 by the W3C, this new standard has caused quite a commotion, especially since, as yet, it has few full-blown applications. XML is a markup language built from the start to be extensible, meaning that you, the author/ creator, can make up any tags you like (so long as you specify them in your XML DTD). XML is designed to enable the use of SGML on the WWW in a more robust manner than was ever possible when using HTML as a Web markup language.

XML offers the following three benefits not found in HTML:

+ **Extensibility**. Because HTML is based on a DTD, HTML does not allow users to specify their own tags or attributes or otherwise semantically qualify their data. Programmers love to create new stuff that's all their own. XML supports this creativity because XML is on the same level of generality as SGML: one creates a DTD and uses whatever codes one wants. An analogy might be a palette that allows painters to create new colors out of the basic set of primary colors. Just think how boring art would be without those mixes!

+ **Structure**. HTML does not support the specification of "deep structures" needed to represent database schemas or object-oriented hierarchies. Ask any developer of a database application about his or her efforts to create a Web-based version of that database, and you will begin to understand the difficulties.

+ **Validation**. HTML does not support the kind of language specification that allows consuming applications to check data for structural validity on importation. This is crucial in all commercial applications and important in database applications as well.

A key element of XML is that it supports Unicode (ISO 10646), the international standard two-byte character set that covers most human written languages. Thus, XML can be written in nearly any language.

SGML is very complex. It's specification manual is nearly unreadable and quite lengthy. The specifications for XML are less than 30 pages (HTML is even shorter!). The learning curve of any authoring tool is closely related to the length of these specifications.

Existing HTML documents can be converted over to XML by following certain rules for the various tags. For example, XML is case sensitive, whereas HTML is not. XML requires that *all* open tags have a closed tag as well. For those of you who code in HTML, think about paragraph <P> and line breaks <BR>. A sloppily coded HTML document will be difficult to convert to XML. XML is positioned to replace HTML as the markup language of choice for developing professional Web applications. As things move towards XML, we will likely see XML-compliant browsers (beginning with Internet Explorer 5.0) surface that are capable of handling both HTML and XML coding. The advantages of XML in handling richer media and databases should serve end users well in future developments.

Unicode

Unicode is a standard developed by the Unicode Consortium intended to provide a unique number for every character, regardless of language, platform, or program. It should facilitate information exchange by enabling a computer to process the text of any language without needing to use numerous, sometimes contradictory, encoding systems. Unicode is currently the standard for Apple, HP, IBM, JustSystem, Microsoft, Oracle, SAP, Sun, Sybase, and Unisys and has been adopted by many vendors. It is also required for de facto standards like HTML 4.0, XML, Java, ECMAScript (JavaScript), and others. Since 1992, it has been kept in sync with ISO 10646 (Information Technology: Universal Multiple-Octet Coded Character Set [UCS]).

One problem of previous encoding systems was that they were too small (generally seven- or eight-bit codes) to accommodate a large number of characters across many languages. Most institutions simply chose the encoding system that accommodated most local need. There are currently efforts being made to map Unicode back to those systems for library applications.

There are several concerns about implementing Unicode, including disk space, how to catalog, data transfer speed, coping with unknown characters, and searching.

Unicode also has some nifty linguistic and technological features, which make it rather useful. One of those features is embedding semantics into the code to provide concept information in addition to the code for the character and how to display it.[19] For more information about Unicode, visit the Unicode Web site at http://www.unicode.org.

THE STANDARDS REALITY

One characteristic of highly technical standards is that the various standards organizations and their voting members constantly scrutinize them to ensure that each is conducive to the realities of the information environment. Information standards are dependent upon the consent of such members and their acknowledgement of the standard's relevance by implementing it on a widespread basis. Even if a standard is recognized by an official organization as furthering the exchange of information, the individual members put it into practice at their discretion—they won't do it if it does not advance their interests or seem to comply with the emerging market. A clear example of this phenomenon identified earlier is the ANSI standard Z39.58, which designates a "Common Command Language" for communication between online bibliographic catalogs. While Z39.50 is a set of rules allowing different computer systems to communicate despite their peculiarities, Z39.58 calls for a universal interface command language that would provide a uniform minimum level of search functionality (the standard does not eliminate existing proprietary search capabilities). This would give end users a respite from the "client software morass" of different interface packages used to access various search services from a single workstation. However, the reality is that the dominance of client/server-distributed computer technology—a reality that has been partially encouraged by Z39.50—increases reliance on Z39.50 for interoperability. In this environment, for-profit database and OPAC vendors perceive a Common Command Language as unnecessary and contrary to their interest in marketing products with distinctive front-end interfaces.

This example illustrates that implementing a national standard is a process that libraries, as primarily consumers of information, sometimes have little control over. While standards that increase access and compatibility between computer systems are beneficial to all parties, the private sector must naturally safeguard its investments. One effort with this intention is the pending Digital Object Identifier (DOI) standard; which was developed to "facilitate electronic commerce and allow publishers to maintain copyright," on information through what may be thought of as "an ISBN for electronic publishing."[20] The DOI has been mandated by the Association of American Publishers under the development of R.R. Bowker and the Corporation for National Research Initiatives. Each DOI is a number consisting of one component given by the DOI Agency (Bowker—for a fee) and another by the publisher for assignment to a specific online article. The DOI thereby distinguishes various forms of content by assigning each a unique number for copyright purposes. Supposedly, whenever a user clicks on a graphic that has been designated by a DOI, that person's e–mail address will be forwarded to the item's publisher. This advantage in identifying their markets, along with copyright protection, gives publishers an incentive to keep their online offerings current.[21] The DOI is set for full implementation next year and foretells a tremendous increase in "the universe of copyrighted, salable objects" on the Internet.[22] Although many publishers remain skeptical of this mechanism's resilience, it is apparent that such a standard is inherently restrictive and could evolve into a measure for transforming much of the National Information Infrastructure into a pay-per-view environment.

RELATED ORGANIZATIONS

Other groups contributing to the compatibility or implementation of information systems in libraries are the Coalition for Networked Information (CNI), the W3C, and the Corporation for National Research Initiatives (CNRI). The CNI is a partnership of the ARL, the Association for Managing and Using Information Resources in Higher Education (CAUSE), and the Inter-University Communications Council (EDUCOM). The coalition was founded in March 1990 to promote the distribution of networked information on the National Research and Education Network (NREN). CNI also has numerous auxiliary members from public libraries and publishers in its Task Force to promote greater communication within higher education on information policies.[23] Although CNI does not regulate or propose standards for information technology, it does provide a forum for communicating on the range of emerging issues in networked information systems.[24]

The W3C is another potential resource that can help libraries stay abreast of trends in online information retrieval. This collection of various organizations is "vendor neutral, working with the global community to produce specifications and reference software that is made freely available throughout the world."[25] Again, W3C does not issue literal standards, but does pass recommendations that have attained "a general . . . consensus among members." Official recommendations start out as working drafts of specifications available for consideration and are then promoted to proposed recommendations by the consortium director before becoming endorsed recommendations.[26] Currently, there are no proposed recommendations under consideration, but there are several consortium-sponsored recommendations and working drafts available for viewing with the intention of contributing to World Wide Web interoperability and information retrieval.

A final organization worth mentioning for its role in the DOI project is the CNRI. Besides its involvement in developing technologies for resolving intellectual property/copyright—as exemplified by the DOI—this non-profit corporation works toward facilitating access to the National Information Infrastructure in general, and claims to have provided technical support to the Library of Congress's National

Digital Library Project, among other efforts for "government, business, and academic institutions."[27]

The obvious importance of library standards requires that librarians and their representative organizations be assertive in conveying their practical priorities and values to these various standards-making organizations. Standards do much more than affect the procedures for retrieving bits of data—they unavoidably define the policies of those information agencies that use them. Therefore, it is only reasonable to conclude that libraries must communicate their concerns to groups such as CNRI if they are to promote a relatively open realm of information. As ANSI declares: "Quite simply, companies [and libraries] that allow key standards issues to be determined by someone else risk being left out in the cold."[28] By contrast, direct involvement within the standards creation process through the above-cited organizations will continue to give librarians leadership opportunity in information access.[29]

SUMMARY

This chapter began with a basic understanding of the role of standards in designing Library Information Systems and closed with a call for professional involvement in developing standards that affect the dissemination of content to end users in increasingly complex technological environments. We examined and profiled several important national and international organizations that support the continued development of standards relating to the processes and services found in most libraries and information agencies. We also examined four categories of formal standards relating to information technology designs. As long as libraries seek to develop and implement new information technologies, they need to be cognizant of the impact standards development has on the processes involved and the services delivered using those technologies.

NOTES

1.   http://www.iso.ch/infoe/intro.html.

2.   Walt Crawford. *Technical Standards: An Introduction for Librarians*. White Plains, NY: Knowledge Industry Publications, 1986.

3.   http://www.niso.org/whatare.htm.

4.   Shirley M. Radack. "More Effective Federal Computer Systems: The Role of NIST and Standards." *Government Information Quarterly*, 7 (1), 1990, p. 38.

5.   Ron Chespesiuk. "Organizing the Internet: The 'Core' of the Challenge." *American Libraries*, 31 (1), January 1999, pp. 59–63. For additional information, visit the Dublin Core Home Page at: http://purl.org/dc/index.htm.

6.   RDF FAQ. Available at: http://www.w3.org/RDF/FAQ. RDF specification. Available at: http://www.w3.org/TR/REC-rdf-syntax/ and http://www.zvon.org/xxl/RDFTutorial/General/book.html. Tim Bray. RDF and Metadata. Available at: http://www.xml.com/pub/a/98/06/rdf.html. Rachel M. Heery. What is . . . RDF. *Ariadne (Online)*, 14, March 1998. Available at: http://www.ariadne.ac.uk/issue14/what-is/. Ora Lassila. Introduction to RDF Metadata. Available at: http://www.w3.org/TR/NOTE-rdf-simple-into.

7.   http://www.oclc.org/oclc/promo/7276z39a/graph.htm

8.   Maribeth Ward. "Expanding Access with Z39.50." *American Libraries*, 25, July/August 1994, p. 640.

9.   Lennie Stovel. "Sidebar 6: Zephyr: RLG's Z39.50 Implementation." *Library Hi Tech*, 12 (2), 1994, p. 20.

10.   http://www.cni.org/pub/NISO/docs/Z39.50-1992/WWW/50.Brochure.part02.html

11.   Malcolm Brown. "What Is SGML?" *Information Technology and Libraries*, 13 March 1994, p. 10.

12.   Anonymous. "SGML in Education: The TEI and ICADD Initiatives." *Computers in Libraries*. 16, March 1996, p. 26.

13.   Ibid., p. 27.

14.   Malcolm Brown. "What Is the TEI?" *Information Technologies and Libraries*, 13, March 1994, p. 8.

15.   Anonymous. "SGML in Education: The TEI and ICADD Initiatives." *Computers in Libraries*,16, March 1996, pp. 27–28.

16.   Clifford A. Lynch. "Text Encoding Initiative: Summary Progress Report." *Bulletin of the American Society for Information Science*, 18, February/March 1992, p. 21.

17.   Marianne I. Gaunt. "Center for Electronic Texts in the Humanities." *Information Technology and Libraries*, 13, March 1994, p. 7.

18.   http://www.w3.org/MarkUp/Activity#current.

19.   Joan M. Aliprand. "The Unicode Standard: Its Scope, Design Principles, and Prospects for International Cataloging." *Library Resources & Technical Services*, 44 (3), July 2000, pp. 160–67.

20.   Norman Oder. "New Online ISBN Moves Ahead." *Library Journal*, 121, October 1, 1996, pp. 15–16.

21.   Calvin Reid. "AAP Unveils DOI at PSP Confab: Publishers Interested But Wary." *Publishers Weekly*, 244, February 24 1997, p. 11.

22.   Ibid., p. 11.

23.   John K. Lippencott. "Change and the Referent Organization: The CNI." *Journal of Library Administration*, 19 (3–4), 1993, pp. 250–52.

24.   Ibid., 254.

25.   http://www.w3.org/pub/WWW/consortium/.

26.   http://www.w3.org/pub/WWW/TR/.

27.   http://www.cnri.reston.va.us/home/cnri.html.

28.   http://www.ansi.org/.

29.   Maribeth Ward. "Expanding Access with Z39.50." *American Libraries*, 25, July/August 1994, p. 641.

Part III
Management Issues

Managing LIS projects is considered by many to be the most important aspect of LIS implementations, and the next six chapters run the gamut from planning to system selection and implementation. Chapter 7 discusses the strategic planning process for information technology and its impact on library staffs. Chapter 8 offers common sense axioms that include guidelines for decision makers. Chapter 9 addresses the impact issues related to technology implementation. Chapter 10 presents an overview of the system reflection process and related implementation issues. Chapter 11 focuses on usability studies. This section closes with a chapter addressing management issues and identifying qualities associated with a systems manager.

Chapter 7

Planning for Information Technology

PLANNING PROCESS

Technology is permeating all aspects of our lives, including the libraries and organizations where we work. The implications of this pervasive force are that we all are constantly coping with and learning new technology skills. Technology has also impacted our social structure as we increasingly use e-mail, electronic greeting cards, online chat rooms, instant messaging, and in some cases, video conferencing, to communicate with our family, friends, and co-workers. Technology has impacted the way we work; information and productivity software collaboration tools are now accessible to all staff members. Technology is infiltrating the marketplace as we increasingly turn to online, Internet-based, e-commerce options to buy things for work and home.

Regardless of the size and type of library, planning for information technology must occur in a broader strategic planning process. Developing a technology plan that is not in concert with the goals and mission of the parent organization is simply an exercise in futility. While the technology plan may be good from a technical point of view, its utility for the library and its parent organization may be negligible if it is not in "synch with the goals of the organization." The purpose of any strategic plan is to set a clear direction that integrates goals, policies, and actions into a cohesive whole.[1]

A strategic library plan works best when the parent organization's mission statement is reflected in the plan. Assessing the suitability of a library plan requires answers to a wide-ranging series of questions. Does the library's vision statement and goals and objectives complement that of the parent organization? Does the library's strategic plan identify the library's core competencies? Is it clear what the library does that adds maximum value? What library services do patrons actually use and, by inference, find to be of value? And what services are used, with and without library assistance? What is the library's role in providing distance services—selecting, acquiring, organizing, and providing access to Internet-based resources? How does the library support these remote users? What kind of training is provided for remote users? If the library's OPAC or Web portal is accessible 24 hours a day, then will additional services, for example, reference, also be available around the clock?[2]

Libraries without a technology plan will experience a much more chaotic life and will require ad hoc purchases of computer equipment and software when something no longer works. Staff will generally feel uncomfortable with and perhaps a bit fearful of information technology because they will have received little or no training. In fact, staff will likely be used to coping with things not working.

Clearly, the preeminent role of library service is to provide access to information—regardless of its actual location. The library's mission is to support the charge of the institution or the interests of the population being served. The preparation of a library strategic plan is an opportunity to consider the unthinkable, to explore options that are outside the box. In some respects, the library should become familiar with the concepts espoused by Michael Hammer and James Champy in their book *Re-Engineering the Corporation.*[3] The term garnered an unfortunate reputation in the early 1990s when it was associated with downsizing. However, re-engineering is not about reducing head count, but rather it is the "fundamental rethinking and radical redesign of business processes to achieve dramatic improvements in critical measures of performance, such as cost, quality, service, and speed."

There are four keywords within this definition. They are:

- **Fundamental**. After it is determined what an organization will do, the focus then shifts to how best to do it. The concentration is on what could be or should be—not what is.

- **Radical**. A radical redesign disregards existing procedures and processes and looks for new ways to accomplish things. Boundaries need to be broken and departments may require re-structuring or destruction.

- **Dramatic**. The focus of re-engineering is to aim for improvements that are an order of magnitude greater than existing processes—improvements on the order of 100 percent, 200 percent, or more rather than incremental improvements.

- **Processes**. A process is a collection of activities that takes inputs and creates an output that is of value to a customer. The focus is not on departments or other organization units. Note that information technology can act as an essential enabler in re-engineering.

The reality today is that information technology increasingly allows a library to change. Moreover, insistent library customers will, in the end, force libraries to change. The speed with which the Web is continuing to change and evolve is a constant fact of life that libraries must reckon with. Yet, the mere fact that technology continues to change at a rapid pace is not sufficient grounds to change the services provided by a library. Rather, the library should be focusing on its users and their needs as the primary motivating factor in any strategic planning process.

During this planning process, the library staff members and decision makers involved in the planning process must question all present practices and assumptions about what the library is and the value it provides to its users.

The goals of a good technology plan, according to March Osten are:

> Strategic technology planning is a dynamic and reflective process that organizations engage in to seize the potential of advanced technologies. Strategic technology plans are grounded in your mission and fully integrated into your overall strategic plan. The strategic technology planning process ensures that you will clarify technological goals and establish priorities, organize relevant stakeholders and create evaluation systems—all before making hardware, software or Internet presence decisions.[4]

A technology plan documents the vision and direction of the library and creates a framework to set goals and identify specific deliverables. Once the plan is in place, it can help library decision-makers measure the costs and success in achieving the plan's goals. Although the plan is a document, it is much more important to recognize that it is also a process to provide staff with a roadmap. The plan connects the library's technology use (current and future) to achieving the library's vision. Not only will the technology plan identify ways to improve the delivery of services, programs, and operations with technology, but it will also include specific outcome measures that can be used to assess the plan's impact in the future.

Frequently at the start of the strategic planning process, the planning team engages in a process to identify strengths, weaknesses, opportunities, and threats (SWOT):

♦ Strengths (what the organization/library currently does well)

♦ Weaknesses (what are the organization's/library's current problems)

♦ Opportunities (forecast future possibilities, in terms of services—not technology—that will benefit the library's users)

♦ Threats (what external pressures could change the competitive landscape).

While a staff member might prepare a SWOT document for discussion purposes, the library's planning team will often simply brainstorm to come up with this information. Regardless of the approach, a SWOT planning document should be prepared that records the perceptions of the library's decision makers.

The library should create or update an inventory of the existing technology that is being used in the library. This inventory should include:

Network Infrastructure (LAN and WAN)

♦ Type of cabling

♦ Location or routes of cabling

♦ Bandwidth capabilities

♦ Internet connection

♦ Wireless service

Computer Hardware (Desktop and Network Level)

◆ Age and performance characteristics of machines

◆ Level of standardization among hardware

Software

◆ Availability of needed software by function

◆ Standardized software

◆ Licenses for all software

Technology Support

◆ User support

◆ Network support

◆ Data backup and virus protection

Staff Skills

◆ Current technology skills among staff

◆ Adequate skills for different job functions

Once the goals have been established and there is a clear understanding of the current situation, a list of projects can be created that will move the library in the direction of achieving its vision (this is sometimes called a gap analysis). The technology plan can establish the natural or preferred sequencing of these projects, but reality would suggest that there needs to be some flexibility—for example, the availability of grant funds may require a project to proceed out of order.

> ⚡ **Tip!** A library information system evaluation checklist is provided at the end of this chapter to help the library decision-makers to better understand and assess the technological capabilities and limitations that currently exist in your library.

An effective strategic planning process helps the library create its own future and is characterized by:

◆ **A customer focus**. How effective is the library in meeting the needs of its users? Effectiveness is answering the question, "Are we doing the *right* things?" Could or should the library be serving more of its potential users? What is the appropriate balance between high-tech and high-touch?

◆ **Maintaining relevant services**. Recognize that the library exists in a competitive landscape and that it must change to remain relevant to its users. One of the major keys to remaining relevant is convenience. Clearly, the convenience of the Web compared to the physical inconvenience of finding and using information in a library must be addressed.

- **Focusing on outcomes**. How does the library impact its users? Impact the community? Impact the parent organization? An attempt should be made to answer the question, "Of what value is the library to _____ (e.g., parent organization, the community)."

- **Examining efficiency**. Examine the internal procedures of the library to determine how efficient its processes and procedures are. Are we doing *things* right? This may involve benchmarking or other data collection and analysis procedures. Could the library outsource some tasks or activities?

- **Exploring the need to provide access to audio, video, images, and other resources beyond text**. Explore the need to provide access to Internet-based electronic resources including indexes and full-text databases (the deep Web), and Internet resources, among other things. The implications of electronic media is that it can be:

  1. Used from a distance
  2. Used by more than one person at a time
  3. Used in a variety of ways.

"Any time anything important changes in an organization by a factor of 10, it is necessary to re-think the whole enterprise."

Andy Grove

"Artifact-based organizations, e.g., libraries, will decline in importance as information escapes the artifact."

Daniel W. Lewis

Once a library has developed its strategic plan, then and only then should it consider developing a technology plan. Prior to starting the planning process, there are some questions that should be addressed:

- What is the involvement of various staff in developing or reviewing the plan? The best plans come from a variety of people who are able to offer diversified opinions.

- What about the involvement of staff outside the library (Chief Information Officer, Chief Technology Officer, IT Manager, and others)?

- To what extent will users be involved in planning and reviewing plans? Will there be user surveys or focus groups?

- Is the library planning to hire a consultant? What is the consultant's appropriate role—facilitator? full team member?

The elements of a good technology plan are few yet they are often overlooked:

♦ **Concise**. The plan itself should be a document that can be read and understood by someone that is not a technology nerd—technological and library jargon should be avoided at all costs. Thus, the plan itself should not be lengthy. In a majority of cases, the technology plan will need to be reviewed and approved by a library board or funding decision makers. In reality, a good technology plan can be a wonderful document to facilitate that review process and serve as a training document for these decision-makers.[5]

♦ **Specific**. The technology plan needs to be an action plan that identifies the tasks to be completed over the next three years. The plan should have specific phased objectives and identify who is responsible for implementing each objective.

♦ **Integrated**. The technology plan needs to have several components including:

> *Infrastructure*. What are the plans for the LAN? What are the bandwidth requirements for the LAN backbone and the backbone to each desktop workstation? What is the current type and speed of the Internet connection? What capacity will be needed in the future for an Internet connection? Is a network diagram included? Is there an inventory of the network-related equipment, such as routers, hubs, cabling, and so forth?

> *Central site equipment*. Do any of the existing servers need to be upgraded or replaced? Do additional servers or disk drives need to be ordered? Is there an inventory of central site equipment?

> *Central site software requirements*. Will the operating systems be upgraded? Are there major upgrades for the library's application software that will need to be installed? Is there an inventory of central site software?

> *Desktop equipment and software requirements*. What portion of the desktop workstations will be replaced (with what speed CPU processor, memory, and disk space,)? Does the desktop operating system need to be upgraded? Is there an inventory of desktop equipment and software? The plan should assume old devices have NO value and that there is a phased equipment-replacement program that is a part of the plan.

> *Standards*. What standards are being used as a planning platform for the library? Standards might include minimum desktop equipment configurations, a specific release of a desktop operating system, Web browser, server hardware & operating system, database management system, LAN communications protocol (e.g., TCP/IP), virus scanning software, firewall software, etc.

> *Web Site Development*. Are the resources needed to maintain and re-design the library Web site identified?

Special Projects. Will the library be engaging in any special projects, such as digitizing historical photographs, technical reports, and other resources? The resources and staffing needed to complete these projects should be identified.

Staffing needs. Are any new positions needed? What are the training needs of the existing technology staff? Is recruiting and retaining technology staff an issue that needs to be addressed? Are any staff members likely to be promoted (in which case the library should be engaged in succession planning)?

Financial Aspects. An effective plan will drive the budget rather than allow the budget to drive the plan. Identify the financial aspects in general terms.

♦ **Foreseeable**. Plan for one to three years ahead. Anything further and the confidence level about future technology developments will decline markedly. The plan should be reviewed annually and updated as needed. Ensuring that the library's decision-makers see the big picture is a better approach than the diffusion of the library's goals that might result should a department-by-department approach be employed.

♦ **Flexible**. Recognize that partial solutions will lead to long-term goals. The plan should have a realistic chance of being attainable, yet require the library to stretch a bit. It is not always possible to achieve each goal in the desired sequence or time frame. However, a number of small interim victories will move the library in the right direction. Technology can change quickly and the library's technology plan needs to have the flexibility to respond quickly to implement and support a new technology when the need arises.

Rather than being a high-tech wish list, a sound technology plan will map the growth of the computer and communications networks that will be needed to support the library's goals. It is vital to recognize that information technology is simply a tool to help the library provide service to its customers. Thus, a technology plan is more than a listing of the hardware and software that currently exists and will be implemented in the coming years. An effective plan is one that demonstrates how effectively using information technology will improve the value of the services provided by the library to its users.[6]

One of the most coherent and compelling technology plans was recently completed at the University of Michigan. This *President's Information Revolution Commission Report* focused on the impacts associated with the information environment and then addressed the needs for infrastructure along with the following related topics: what we should teach, how we should teach, our research agenda, and outreach and the new learning community.

✎ **Tip!** A copy of the University of Michigan's *President's Information Revolution Commission Report* is available at http://www.umich .edu/pres/inforev.

Outline of a Technology Plan

- Executive Summary
- Description of the Library
- Assessment of Challenges Facing the Library
- The Current Technology Environment
- Assessment of the Current Technology Environment
- Assessment of the Library's Web Site
- Plan of Action Including Timelines and Budgets
- Plan for Revisions
- Appendixes (as needed)

STAYING CURRENT

What can a library staff member do to keep current with the rapidly changing technology field? Oh, so many resources and so little reading time! Subscribing to a number of print or electronic library and technology resources is a good starting point. Scanning these publications will provide a general overview of what is happening in the computer and communications technology arenas. Subscribing to an alert service that provides summaries of articles is another really useful strategy to cope with information overload. The trick is not to get immersed in the details, but rather to focus on the horizon to see the big picture. When reviewing an article:

- Consider how the technology could improve service to the library's patrons or its staff members.
- Recognize that some industry players, by their immense size, will have a disproportionate impact on the marketplace. Some of the vendors who fall into this category are Microsoft, Oracle, Sun, or Cisco. Thus, be cautious about betting against one of these firms.
- Clearly identify those areas that you can control, as well as those technology components that are outside your control.

At conferences, online discussion groups, and other forums, make sure you chat with your peers about the direction they are moving and new technologies they are implementing.

IMPACT OF INFORMATION TECHNOLOGY ON LIBRARY STAFF

Information technology is unmistakably having a major impact on staff members at all levels within the library, whether professional, para-professional, or clerical. There are six major implications concerning the use of information technology for library staff members:

- **Increasing workload**. While access to computer resources throughout the organization improves the staff's overall productivity, this accessibility also means that the staff's workload is increasing. The technology now means that each staff member not only needs to do his or her normal duties in a shorter period of time, but are also being called upon to respond to e-mails and other communications from individuals both within and outside the organization.

- **Staff is not being reduced**. One of management's original expectations concerning information technology was that staff could potentially be reduced. Some libraries have been able to cope with a doubling or tripling of the workload without increasing staff by more effectively using the tools provided by information technology—such tools as a LIS, Microsoft Office, and e-mail. However, the mix of staff is changing because of the drift-down principles:[7]

  1. Nothing should be done by a professional that can be done by a technician

  2. Nothing should be done by a technician that can be done by a clerk

  3. Nothing should be done by a clerk that can be done by a machine.

- **Computer workstations require care**. The workstations attached to the LAN within the library require periodic care and feeding. Problems will inevitably crop up that need to be resolved, such as installing a new software driver on each desktop workstation once a new printer has been installed, installing a new desktop operating system, repairing a corrupted disk drive, or installing a new version of a Web browser and associated plug-ins.

- **Need to upgrade skills**. When confronted with a plethora of new software versions or new application software, staff members are faced with the need to upgrade their skills so they can effectively use the available information technology. We have all been bombarded with technology-related jargon. For example, just a few years ago, most of us probably did not know what PDF, Perl, CGI, EAD, and TEI actually meant and how they might be used in a library.

- **Forget some skills/knowledge**. Conversely, staff members occasionally need to forget some skills that worked in the past when there was a slower pace of life and we had less to do each day. Trying to stay current with several professional discussion groups (and the associated blizzard of e-mails) is a nice objective, but seldom attainable.

◆ **Jobs are automation dependent**. Clearly, with almost all staff members having access to and expected to be comfortable with computer technology, staff does need to be comfortable entering information into a variety of applications or surfing the Internet. Ironically, one of the reasons some librarians chose their profession is that they did not want to have a career that required "typing skills."

SUMMARY

The importance of preparing a technology plan cannot be over-emphasized. However, this technology plan should be based on the requirement that technology should only be contemplated after the library has a clear understanding of the mission and goals of its parent organization.

Evaluating Your Library Information System

For each option, choose the appropriate value reflecting the situation in your library and enter the score to the right.

Your Score

Technology Planning   _____

No Technology Plan exists for the library	0
"Techno-centric" Plan exists	2
Organization "mission-focused" Plan	5
Organization "mission-focused" Plan w/ budget	10

Infrastructure

Speed of LAN   _____
1 Mbps	1
10 Mbps	5
10/100 Mbps	9
Faster	10

Communications protocol   _____
TCP/IP supported	10

How frequently does the LAN fail?   _____
Several times a week	1
Once a month	5
Once every 6–12 months	9
Once a year	10

Speed of the Internet connection   _____
Dial-up modem	1
1.5 Mbps (T-1 line)	5
45 Mbps (T-3 line)	9
Faster	10

Budgets for replacement of computers   _____
Never—they last a long time	0
Only if they can't be repaired	2
On a regular 3–4 year cycle	10

Infrastructure Subtotal   _____

Evaluating Your Library Information System

		Your Score
Type of System		_____
Character-based	1	
Client/Server-based	5	
Web-based	10	
Age of System		_____
More than 7 years	1	
5–7 years	5	
3–5 years	7	
Less than 1 year	10	
Z39.50 (Version 3)		_____
Server supported	10	
Client supported	10	
Searching		_____
Browse/keyword indexes	5	
Browse/keyword indexes +		
Automatic synonym searches	10	
OPAC (add scores of multiple choices)		_____
Library catalog	1	
Hypertext linking of URL's	3	
Web-based OPAC accessible	3	
via the Internet		
Access to electronic resources—		
indexes, abstracts, full-text	5	
Access to images, audio and		
video files	5	
Display of book jacket images,		
book reviews, author bios, etc.	7	
Full-text access to word processing,		
PowerPoint, and spreadsheets	7	
Personalization of the OPAC	10	
Acquisitions		_____
MARC-based EDI transactions	1	
X.12-based EDI transactions	5	
XML-based EDI transactions	10	

Your Score

Serials   _____
    MARC-based EDI transactions   1
    X.12-based EDI transactions   5
    XML-based EDI transactions   10

API Interfaces (add scores of multiple choices)   _____
    Automatically move data between:
    Employee file   5
    Campus student registration file   5
    Organization's accounting system   10

    Library Information System Subtotal   _____

Operations

Technology Training for Staff   _____
    None   0
    Informal   3
    As needed   5
    Formal technology training plan for
        each staff member   10

Back-Ups   _____
    None   0
    Sporadically   3
    Done on a regular schedule   7
    Done on a regular schedule with off-site storage   10

Anti-Virus Detection   _____
    None installed   0
    Updated sporadically   3
    Updated on a weekly basis   5
    Updated daily   10

Software Application Updates   _____
    Done sporadically   0
    Done when needed to correct a problem   3
    Done or a regular schedule   10

    Operations Subtotal   _____

Database (total of all categories)   _____

If a category has 0% machine-readable records, assign a 0 rating.
If a category has 50% machine-readable records, assign a 5 rating.
If a category has 100% machine-readable records, assign a 10 rating.

> Books
> Serials (Titles)
> Audio/Visual
> Images
> Technical Reports
> Patents
> Government Documents
> Other

TOTAL SCORE   _____

If your LIS evaluation score is less than 100, then you need to immediately start planning to install a new system or upgrade your network infrastructure, or both.

If your LIS evaluation score ranges from 100 to 150, then you need to work with your LIS vendor and the vendor's Users Group to add some significant enhancements. You should also consider making improvements to your infrastructure.

If your LIS evaluation score is more than 150, then you can relax a bit as you are obviously on the leading edge (but not the bleeding edge) of technology. However, you should carefully review areas in which you might want to make some improvements.

SUGGESTED READINGS

Anderson, Larry, and John Perry. *Technology Planning: Recipe for Success*. March 1994. Available at: http://www.nctp.com/html/tp_recipe.html.

Bocher, Robert. *Writing Public Library Technology Plans*. 2000. Available at: http://www.molo.lib.oh.us/wnew/referen/techplan.htm.

Boss, Richard W. "Introduction: Information Technology Overview and Trends." (Model Technology Plans for Libraries, Part 1). "Information Technology Plan for a Single Facility." (Model Technology Plans for Libraries, Part 2). "Information Technology Plan for a Library System." (Model Technology Plans for Libraries, Part 3). *Library Technology Reports*, 31 (1), January/February 1998, pp. 5–69.

Cohn, John N., Ann L. Kelsey, and Keith Michael Fiels. *Writing and Updating Technology Plans: A Guidebook with Sample Policies on CD-ROM*. New York: Neal-Schuman, 1999.

Cravens, J. *Introducing New Technology Successfully into an Agency and Why Your Organization Needs a Technology Plan*. Last revised May 14, 2000. Available at: http://www.coyotecom.com/database/techbuy.html.

The Library Network. *Technology Planning*. 2001. Available at: http://northville.lib.mi.us/tech/techplan.htm.

Mayo, Diane, and Sandra Nelson. *Wired for the Future: Developing Your Library Technology Plans*. Chicago: American Library Association, 1999.

Osborne, David, and Ted Gaebler. *Reinventing Government: How the Entrepreneurial Spirit Is Transforming the Public Sector*. New York: Addison-Wesley, 1992.

See, John. *Developing Effective Technology Plans*. July 17, 2001. Available at: http://www.nctp.com/htm/john_see.html.

Sweeney, R. T. "Creating Library Services with WOW! Staying Slightly Ahead of the Curve." *Library Trends*, 46 (1), 1997, pp. 129–51.

Wisconsin Department of Public Instruction. *Library Technology Planning: An Outline of the Process*. July 2000. Available at: http://www.dpi.state.wi.us/dpi/dltcl/pld.planout.html.

SUGGESTED WEB RESOURCES

Eau Claire Area School District—Department of Technology (ECASD) Technology Plan
http://www.ecasd.k12.wi.us/departments/technology/21stcentury/default.htm

Helping (technology planning for non-profits)
http://www.helping.org

Kansas City Public Library Long-Range Technology Plan for 2001–2005
http://www.kclibrary.org/kcpl/techplan/default.htm

NPower (technology planning for non-profits)
http://www.npower.org

Ramapo Catskill Library System Technology Plan 2001–2004
http://www.rcls.org/techplan.htm

TechSoup (technology planning for non-profits)
http://www.techsoup.org

NOTES

1.   Valerie Feinman. "Five Steps toward Planning Today for Tomorrow's Needs." *Computers in Libraries*, 19 (1), January 2000, pp. 18–21.

2.   Rebecca Jones. "Business Plans: Roadmaps for Growth & Success." *Information Outlook*, 4 (12), December 2000, pp. 22–29.

3.   Michael Hammer and James Champy. *Re-Engineering the Corporation: A Manifesto for Business Revolution.* New York: Harper Business, 1993. See also the more recent and pragmatic book by Michael Hammer. *The Agenda: What Every Business Must Do to Dominate the Decade.* New York: Crown Business, 2001.

4.   March Osten. "Strategic Technology Planning: What is it?" January 4, 2001. Available at: http://www.techsoup.org/articlepage.cfm?ArticleId=267&topicid=11.

5.   Michael Schuyler. "Life Is What Happens to You When You're Making Other Plans." *Computers in Libraries*, 20 (4), April 2000, pp. 54–55.

6.   Jan A. Baltzer. "Consider the Four-Legged Stool As You Plan for Information Technology." *Computers in Libraries*, 20 (4), April 2000, pp. 42–45.

7.   Michael Gorman. "The Organization of Academic Libraries in the Light of Automation." *Advances in Library Automation and Networking*, 1, 1987, p. 152.

Chapter 8

Basic Technology Axioms

This chapter presents several axioms that appear to have a high degree of relevance or "truism." You might think of them as guiding principles (i.e., these axioms are frequently found in most situations where library professionals cross paths with information and communications technologies).

The dictionary specifies an axiom to be: "1. A self-evident or universally recognized truth; 2. An established rule, principle or law." In mathematics, an axiom is a truth. Such truths rarely exist in the world of LIS, but there is a world of experience, both positive and negative, in libraries and in other organizations, that allow us to formulate the axioms discussed in this chapter.

These principles, or axioms, deal with such things as:

- Standards
- Information Databases
- Hardware Platforms
- Applications Software
- Decision Making
- Management

They do not necessarily deal with the functional or performance issues associated with information technology applications in libraries. After their initial presentation, most of these axioms will seem "self-evident." They become important when considering various strategies for implementing technology applications in libraries and related information agencies.

AXIOM 1: THE DECISION TO AUTOMATE IS IRREVERSIBLE

For centuries, libraries have played the primary role in providing access to knowledge records. These records have predominantly been kept in print form. Using computers to automate certain processes represents a modernization of the library, and in certain cases has resulted in a rather dramatic change in the attitudes and expectations of librarians and users alike. Previously, professional librarians were concerned with the impact of technology on their positions, as they had been defined in that era. Further development resulted in the widespread realization that information technologies could be used to streamline certain routine tasks and procedures, freeing librarians to do more professional tasks, such as providing increased services to end users. As users have become better acquainted with the information technologies, expectations have risen. Users often feel that libraries can or should be the key access point to all sorts of information, whether held physically in the library or not.

As librarians realize the benefits of automating certain backroom technical services, and as users continue to expect increased information services from libraries, the lure and hold of the information technologies appears to be irreversible. Once the individual librarian or the user samples the fruits of technology, there appears to be no going back to "how things were."

Libraries will continue to acquire books, periodical titles, maps, microforms, and other print-based resources. In many cases, this is the preferred format, and both professionals and end users have much invested in these resources. Increasingly, however, informational materials are appearing primarily or first in digital form, with a printed document being a by-product or personal rendering of that content. Some content will be accessed and distributed via this digital format. The two formats will coincide in libraries, as some content will be rendered in one form or the other. In some cases, multiple formats for identical information will be the norm.

Libraries that have incorporated technology to improve access to their collections will not find it easy to return to previous print-based and mechanical means of providing access. Libraries that adopted these information technologies early have by and large moved on to experiment with other digital formats—images, audio, and video files. The moral of the axiom lies in this irreversibility. If technology is, in fact, not an easily reversed decision, then one must carefully consider the consequences of making that decision in the first place. The various options that are available today must be carefully considered, keeping an eye out for future advances that may replace or extend those options.

AXIOM 2: STANDARDS ARE CRITICAL

Standards are important when applying technology to library processes and supporting the provision of services. Chapter 6 discussed the role of information standards and the associations that administrate formal standards. In this chapter, we only consider the concept of standards as a critical component in identifying, selecting, and implementing a library information system.

Picture the situation where a professional librarian begins to define those fields that might be incorporated into a database design used to represent bibliographic objects. The individual must specify such attributes as field name, length of field (number of characters), type of characters allowed in each field, the order of the occurrence of each field, and related details. Clearly, if left to design such a structure in a vacuum, each professional would come up with a unique design that emphasizes one or more attributes, orders fields differently, excludes certain fields, or assigns different characteristics to various fields identified for use in each specific instance.

Now imagine if all libraries had their own proprietary design for a bibliographic record. Quite possibly one might have a slight advantage over the next, but none of the institutions would be capable of communicating with each other: their record structures would be incompatible. They would be unable to identify works held in common, or resources held uniquely (for purposes of reciprocal borrowing). In addition, they would not able to share cataloging records, OPAC access, conduct bibliographic verification, and many other technical and public service tasks commonly associated with cooperating libraries. In essence, they would be operating as independent agencies in the information world.

The agreement among various libraries to adhere to and comply with various standards allows the development and refinement of cooperative services to occur. There are many standards in the areas of libraries, information services, and the database industry, but the most important ones relating to technology are standards that address communications structures and interoperability issues.

The primary standards for communications include those identifying the MARC bibliographic record, along with the patron, transaction, and holdings file record structures. Z39.50, the standard that addresses interoperability of diverse computing platforms, is the predominant development standard of interest to systems designers attempting to connect formerly disparate systems. Adherence to standards is a most important axiom, worthy of serious professional consideration.

AXIOM 3: THE CONVERTED DATABASE IS THE MOST IMPORTANT ASSET

Many professionals who become involved in selecting an integrated library system focus a significant amount of their decision-making energies on the hardware and software choices associated with a given system. Decision-making groups need to recognize that the hardware base and its accompanying applications programs (e.g., circulation control, cataloging modules, online public access catalogs, and so forth) will be continually upgraded and eventually replaced after some period of time. This is not to say that system functionality is not an important issue. Many library institutions maintain a specific vendor's system for up to 10 years, and it is important to have a reliable and fully functional system in place. However, it is the data stored within these systems that will be carried over to whatever hardware or software system is chosen to upgrade or replace the current system.

After the irreversibility and the standards axioms, the focus shifts to data stored as records. Collectively, these records form a set of databases representing various objects of interest to librarians in support of technical, public, and administrative services. These records represent things like bibliographic data, patron data, holdings information, and transaction data. The creation and ongoing maintenance of these various databases is extremely time consuming and fraught with detail.

For these reasons, the portability of data stored as records becomes a very important consideration. Portability is enabled by two important attributes: ownership and adherence to standards. First, the library must retain ownership of its internal records; second, adhering to standards specifying nationally recognized data and record structures ensure that those owned records can be migrated to newer systems should that be necessary. Failure to follow standards results in the need to re-convert or re-enter records, which is a costly and time-consuming (and not terribly exciting) process. Databases that adhere to national and international standards are important considerations in your decision-making process.

AXIOM 4: CONVERSION, MAINTENANCE, AND TRAINING ARE ALWAYS UNDERESTIMATED

Historically, hardware and software costs overshadow the costs associated with other considerations that are part of the entire integrated library system. A decade ago, hardware was the most expensive component in the cost mix; in some cases, as much as three out of every four dollars spent was associated with hardware. The mass production and distribution of small but powerful distributed computing systems has shifted the dominance of costs towards the development of sophisticated software that provides the functionality of any successful implementation. Currently, 45 percent of the revenues of library system vendors originate from that applications software base. So it is not unexpected for decision-making groups to place a greater emphasis on the software and less on the hardware that runs those applications.

So much emphasis and planning surrounds these critical decisions resulting in functional systems that other, very important considerations can go either unnoticed or unplanned. Converting data, maintaining systems (including hardware and software), and training staff are examples of such a lack of consideration or preparation in planning.

As mentioned earlier, conversion is an important consideration that is often difficult to plan and estimate. It also is not an exciting task from an administrative perspective. Converting records in accordance with standards represents a large commitment of technical service effort, and often does not attract much of the technology spotlight. In some cases, decision-making groups have actually failed to recognize or budget for the costs to migrate existing records from either print or existing digital representations.

The maintenance associated with hardware and software is a negotiated point between the library and the selected vendor. Hardware maintenance can range from 8 percent to 12 percent of the cost of the system per year.[1] Over a 10-year life span, the cost to maintain a system can exceed the cost to purchase that system. Some vendors build the cost of software maintenance into the purchase price, while others offer new releases at upgrade prices, less than the cost of new or replacement software solutions. Currently, vendors' revenues include approximately 29 percent from service and maintenance agreements.[2]

Maintenance includes both replacement and upgrade of initial hardware and software. As many professionals have experience with personal computing systems and forego services associated with hardware maintenance, this experience often translates into a less than full interest in providing such services for their LIS solutions. When one considers the impact of such a decision on the public user base, the results can be disastrous. Replacement is also a consideration that needs to be planned for. At some point new solutions are needed, and whether the current vendor is the source or whether a new procurement is called for, these replacement costs are often left unplanned.

A perfectly configured system with excellent functionality and quality-controlled databases are only as good as those who seek to use that system. Library professionals, para-professionals, clerical staff members, and the end user need to be trained in properly using the new system. Corporate America spends a significant portion of its revenues on developing and training its employee base. In many libraries, such training is often done by injection, osmosis, or, worse, not done at all. Injection training occurs at one time when the system is first installed. This may be successful for those present at the training, but doesn't help those who were not invited or not on staff at the time. Osmosis training occurs when learning is absorbed from others over time. It can be an effective approach if properly planned and coordinated. Vendors will "train the trainers," who then pass their knowledge on to their colleagues. Lack of training is inexcusable, but does occur in some instances. Costs can exceed budgeted amounts, and training is often the first to be sacrificed.

Imagine the reaction of the patron who finds that the reference librarian doesn't know every trick and nuance in searching the online catalog. Why would he or she bother to ask for help in subsequent situations? What is the net effect of such an event on the relationship between the librarian and the patron?

AXIOM 5: USE OF TECHNOLOGY WILL GROW TO FILL THE AVAILABLE CAPACITY

The classic line uttered by the police chief in the original 1973 *Jaws* movie occurred when the chief saw the shark up close for the first time. Just after slinging some chum over the side, the shark burst out of the water, surprising the chief into proclaiming to the captain, "You're going to need a bigger boat."

The experts knew a lot about the shark: his type, his bite size, his feeding habits, and so forth, but they hadn't seen the creature up close and personal as the chief had. This can be the case with information technologies as well. Most of us are familiar with desktop devices, networked workstations, and the like arranged in rather small settings with limited numbers of concurrent users.

Library information systems have the potential to provide access to tremendous amounts of bibliographic and full-text information to large numbers of users, many operating concurrently and in a remote, distributed fashion. The success often associated with introducing a new library information system, whether new or a replacement, often leads to an increase in the use of that service or system. It is most difficult to estimate the growth in use, but a common rule of thumb is to build a system capable of expansion without having to replace the initial central computing resources. One might also plan on increasing access to the new system, in terms of additional terminals or local workstations (within the library) or with high-speed lines supporting external connectivity to end users distributed geographically.

The key is to be able to reconfigure the initial system to accommodate increased demand, should that be the case. The experience in most libraries is that their disk storage space fills faster than expected; there is an almost constant pressure to add workstations for the library's customers to use. And the shark looks larger than life!

AXIOM 6: INFORMATION TECHNOLOGY IS THE CENTRAL NERVOUS SYSTEM OF STRATEGY

Information technology has become a core function within the library. The library needs to have a LIS that provides all of the functional richness to help staff complete their jobs in a productive manner, and support users in their quest for information. At the same time, the standards-based LIS needs to be flexible enough so that it can quickly incorporate new technologies, as well as communicate with a diverse set of other systems—both within the parent organization and also with other libraries and organizations outside the library.

The time is long past for a LIS to act like a stand-alone system or "silo" and ignore the need to communicate with other libraries and other systems.

AXIOM 7: THE NETWORK REALLY MATTERS

The most significant development in information technology over the last decade or so is networking. Everyone is part of a network, and now almost all networks are connected. What this means is exponential connection and the power that connectivity brings. The network is global and the Internet is global. And your neighborhood is the network. Thus, your network needs to be able to support not only the anticipated volume of transactions based on your existing types of applications, but it must be able to grow to support images, audio, and video streaming applications, as well as interactive events. Just as information technology is the heart of the system, so is networking the key to connecting lifelines across great distances.

AXIOM 8: SUPPORT COSTS FOR TECHNOLOGY SOURCES AND SERVICES WILL BECOME A SIGNIFICANT PART OF A LIBRARY'S BUDGET

The cost to acquire technology is often given prime consideration when planning for technology innovations within the library. In some cases, initial cost becomes a key decision point for both administrators and members of the decision-making team. What is often neglected or under-emphasized is the fact that after a new system or service is first installed, much remains to be done in terms of supporting the continued successful use of that existing technology base.

Just as the initial purchase of a vehicle or a house does not signal the end of expenditures of time, effort, and monies, so too is the attention needed to support the installed LIS solution. Axiom 5 stated, "the use of technology will grow to fill the available capacity." This means that somewhere along the line, new resources will need to be committed to sustaining and growing the network infrastructure and the services behind that technology. This includes developing and training staff to maintain the new system, training staff to teach others how to maximize the capabilities of the system, and paying continued attention to upgrading components contained with the new system.

There are costs associated with all of these new ventures, and funds must be established and set aside for future needs, such as installing new desktop workstations, upgrading network connections to higher speeds, and upgrading servers to support increased demand for services. You might expect to keep your car for up to 10 years, but you will be changing your fluids, adjusting mechanical components, replacing brake parts, and doing tune-ups all along the way. A good long-term plan identifies likely commitments and injections of funds to support such maintenance requirements. Be prepared to respond to demands for support and for new services that were not originally thought of during the initial planning stages of the project.

SUMMARY

We hope this short list of essential axioms will prepare you and your institution to tackle the difficult challenges associated with implementing technology solutions within the context of your library institution. Your own experiences will allow you to add your personal reflections to this beginning list.

NOTES

1.   Review of numerous vendor proposals over the last 10 years.

2.   John Barry. "Closing in on Content: Automated System Marketplace 2001." *Library Journal*, 126 (6), April 1, 2001, pp. 46–58.

Chapter 9

The Impact of Technology on Library Services

Information technology has had a clear and persuasive impact in almost every area of the library, be it the online catalog used by a library customer, in technical services, or in administrative services. This chapter explores the effects that communications technology and computer-based systems have had in each of these functional areas.

POSSIBLE BENEFITS

Given the widespread adoption of information technology in the daily lives of almost every end user, it is no longer appropriate to consider whether a library should incorporate information technology, as was discussed in the literature during the 1960s and 1970s, but rather to recognize some of the major consequences of library information systems.

Cliff Lynch suggests that technology incorporates within it two "cultures of change": innovation, where the application of technology improves what is currently being done, and transformation, where technology changes "fundamentally what is done, or is applied to new things."[1]

"There will always be unintended effects of new technologies. Some of these unintended effects will be fortuitous and some less so."

Bonnie Nardi and Vicki O'Day

There are several possible benefits that may accrue to a library as the result of using network and information technologies. These benefits will vary depending upon the functional area and how well the library has revised its manual procedures and processes to complement the automated system. Among these possible benefits associated with ILS are:

- **Improved productivity**. Existing staff members are able to cope with increased workloads or take on additional responsibilities, or both, as the result of the library having installed an ILS. Based on an initial survey (and a follow-up survey 10 years later), library staff members generally feel that automation has increased their workload and responsibilities.[2]

- **Reduce staff**. In a few cases, libraries were able to reduce staff that was involved with labor-intensive, manual processes with high volumes of activity once the ILS had been installed. However, for a majority of libraries, there has been little or no reduction in the number of overall staff as the result of automation (many staff members have been moved to public service positions).

- **Reduce unit cost of operation**. The efficiencies that can be achieved with an ILS allow a library to reduce the costs associated with a particular activity. For example, sharing cataloging data through a bibliographic utility such as OCLC allowed libraries to avoid duplicating the effort associated with creating original cataloging records. This reduced the number of professional staff and resulted in delegating work to lower-skilled and lower-paid staff.[3]

- **Improve control**. An ILS will accurately record the status and location of all items that are maintained in its database. Thus, rather than having silos of paper records found only in one department, the online system allows every staff member to learn about and update information associated with a particular item or record.

- **Reduce errors**. Using an ILS means that the number of errors that would have occurred in a manual system are significantly reduced, because the majority of systems use barcode scanners to uniquely identify an item.

- **Improve speed**. Using an automated system means that a variety of activities are completed in a timelier manner. For example, materials are getting on the shelves faster, circulation-related transactions happen quicker, and so forth.

- **Improved access**. Because the majority of library staff members have desktop workstations that are connected to the ILS, they each have access to the latest information about an item or record. In addition, the LIS will typically provide several indexes to the library's database (e.g., keyword indexes) that are not available with manual systems.

- **Increase range and depth of service**. An ILS, especially a system that is accessible via the Internet, allows the library's customers to access the library's collection and other information resources 24 hours a day, 7 days a week. In addition, most systems will allow library patrons to view portions of their record, place holds, or be alerted when an item is available. Thus, the library patron is no longer constrained to visiting the physical library in order to receive services.

♦ **Facilitate cooperation**. The ability of an ILS to export standard MARC records allows libraries to participate in various cooperative projects (building local, regional, and state databases; lists of serials owned by participating libraries; and so forth).

♦ **By-products**. An ILS allows a library to examine, by using a variety of historical statistical data gathered by the automated system, the range and quality of services it provides to its customers. For example, some libraries have examined the actual usage of its collection in an effort to understand the needs of its customers better.

The impacts of automated technology on the library patron using an OPAC, online databases, and reference services will be explored prior to examining the implications in technical services.

IMPACTS ON OPACs

With the introduction of the OPAC in the early 1980s, several studies have been conducted to identify the problems encountered by OPAC users, as well as to make suggestions for improving the OPAC experience.[4] Initially there were three main benefits that resulted when an OPAC was introduced into a library. These benefits included:

♦ **Reduced costs to provide a library catalog**. No more filing cards! Because the largest component of the average library's budget is for personnel costs, eliminating the time it took to maintain and file cards in the library's card catalog resulted in significant savings. These cost savings accrue to the library on an annual basis, although this is frequently overlooked by a number of library managers and funding decision makers.

♦ **Improved access to the collection**. The OPAC provides not only were card catalog-like browse indexes (left-to-right, character-by-character); it also provides keyword indexes, often with Boolean limiting capabilities. In some cases, even more sophisticated search tools, such as automatic synonym searching, were also provided to patrons. As the World Wide Web spread through the 1990s, libraries moved to provide local dial-in modem access. Thus, library patrons now had around the clock access to the library's collection from their home, office, or dormitory.

♦ **Immediate access to location and status information**. Given the remote access to the library's collection and other information resources, one of the real benefits for the patron is being able to determine whether an item of interest can be found on the shelves or if it is checked out or missing. This allows the patron to discover the status of an item before making a trip to the library.

Yet, despite the ubiquitous nature of the OPAC, problems associated with it persist even today.

OPAC Problems

Christine Borgman[5] has suggested that there are three layers of knowledge required for successful online catalog searching:

- Conceptual knowledge of how the information retrieval process works—how to translate an information need into a search query. Problems arise in this area because people arrive at a catalog with incomplete information for any of the indexes provided by the catalog.[6]

- Semantic knowledge of how to formulate a search query—how and when to use different search features. In a manual catalog, the user is expected only to recognize the entries while in an automated catalog, the user is expected to formulate queries.

- Technical skills in conducting a search query—having a basic knowledge of computing skills and any required syntax for entering a specific search query.

OPAC users can experience a wide variety of problems. These problems will be grouped using the above three categories.

Conceptual Knowledge

- Searching by subject is the predominant use, yet users experience trouble conducting these searches. They fail to match search requests with subject vocabulary (keyword LCSH search successful only 50% of the time).[7] It is well known that users have greater success when they are able to browse subject headings, especially when they are shown the syndetic structure of subject headings—broader headings, related headings, and narrower headings.[8]

- Subject lists or subject headings in some LIS are constructed from headings found in the bibliographic records and, on average, these bibliographic records contain less than two subject headings.

- Users enter terms that are too broad or too narrow.

- Arranging subject terms alphabetically tends to scatter related terms and can sometimes lead the OPAC user astray (if no authority records with their associated cross-references are included in the OPAC).

- Cross-references are limited and weak. Following cross-references will often lead the user away from his or her search focus.

- Using authority control provides real benefits. Recall is increased (find everything on a subject) and precision is also increased (exclude material on other topics using homonyms).

Semantic Knowledge

- Too many failed searches—no records found, or users simply give up.[9]

- Retrieval of a large number of records.

- A missed opportunity (e.g., a keyword search is not followed up with a hypertext subject search or call number search).[10]

- Boolean operators are not understood and are rarely used. Users often use "and" and "or" backwards. To make matters worse, some systems use an implied Boolean "and" when a user enters multiple keywords, while other systems use an implied Boolean "or."

- Lack of user perseverance.[11] Users are not inclined to try multiple indexes if their first attempt fails.

- Most online catalogs place the burden on the user to reformulate and re-enter queries until success is achieved—the paradox of information retrieval.

- Finding something of relevance as the result of searching the OPAC. In one recent study, relevance was defined as whether the user saves, prints, emails, or downloads a citation. Approximately 18 percent of all search sessions were determined to be relevant.[12]

- Keyword search failures are related to linguistic problems. That is, in some cases different words have the same meanings while, in other cases, the same word will have different meanings.[13] Also, from a pragmatic perspective, formulating a search request (e.g., "disease medication" vs. "medication side effects") will retrieve a different set of records.

- Domain specificity. The vocabulary in various domains is often jargon filled, specialized, and unique. If users have no experience in or knowledge of this specialized domain vocabulary, the search results will likely be quite poor—even if they retrieve records and feel like they have been successful.

- Problems associated with displaying information and using library jargon to identify data fields.[14]

Technical Skills

- Basic computer skills are often lacking in novice OPAC users—they are challenged by a range of difficulties, such as using a mouse, or entering a search request using a required syntax.

- Navigational frustrations (e.g., Where am I? What should (can) I do now?).[15] Interestingly, a review of the OPAC user log files indicates that if users make an error, they will more than likely repeat the same action (and obtain the same error message a second time—almost as if they don't believe they could make an error or they are just double-checking the machine).

Given these problems, what then can a library do to improve their OPAC?

- **Improve the library's database**. If your bibliographic records have not been cleaned up, do so. Use authority control records and add cross-references on an ongoing basis. Review the frequency of subject headings in your library's catalog (a subject heading linked to a few or a very large number of bibliographic records is not likely to be of value to the library's customers). Consider adding enhanced MARC records to the library's database.[16] These initiatives were discussed in greater detail in Chapter 4.

- **Vendor improvements**. Library customers, through a Users Group, can ask for specific enhancements to the OPAC. Among the suggestions that researchers have made for improvements are: providing an option for a step-by-step approach to conducting a search, adding search assistance tools to help the user, as well as suggesting re-directed searches (e.g., from a keyword search to a subject browse search).[17] David Thomas found that if subject-rich content (subject headings and summaries) were added to brief record displays, then the need to display full MARC records would be reduced significantly.[18] Given this plethora of research about how to improve the OPAC, it is a bit discouraging to see that most vendors have not done much on their own to improve the end user searching capabilities of their OPACs.

- **New initiatives**. Several vendors have added optional features to their Web-based OPACs so the user can view the book jacket, peruse book reviews, read a summary of the book, and examine a biography of the author (e.g., see Epixtech's iCat and Sirsi's Bistro). Several researchers have suggested using information visualization software (e.g., when the user is browsing the thesaurus structure of subject headings).[19] Others have suggested providing some navigation assistance to help the user understand the information domain prior to actually performing a search (e.g., a front-end database or a meta database that might include dictionaries and thesauri—perhaps a site map as many Web pages offer?).[20] Others have suggested providing access to classification information as a part of the OPAC.[21]

Amanda Spink and her colleagues found that the searching experience of OPAC users is almost identical to users searching the Web. That is, most people use few search terms, make few modified queries, rarely use advanced search features, and only view a few Web pages.[22]

Given the importance of the OPAC for a library, it is clear that libraries should be asking their LIS vendor to work on major enhancements to the OPAC, especially Web-based OPACs. The OPAC must inform the user about the diversity of information resources available to them—what the library physically contains, what the library can obtain for them, and links to Internet resources that the user can trust.[23]

"We need to change the definition of the catalog from what we (librarians) **THINK** it is to what our users **WISH** it were!"

"Our catalog should represent everything we have **AND** the things that we have access to elsewhere."

Shirley Baker

IMPACTS OF ONLINE DATABASES

The database industry is one that is strong and growing. Vendors provide access to a variety of data—text, numeric, images, sound, and video files. A rich diversity of databases exists: 71 percent are word-oriented, 17 percent are number-oriented, and 7 percent are image/picture-oriented. Database producers who create and provide these databases might be the primary publisher or a secondary publisher. Secondary publications include citations, abstracts, or other materials descriptions created by the primary or original publisher. In some cases, several databases are gathered together by a database distributor (e.g., Lexus/Nexus, ProQuest, or Dialog). In other instances, a database is only accessible via the primary publisher. Traditionally, librarians have provided a value-added service by providing search intermediation services. Currently, end users seek direct access to these resources, which are often licensed by the library for use by its customer base (i.e., as a sort of Intranet).

When an online database publisher or distributor creates and maintains a database, it provides a value-added service that is involved with creating, editing, indexing, distributing, and archiving the database. The traditional distribution channels used by online database publishers are evolving with the availability of the Internet. Some publishers and database distributors are exploring how to provide direct end user access to the database, bypassing the library.

Most libraries are moving away from subscribing to a database via CD-ROM and are moving to providing access via the Internet. Few of these databases support Z39.50 interoperability, although each year more publishers are starting to support this standard. In many cases, access to the online database is not well integrated into the library's OPAC, and users must learn a new interface for each database they use. In addition, each database supports a unique set of controlled vocabulary terms and search syntax, which adds some complexity for the user who is conducting a search. Keyword searching dominates, and the majority of searches by end users are simple. Clearly, the multiplicity of databases is still a major problem for searchers.

As shown in Table 9-1, the Internet has been used to provide far greater access to an increasing number of full-text databases.

Table 9-1. Online Database Use and Revenues

	1978	**1994**
Connect hours	780 K	8.5 M
Revenues	$40 M	$1.2 B

When evaluating possible databases to license for use, a library should consider:

- **Subject**. Is the subject area covered by a database appropriate for the users of this library?

- **Technical Issues**. Who are the users? Will they be able to understand and use the service given the user interface that is provided?

- **Types of Publication**. Are the publications included in this database appropriate and will the information meet the needs of the library's customers?

- **Cost**. Will the library customers receive value given the cost to license access to the database?

- **Currency of Information**. How frequently is the database updated? What is the time range coverage of the database?

- **Full Text**. Does the end user have access to full-text materials from the database, or does the library need to provide document delivery services to support access?

IMPACTS ON REFERENCE

Online catalogs may have started displacing physical card catalogs in the 1980s, but mediated online searching, typically performed by reference librarians, was added to extend, not replace, the print collection. CD-ROM workstations and locally loaded databases that were added in the 1980s were intended to complement the resources available in the library. Then came the increase in Internet use in the 1990s and the access to online databases and other information resources that it provided. These newer technologies seldom replace the technologies already in place, but more often are likely to coexist with those prior services.[24]

Today, reference librarians have access to the Internet and a variety of other information resources. Yet, these highly trained professionals are called upon to help users cope with technology—from formatting a diskette, fixing printer paper jams, restoring frozen workstations, explaining rank order retrieval systems, and so on.[25]

Anne Lipow suggests that there are four trends contributing to instability in the reference environment:[26]

- ◆ As Internet use increases, use of reference services in the library decreases.

- ◆ Many patrons feel that they don't need a librarian due to the Internet.

- ◆ Reference librarians can't keep up with all of the new Internet resources that are appearing daily.

- ◆ Commercial services are providing satisfactory information resources at the end user's point of need.

Some libraries have begun providing reference services through some electronic means—e-mail, chat, instant messaging, or submitting a Web form—rather than in person or over the telephone. The experience of libraries providing these new reference services suggests that, while the demand is not heavy, library patrons are satisfied with the service.[27]

Given the "always on" nature of the Internet, individual libraries, consortiums, the Internet Public Library, and the Library of Congress are experimenting with providing around-the-clock reference services. The Metropolitan Cooperative Library System in Southern California has been providing a "24/7" reference service with live interaction and call routing to a network of subject specialists. The intent is to offer an experience that is similar to a telephone reference call but uses the advantages of Web technologies.[28] The Library of Congress experimental Collaborative Digital Reference Service (CDRS) is designed to provide a professional reference service to users anytime, anywhere through an international library network. In collaboration with OCLC, the Library of Congress will design a new reference service based on this CDRS project.[29]

Libraries should also recognize that they are competing with Web-based commercial "Ask A . . ." services. Some of these 24/7 commercial services are shown in Table 9-2. Three categories of commercial services are available: the user asks a question in natural language, and a computer system responds; the user is linked to a professional searcher; and the software links a question to an appropriate "expert" from among a network of volunteer experts.[30]

Clearly, the convenience of this kind of service is appealing—the Web is more accessible and less intimidating than physically visiting a library to consult a reference librarian. Typically, though, these services only search the Internet and not the collections in libraries or information resources to be found in online databases. Thus, to compete, libraries must move beyond providing service that is confined to a physical location.[31]

Table 9-2. Commercial "Reference" Services

Service	URL	Price	Comments
Abuzz	www.abuzz.com	Free	
All Experts	www.allexperts.com	Free	Limited to music questions.
Ask an Expert	www.askanexpert.com	Free	Experts need to have established a Web site for a particular subject.
Ask Jeeves	www.ask.com	Free	Computer responds to questions (goal is to answer 20% of the questions 80% of the time using a knowledge base of 10 million answers). Ask Jeeves handles about 3 million queries a day.
Ask Me	www.askme.com	Free	
Atomica	www.atomica.com	Free	Formerly GuruNet.
EXP	www.exp.com	Expensive	Can rate the experts answer.
Expert Central	www.expertcentral.com	Fee	More than 5,000 experts available to respond to your question.
Expert City	www.expertcity.com	Free	Limited to computer questions.
Experts	www.experts.com	Fee	Registry of professionals who serve as expert witnesses.
Keen	www.keen.com	Fee	Ask question via the Web and talk via telephone with an expert to get the answer.
Know Post	www.knowpost.com	Free	Answers by experts earn credits.
Web Help	www.webhelp.com	Fee	People respond to questions.

Unfortunately, to date, there has been no systematic evaluation of the quality and timeliness of commercial reference services compared to online reference services (e-mail or chat) provided by public and academic libraries.

The bottom line is that the Internet changes the scope and dynamics of reference services and allows the library to provide an information portal that leads in and out of the library. In a collaborative environment, the range and quality of reference services is no longer constrained by the size of a library's reference collection or the subject expertise of its reference staff.

> ⚡ **Tip!** Librarians may want to participate in a discussion group about digital reference services. Two such groups are:
> http://www.vrd.org/Dig_Ref/dig_ref.html
> http://www.groups.yahoo.com/group/livereference

IMPACTS ON DOCUMENT DELIVERY

Historically, document delivery options have been evaluated based on four factors:

- **Coverage**. What types of documents are available from the document delivery service—copies of journal articles, technical reports, marketing reports, standards, and so forth?

- **Cost**. What is the cost for delivering a specific document? Does price vary based on the size of the document? Is there a discount for an increasing volume of purchases?

- **Speed**. How fast is the document delivered on average? What is the range of service delivery—shortest, longest?

- **Delivery options (document formats)**. What are the different ways in which the document can be delivered—e-mail, fax, download via the Internet, snail mail? Can the document be delivered in an electronic format (e.g., Word document, PDF format, and so forth)? Will the document be delivered to the library or directly to the end user?

Documents can now be delivered in a matter of days for print materials and hours for electronic materials. Depending upon the source, document delivery can be very expensive. Document delivery has become a component of the acquisitions budget for some libraries. After all, with document delivery, the library is assured that the item will be used by at least one user rather than being a "just in case" book or another item that is purchased by the library hoping it will be used by a library patron sometime in the future.

IMPACTS ON INTERLIBRARY LOAN

While interlibrary loans (ILL) amount to a tiny fraction of a library's annual circulation, it is still an important library service. Libraries in North America and Europe loan millions of items annually to other libraries. Rather than requiring a library customer to fill out a manual form that is submitted to a library staff member for review and follow-up action, some libraries have found that patron-initiated interlibrary loan requests using an automated system provides better service and lower costs.

When evaluating interlibrary loan services, four factors are usually considered: What types of requests are being made (by subject area)? What is the fill rate (what proportion of requests are actually filled)? What is the service level (time from request being made to the library receiving the item)? What does the service cost?

Interlibrary loan costs are not inexpensive. When borrowing an item, a library can expect to incur average costs of $18.62; while lending an item will cost the library $10.93.[32] Some libraries have used ILL data to calculate the cost of providing access to articles from cancelled journals and identifying journals for reinstatement.[33]

Clearly, services such as OCLC's interlibrary loan module, as well as state and regional interlibrary loan systems run by cooperatives (which usually by-pass the OCLC system) have done much to reduce the costs associated with providing an interlibrary loan service. The requesting library's ability to identify a lending library, confirm the loan of a book, and, in some states, use a fairly fast delivery service means that the patron receives the desired item much faster than even 10 years ago.

The lending library can photocopy an article and deliver it directly to the patron or library using a delivery service, fax, e-mail, Ariel, or snail mail. The net impact for the patron is that he or she receives the article in a matter of days rather than weeks.

IMPACTS OF ELECTRONIC JOURNALS

Increasingly, publishers are providing access to the full-text contents of their journals in electronic format, sometimes called eJournals. In some cases, libraries are eliminating some of their print journals and relying on electronic access. For OPAC users, this means that they now have the opportunity to do full-text searching on the contents of these journals rather than relying solely on citations and abstracts.

While the subscription cost per journal title is less than the printed version, there are a variety of other cost impacts for a library to consider. Typically, access to a specific set of eJournals are bundled with other eJournals, so the library may actually increase access to the number of journals for their end users. The net impacts for a library would appear to be mixed—that is, staffing or costs increase or decrease, depending upon the area being considered. The implications for using electronic journals within a library are shown in Table 9-3.[34]

Table 9-3. Net Impacts from Use of Electronic Journals

Activity	Net Impacts
Infrastructure/Systems	Increased staffing and costs
Administration	Increased staffing and costs
Technical Services	Mixed impact on staffing and costs
Circulation	Reduced staffing
Reserves	Reduced staffing
Document Delivery	Reduced staffing and costs
Reference Services	Unclear

IMPACTS ON ACQUISITIONS

Automation has had several important impacts on acquisitions:

♦ Reduction of paper and filing costs

♦ Eliminate duplicate orders by checking an on-order file and the library's catalog

♦ Able to download MARC records at time of order, which reduces time, costs, and occurrence of error

♦ Access to easy-to-use currency conversion tables

♦ Management reports to monitor vendor performance

♦ Tools to track the spending of the library's entire materials acquisitions budget

♦ Limited access to online reviews, although this is improving each year.[35]

A LIS is designed to provide a single set of files that the library maintains. If the system does not provide an interface to a book or serials jobber, then the library must decide whether to maintain two sets of records (one in the LIS and one at the jobber) or rely on the jobber-provided system. In most cases, it should be noted, the jobber-provided system is designed to lock in the library. Thus, with these vendor-provided systems, there are generally no opportunities to compare prices between vendors. To date, little use of electronic data interchange (EDI) has occurred—but XML is coming, which should help.

Libraries have been shifting their focus from ownership to access. Online access to journals, newspapers, and other information resources has opened up a library's limited physical collection to an almost limitless set of possibilities. Libraries are turning to consortiums to help negotiate licenses to access online content.[36]

IMPACTS ON SERIALS

Managing serials is an important task that can consume significant staff resources in a non-automated setting. The ordering, renewal, invoicing, check-in, claims, binding, and dealing with cancellations are all processes that require attention to details. While a majority of systems support the receipt of journal issues and allow the library to define a variety of arrival predication patterns, few systems support the MARC Format for Holdings at both the detail and summary holding levels. The CONSER (CONversion of SERials) Project has helped libraries build a database of serials-related bibliographic records.[37]

Among the benefits of automating serials are:

◆ Increased control over receipt of issues. This allows the journal issues to get into the hands of the end user sooner. It also allows for the more timely and accurate claiming of issues that do not arrive.

◆ Production and maintenance of routing lists.

◆ Production of local, regional, and state serial holding lists.

◆ Management reports about the usage of each serial title.

IMPACTS ON CATALOGING

Automating cataloging was the first step to create a library's machine-readable database around which other modules and services could be built. Reference, resource sharing, serials control, acquisitions, circulation control, and collection development are all dependent upon the availability of the core-cataloging database.

The availability of MARC records and linking computer terminals using telecommunications have allowed catalogers to share bibliographic cataloging records. OCLC's union catalog (now called WorldCat) grew fairly rapidly because, as more records were added to its database, more libraries were drawn to participate. While clearly helping libraries reduce or control cataloging costs, the majority of library online catalogs simply replicate the card catalog format on a computer screen.[38]

Among the other impacts of automation on cataloging are:

◆ Lower costs incurred by substituting para-professionals for librarians. Average cost of copy cataloging is $16.25 per hour.[39]

◆ More use of copy cataloging, which helps to lower costs. Copy cataloging, while requiring some training, experience, and common sense, does not require an MLS degree. As the use of para-professionals increased, fewer professionals chose to pursue a cataloging career, which has resulted in a shortage of cataloging librarians.[40]

◆ Elimination of card catalogs and their attendant filing and maintenance costs.

◆ Change in workflow has a big impact on productivity. Minimizing the number of times an item is handled helps reduce costs.

- Management expectations set original cataloging rates.

- The cost of a cataloging record varies, depending upon the source.

- The Z39.50 standard returns a MARC record to the requesting library. Some libraries are using this fact to add bibliographic records to their database instead of using the more traditional sources of cataloging records.

Besides cataloging print and other materials found in its collection, the library is faced with deciding whether to catalog information resources that may be found in other locations (i.e., on the Web). For some libraries, the catalog has exceeded its traditional role. Rather than being an inventory of what the library owns, the catalog facilitates access to a wide variety of materials, regardless of their location.[41] Libraries are also confronted with the decision of whether to use a MARC bibliographic record or a metadata standard such as the Dublin Core. Some have found it difficult to accurately and completely describe an Internet resource using a bibliographic record. This difficulty is further compounded by the fact that Web resources vary greatly, which makes the descriptive process even more problematic. Most librarians see classification as a valid subject approach for all the materials in the library's collection or Internet-based resources accessible to the library patron using the library's online catalog.[42]

IMPACTS ON CIRCULATION

Vendor-provided automated circulation systems, first introduced in the early 1970s, support a wide range of circulation-related activities. These systems introduced libraries to the concept of using barcodes as a way to uniquely identify each item in the collection. Using barcode scanners at the circulation desk speeded up the checkout and check-in process. The net effect of an automated circulation system is improved control over the library's collection and increased staff productivity.

Among the benefits noted by several libraries with automated circulation systems are:

- No staffing increases are required to cope with increased circulation levels. The improved productivity means that libraries have not had to increase staff even in the face of increased demand for services (annual circulation statistics are increasing).

- Generating timely overdue notices means faster return of overdue items. In some cases, libraries found they had a higher postage cost because overdue notices went out on time rather than being dribbled out using a manual process. Postage costs are reduced with e-mail delivery of overdue and other types of notices.

- Fine revenues go up. There is less discussion about library fines since the computer tracks the checkout, renewal, and return dates.

- Items lost through the circulation system are reduced (i.e., an item checked out but never returned by the patron goes down). Generally, with an automated system, the number of items borrowed but not returned is less than one-half of one percent of annual circulation.

- Patrons are usually able to view their own patron record, determine the status of a hold request, place a hold, and perform other activities remotely by using the library's Web-based OPAC linked to or integrated with the circulation module.

- Some libraries have installed self-checkout machines to provide additional service points at the circulation desk.[43] This reduces staffing requirements at the circulation desk.

Given the reliability of today's computer hardware, circulation desk problems that were previously experienced as a result of system down time are no longer a major concern.

Reserve Book Room (RBR) modules, especially those that have been recently introduced and help the library control and resolve intellectual property issues, have been well received by libraries, as well as library users. In some academic libraries, the RBR is the most intensively used information resource within the library. For users, gaining access to the RBR module means that they can download and print articles anytime, rather than having to deal with queues and copies of damaged articles.[44]

SUMMARY

Clearly the impact of automated systems in libraries has been pervasive and significant. The benefits that have resulted from automation depend, in part, on the efficiency of the library before it was automated, how well the automated system has been integrated into the library's work flows, and which functional area within the library is being considered.

SUGGESTED WEB RESOURCES

Library of Congress Collaborative Digital Reference Service
http://www.loc.gov/digiref/

MCLS 24/7 Reference Service
http://www.247ref.org/

NOTES

1.   Clifford Lynch. "Serials in the Networked Environment." *Serials Librarian*, 28 (1/2), 1996, p. 119.

2.   Dorothy E. Jones. "Ten Years Later: Support Staff Perceptions and Opinions on Technology in the Workplace." *Library Trends*, 47 (4), Spring 1999, pp. 711–45.

3.   Michael Buckland. *Redesigning Library Services: A Manifesto*. Chicago: American Library Association, 1992. Michael Gorman. "The Organization of Academic Libraries in the Light of Automation." *Advances in Library Automation and Networking*, 1, 1987, pp. 151–69. Karen L. Horney. "Fifteen Years of Automation: Evolution of Technical Services Staffing." *Library Resources and Technical Services*, 31, Winter 1987, pp. 6–76.

4.   The largest survey of OPAC users and non-users was sponsored by the Council on Library Resources during the early 1980s. See Joseph R. Matthews, Gary S. Lawrence, and Douglas K. Ferguson. *Using Online Catalogs: A Nationwide Survey*. New York: Neal-Schuman, 1983. Joseph R. Matthews, ed. *The Impact of Online Catalogs*. New York: Neal-Schuman, 1986.

5.   Christine L. Borgman. "Why Are Online Catalogs Still Hard to Use?" *Journal of the American Society for Information Science*, 47 (7), 1996, pp. 493–503, and Christine L. Borgman. "Why Are Online Catalogs Hard to Use? Lessons Learned from Information Retrieval Studies." *Journal of the American Society for Information Science*, 37 (6), 1986, pp. 387–400.

6.   Christine L. Borgman and S. L. Siegfried. "Getty's Synoname and Its Cousins: A Survey of Applications of Personal Name Matching Algorithms." *Journal of the American Society for Information Science*, 43, 1992, pp. 459–76. H. Chen and V. Dhar. "User Misconceptions of Information Retrieval Systems." *International Journal of Man-Machine Studies*, 32, 1990, pp. 673–92. A. G. Taylor. "Authority Files in Online Catalogs: An Investigation of Their Value." *Cataloging & Classification Quarterly*, 4 (3), 1984, pp. 1–17.

7.   Bryce Allen. "Individual Differences, Values and Catalogs." *Technicalities*, 11 (7), 1991, pp. 6–10. Rosemary Thorne and Jo Bell Whitlatch. "Patron Online Catalog Success." *College & Research Libraries*, November 1994, pp. 479–97. See also Bates (1986) Op. Cit. Carlyle (1989) Op. Cit. Drabenstott and Weller (1996) Op. Cit. and Markey (1984) Op. Cit.

8.   Carol A. Mandel and Judith Herschman. "Online Subject Access—Enhancing the Library Catalog." *The Journal of Academic Librarianship*, 9(3), 1983, pp. 148–55.

9.   Allyson Carlyle. "Matching LCSH and User Vocabulary in the Library Catalog." *Subject Control in Online Catalogs*, 1989, pp. 37–63. Karen M. Drabenstott and Marjorie S. Weller. "Failure Analysis of Subject Searches in a Test of a New Design for Subject Access to Online Catalogs." *Journal of the American Society for Information Science*, 47 (7), 1996, pp. 519–37. Charles R. Hildreth. "The Use and Understanding of Keyword Searching in a University Online Catalog." *Information Technology and Libraries*, 16 (2), June 1997, pp. 52–62. Rhonda A. Hunter. "Successes and Failures of Patrons Searching the Online Catalog at a Large Academic Library: A Transaction Log Analysis." *RQ*, Spring, 33 (1), 1991, pp. 395–402. Ray R. Larson. "The Decline of Subject Searching: Long-Term Trends and Patterns of Index Use in an Online Catalog." *Journal of the American Society for Information Science*, 42 (3), 1991, pp. 197–215. Ray R. Larson. "Classification Clustering, Probabilistic Information Retrieval and the Online Catalog." *Library Quarterly*, 61, 1991b, pp. 133–73. Ray R. Larson. "Between Scylla and Charybdis: Subject

searching in the online catalog." *Advances in Librarianship*, 15, 1991c, pp. 175–236. Karen Markey. *Subject Searching in Library Catalogs: Before and After the Introduction of Online Catalogs*. OCLC Library, Information, and Computer Science Series. Dublin, OH: Online Computer Library Center, 1984. Karen Markey. "Users and the Online Catalog: Subject Access Problems." *The Impact of Online Catalogs*. Joseph R. Matthews, ed. New York: Neal-Schuman, 1986, pp. 35–69. Karen Markey. *Dewey Decimal Classification Online Project: Evaluation of a Library Schedule and Index Integrated into the Subject Searching Capabilities of an Online Catalog*: Final Report to the Council on Library Resources. OCLC Research Report No. OCLC/OPR/RR-86/1. Dublin, OH: Online Computer Library Center, 1986b. Ann O'Brien, "Online catalogs: Enhancements and developments." *Annual Review of Information Science and Technology*. Martha E. Williams, ed., 29, 1994, pp. 219–42. Thomas A. Peters. "When Smart People Fail: An Analysis of the Transaction Log of an Online Catalog." *The Journal of Academic Librarianship*, 15 (5), 1989, pp. 267–73. Thomas A. Peters. "The History and Development of Transaction Log Analysis." *Library HiTech*, 11 (2), 1993, pp. 41–66.

10.   John Tolle. "Transaction Log Analysis: Online Catalogs. Research and Development in Information Retrieval." *Sixth Annual International ACM SIGIR Conference*, 17 (4), 1983, pp. 147–60. Stephen E. Wiberley Jr., Robert Allen Daugherty, and James A Danowski. "User Persistence in Scanning Postings of a Computer-driven Information System: LCS." *Library and Information Science Research*, 12 (4), 1990, pp. 341–53.

11.   See for example Drabenstott and Weller (1996) Op. Cit. Matthews et al. (1983) Op. Cit. Tolle (1983) Op. Cit. Hjerppe (1985) Op. Cit.

12.   Michael D. Cooper and Hui-Min Chen. "Predicting the Relevance of a Library Catalog Search." *The Journal of the American Society for Information Science and Technology*, 52 (10), August 2001, pp. 813–27.

13.   C. B. Lowry. "Preparing for the Technological Future: A Journey of Discovery." *Library HiTech*, 13 (3), 1995, pp. 39–54.

14.   Virginia Ortiz-Repiso and Purificacion Moscoso. "Web-Based OPACs: Between Tradition and Innovation." *Information Technology and Libraries*, June 1999, pp. 68–77. Martha Yee. Op. Cit.

15.   See for example, Drabenstott and Weller (1996) Op. Cit. Hunter (1991) Op. Cit. Matthews et al. (1983) Op. Cit. Larry Millsap and Terry Ellen Ferl. "Search Patterns of Remote Users: An Analysis of OPAC Transaction Logs." *Information Technology and Libraries*, 12 (3), 1993, pp. 321–43.

16.   Pauline Atherton. *Books Are for Use: Final Report of the Subject Access Project to the Council on Library Resources*. Washington, DC: Council on Library Resources, 1978.

17.   Karen Markey. "Alphabetical Searching in an Online Catalog." *The Journal of Academic Librarianship*, 14 (6), 1989, pp. 353–60. Tamas E. Doszkocs. "CITE NLM: Natural-language Searching in an Online Catalog." *Information Technology and Libraries*, 2 (4), 1983, pp. 364–80.

18.   David H. Thomas. "The Effect of Interface Design on Item Selection in an Online Catalog." *LRTS*, 45 (1), 2001, pp. 20–46.

19.   Check issues of the *IEEE Transactions on Visualization & Computer Graphics* and the annual proceedings of the *International Conference on Information Visualization* for examples of how visualization software could be adapted for an OPAC.

20.   Marcia Bates. "Rethinking Subject Cataloging in the Online Environment." *LRTS*, 33(4), 1989, pp. 400–412. Marcia Bates. "Subject Access in Online Catalogs: A Design Model." *Journal of the American Society for Information Science*, 37, 1986, pp. 357–76. Karen M. Drabenstott. "Enhancing a New Design for Subject Access to Online Catalogs." *Library HiTech*, 14 (1), 1996, pp. 87–109. Karen M. Drabenstott and Marjorie S. Weller. "Testing a New Design for Subject Searching in Online Catalogs." *Library HiTech*, 12 (1), 1994, pp. 67–76. Charles Hildreth. "Pursuing the Ideal: Generations of Online Catalogs." *Online Catalogs, Online Reference: Converging Trends. Proceedings of a Library and Information Technology Association Preconference Institute, June 23–24, 1983*. Brian Aveney and Brett Butler, eds. Chicago: American Library Association, 1984, pp. 31–56. Charles Hildreth. *An Evaluation of Structured Navigation for Subject Searching in Online Catalogs*. Unpublished doctoral dissertation, Department of Information Science, City University, London, UK, 1993. E. N. Efthimiadis. "User Choices: A New Yardstick for the Evaluation of Ranking Algorithms for Interactive Query Expansion." *Information Processing and Management*, 31 (4), 1995, pp. 237–47. S. E. Robertson and M. M. Hancock-Beaulieu. "On the Evaluation of IR Systems." *Information Processing and Management*, 28 (4), 1992, pp. 457–66. S. Walker and M. M. Hancock-Beaulieu. *OKAPI at City: An Evaluation Facility for Interactive IR*. British Library Research Report No. 6056. London: British Library, 1991.

21.   See for example Drabenstott and Vizine-Goetz (1994) Op. Cit. Elaine Servenious. "Use of Classification in Online Retrieval." *Library Resources & Technical Services*, 27 (1), 1983, pp. 76–80.

22.   Amanda Spink, Dietmar Wolfram, Major B. J. Jansen, and Tefko Saracevic. "Searching the Web: The Public and Their Queries." *Journal of the American Society for Information Science*, 52 (3), February 1, 2001, pp. 226–34.

23.   Jane E. Hughes. "Access, Access, Access! The New OPAC Mantra." *American Libraries*, May 2001, pp. 62–64.

24.   Carol Tenopir and Lisa Ennis. "The Impact of Digital Reference on Librarians and Library Users." *Online*, 22 (6), 1998, pp. 84–86.

25.   Barbara Campbell. *Impact of Technology on Library Reference Services*. 2000. Available at: http://home.att.net/~barbcampbell/lecure/impact.htm

26.   Anne Lipow. " 'In Your Face' Reference Service." *Library Journal*, 124 (13), 1999, pp. 50–52.

27.   K. Broughton. "Our Experiment in Online, Real-Time Reference." *Computers in Libraries*, 21 (4), April 2001, p. 26. Beth Garnsey and Ronald Powell. "Electronic Mail Reference Services in the Public Library." *Reference & User Services Quarterly*, 39 (3), 2000, pp. 245–54. Theodore Hull and Margaret Adams. "Electronic Communications for Reference Services: A Case Study." *Government Information Quarterly*, 12 (3), 1995, pp. 297–308. Joseph Janes, David Carter, and Patricia Memmott. "Digital Reference Services in Academic Libraries. *Reference & User Services Quarterly*, 39 (2), 1999, pp. 145–50. Joseph Janes and Charles McClure. The Web as a Reference Tool: Comparisons with Traditional Sources." *Public Libraries*, 38 (1), 1999, pp. 30–33. Nancy O'Neill. "E-mail Reference Service in the Public Library: A Virtual Necessity." *Public Libraries*, 38 (5), 1999, p. 302+.

28.   Susan McGlamery and Steve Coffman. "Moving Reference to the Web." *Reference & User Services Quarterly*, 39 (4), 2000, pp. 380–86.

29.   Laverna Saunders. "IT Report from the Field: Building the Virtual Reference Desk." *Information Today*, 18 (3), 2001, pp. 25–26. Diane Nester Kresh. "Offering High Quality Reference Service on the Web—the Collaborative Digital Reference Service (CDRS)." *D-Lib Magazine*, 6 (6), June 2000. Available at: http://www.dlib.org /dlib/june00/kresh/06kresh.html.

30.   S. Feldman. "Find What I Mean, Not What I Say." *Online*, 24 (3), 2000, pp. 49–56. N. G. Tomaiuolo. "Ask and You May Receive: Commercial Reference Services on the Web." *Searcher*, 8 (5), May 2000, p. 56.

31.   Amy M. Kautzman. "Digital Impact: Reality, the Web, and the Changed Business of Reference." *Searcher*, 7 (3), March 1999, p. 18+. Mary E. Ross and John R. M. Lawrence. "Internet Reference: Boon or Bane?" *American Libraries*, 30 (5), May 1999, p. 4.

32.   Mary E. Jackson. *Measuring the Performance of Interlibrary Loan and Document Delivery Services.* 1997. Available at: http://www.arl.org/newsltr/195/illdds .html

33.   Mary Dabney Wilson and Whitney Alexander. "Automated Interlibrary Loan/Document Delivery Data Application for Serials Collection Development." *Serials Review*, 25 (4), 1999, pp. 11–19.

34.   Carol Hansen Montgomery and JoAnne Sparks. "Framework for Assessing the Impact of an Electronic Journal Collection on Library Costs and Staffing Pattern." Available at: http://citeseer.nj.nec.com/390517.html.

35.   Richard W. Boss. "Options for Acquisitions and Serials Control Automation in Libraries." *Library Technology Reports*, 33 (4), July–August 1997, pp. 403–95.

36.   Catherine Moffat. *The Future of Library Acquisitions.* Available at: http:// Pandora.nla.gov.au/nph-arch/01998-Feb-16/. Glenda A. Thornton. "Impact of Electronic Resources on Collection Development, the Role of Librarians and Library Consortia." *Library Trends*, 48 (4), 2000, pp. 842–51.

37.   L. K. Bartley and R. R. Reynolds. "CONSER: Revolution and Evolution." *Cataloging and Classification Quarterly*, 8 (3), 1989, pp. 47–66.

38.   Roy Tennant. "21st Century Cataloging." *Library Journal*, 123 (7), April 15, 1998, pp. 30–31.

39.   Dilys E. Morris and Gregory Wool. "Cataloging: Librarianship's Best Bargain." *Library Journal*, 124 (1), January 1999, pp. 44–46.

40.   Kenneth Furuta. "The Impact of Automation on Professional Catalogers." *Information Technology and Libraries*, 20 (1), September 1990, pp. 242–52.

41.   Mary Beth Weber. "Factors to be Considered in the Selection and Cataloging of Internet Resources." *Library HiTech*, 17 (3), 1999, pp. 298–303.

42.   J. McRee (Mac) Elrod. "Classification of Internet Resources: An AUTOCAT Discussion." *Cataloging & Classification Quarterly*, 29 (4), 2000, pp. 19–38.

43.   William Saffady. "The Status of Library Automation at 2000." *Library Technology Reports*, 36 (1), January/February 2000, pp. 3–97.

44.   Richard J. Goodram. "The E-RBR: Confirming the Technology and Exploring the Law of 'Electronic Reserves': Two Generations of the Digital Library System at the SDSU Library." *The Journal of Academic Librarianship*, March 1996, pp. 118–23.

Chapter 10

System Selection and Implementation

This chapter presents an overview of the system selection process and implementation issues associated with installing an automated library system. We begin by reviewing the system options available to libraries and then proceed to discuss a variety of issues associated with selecting and installing a library information system.

Functionality within a LIS can be considered from many perspectives. Initially, the professional librarian and decision maker would need to be aware of the various processes conducted and services provided that are in some fashion supported by technology. These professionals would also need to know the overall status of the developments within a LIS.

PROCESSES AND SERVICES

The processes and services provided by libraries and librarians can be viewed as being a part of technical services, public services, or administrative planning and decision-making. Arguably, some processes or services cross one or more of these artificial boundaries, but that is not our point here. For the moment, let us consider these divisions for the purposes of examining technology applications to library-related processes and services.

Technical Services

Technical services include those backroom tasks conducted by professional librarians that often go unnoticed by patrons and others unfamiliar with library procedures. In fact, many of these tasks include the most important decisions to be made by the professional librarian! While collection development can arguably be considered primarily a professional task, and while technology will never completely replace a professional in this important decision-making process, certain aspects of that decision, and subsequent procedures related to those decisions, can be supported by technology (e.g., Google, the Internet search engine, uses strength of linkage for relevance, a form of collection development). Having made a decision to purchase a particular document, whether it is a monograph, serial, or other material, the task of managing the acquisition of that object becomes paramount. This task might be considered somewhat repetitive in nature, making it a good candidate for using technology (criteria for automation: tasks that are detailed, form driven, and repetitive). Acquisition systems are important components within the overall LIS.

Cataloging is that important intellectual task, performed by librarians, that places the acquired object within the context of the physical collection held by that library system (a major problem in today's library is integrating across all formats, most particularly electronic). While once a rather solitary practice, cataloging is now primarily a shared or collaborative process, with authoritative standardized bibliographic records being readily available (in most instances) for particular knowledge records. In the 1960s, the Library of Congress undertook a massive bibliographic project that resulted not only in the international standardization of the bibliographic record known as MARC (ANSI/NISO Z39.2-1994, the Information Interchange Format), but spawned the development of large centralized bibliographic databases such as OCLC. These bibliographic utilities provided a centralized means for sharing cataloging records across thousands of library institutions.

Nearly all libraries circulate their materials, thereby necessitating a need to control their inventory of books, periodicals, and other media. Circulation control, once done by hand, then later using punched card technologies, is now primarily done using software applications capable of handling millions of transactions and correctly identifying those materials checked out by patrons that might be overdue. While smaller libraries may still manage this process manually, libraries checking out more than 50,000 titles annually benefit from these applications, which streamline a process that is form-driven, detailed, tedious, and primarily administrative. In fact, circulation systems solutions were the first applications leading to the development of the library systems marketplace some 30 years ago.

Additional processes within technical services include serials control, materials booking (holds and reserves), and interlibrary loan, all of them sharing with circulation the same properties that make them ideal candidates for technology solutions.

Public Services

Public service functions within the library include those services provided by both the collection and library professionals to the end user. Technology applications in the 1980s modernized the former card catalog into what is called the online public access catalog (OPAC). New developments have pushed that envelope even farther, transforming the online catalog into a one-stop service that can access not only the collection of materials held by the local library, but can also provide access to the collections in other libraries, as well as to materials located on the Internet. Initially intended to provide access to union catalogs across libraries within an institutional library system, online catalogs now extend to provide access to collections around the world, in some cases extending reciprocal borrowing privileges to end users seeking to borrow materials from other library systems.

Online databases that were once separate resources are now licensed by a specific library or group of libraries and made available directly to end users with appropriate password access. The online database industry grew out of the need to organize the various subject literatures, many of which were published within the journals of various government agencies (e.g., ERIC and Medline), professional societies (e.g., Chemical Abstracts), and for-profit organizations (e.g., LEXIS/NEXIS, WestLaw). This was not a new idea, as the profession had been crafting print-based secondary publications for nearly a century (e.g., Medline arose from the print publication Index Medicus, put out by the National Library of Medicine). What is remarkable is the explosive growth that has occurred in the database industry. For many years, this industry was treated as a separate entity, as if it had a different set of users, a different audience. In addition, many database providers sought cost recovery for their value-added commitment to organizing the various subject literatures, and these costs posed a challenge to library organizations in terms of how to account for the use of such licensed resources. In the 1970s and 1980s, libraries used to owning physical objects struggled with the notion of licensing information that had costs associated with it and could not be owned.

Now libraries face the challenge of tying these and other information services together into a neatly designed set of public service offerings. The new kid on the block involves Web-based information content. Note that this type of content differs from Web-based services, which libraries have designed to offer both online catalogs and online databases. In these cases, the Web is an access and delivery tool, not a vehicle for content. As the Web has grown, not just in popularity and use, but also in content, librarians in the quest to meet the needs of end users have identified new resources. These have been incorporated into the overall service package proffered by certain libraries. Often the end user is quite unaware that the various information services offered by these libraries involve sources from distinctly different origins. In a sense, that is the beauty of the Web. Link pages can be designed to mask the distinctions between various resources—some owned, some licensed, and some freely available.

One problem associated with providing links to licensed information is that not all sources are full text. In the instances where the user identifies a resource—say a particular issue of a journal or an article within that issue—the library must attempt to provide that information object to the end user in some convenient fashion. An entire industry surrounding document delivery has sprung up from this demand. While these delivery systems have been in place for some time, the industry's growth is directly related to the increase in access to remotely owned information resources by end users.

For years, libraries have built special collections and made them available to end users who have visited the locations specified by the local library. Increasingly, however, end users are interested in accessing these materials from remote locations outside the library, at times when the library doors may not be open. Some collections, or important portions of these special collections, have been captured using digital tools and made available to patrons around the world. These digital collections are increasing in size and number, and are often available to users via the Web. Often these are referred to loosely as digital libraries, a term and a concept we will cover later. In many cases, these are special digital collections, but the term has taken on new meaning and served to heighten end users' expectations that all print resources can and will be digitized.

One troublesome problem for libraries in providing robust and effective access to Web-based resources has been the problem of linking. The Web, despite its utility and ubiquity, is nonetheless quite primitive when it comes to linking. Generally, links are static (point to one hard-coded location) and singular (unable to point to multiple destinations). OpenURL, a NISO standard, is a way to encode links for bibliographic resources that enables richer linking services than is generally possible. It is designed to solve one problem (the issue of sending the user to the copy of an item a library has licensed rather than to one it has not—also called the "appropriate copy" problem) and provide opportunities for adding other linking services (such as looking up other articles by the same author). Given today's complex electronic publishing environment, constantly changing URLs don't scale up well for article reference linking purposes. To deal with this problem, publishers have adopted DOIs as stable article identifiers. To help publishers locate DOIs for articles in journals published by other companies, CrossRef was established to allow for DOI retrieval based on metadata, such as author name. SFX, a proprietary product that uses OpenURL, allows libraries to define rules that allow SFX to dynamically create links that fully integrate their information resources regardless of who hosts them—the library or external information providers. The user is presented with context-sensitive links that are dynamically configured on the basis of the institution's e-collections.

Thus, OpenURL, CrossRef, DOI, and SFX represent a new generation of technology, even a new approach to solving library problems based on the Web as an enabling technology.

Administrative Planning and Decision-Making

To librarians, technical services are the most important set of professional tasks. To end users, public services are the most visible part of the library. Both groups might forget that library administration is also an important consideration in the context of library information systems.

Management is responsible for drafting service goals for the library. These goals include things like maintaining and strengthening excellent customer service; providing access to accurate, timely information for all patrons; and keeping pace with technology innovations. When these goals are established, the library then needs to keep track of data that provide insight as to whether or not these goals are being met. The quantification of such data, and the reporting structures that gather and summarize data relating to these goals, can be derived from the actual subsystems used to provide services and support processes within the library. Library administrators (and policy and decision-making library boards) work from general reports that reveal patron usage, collection usage, valuation of specific services, and so forth. In a sense, this data can be viewed as a byproduct of the various applications we have discussed under technical and public services. It is important to point out that this information can be extracted from these various subsystems, and that administrative responsibilities require that such data be gathered and analyzed in an attempt to improve overall service to the end user.

Management is also responsible for ensuring that the necessary infrastructure is put into place and is well maintained to support the LIS. The infrastructure includes cabling, hardware, and software that is installed or upgraded with sufficient bandwidth to support the many different kinds of users that will be using the LIS.

SYSTEM SELECTION

Historically, the process recommended to librarians is that they employ a Request for Proposal process to select a LIS.[1] An overview of the selection and implementation process suggests that five steps should be employed:

1. Identify a library's needs

2. Document the library's needs

3. Evaluate alternatives

4. Prepare written agreements

5. Begin implementation process.

This chapter also deals with three other very important issues. First, what are the professional and personal competencies of librarians that allow them to be of value to their customers? Second, what are the information literacy skills a library staff member or individual needs today to recognize when information is needed and to know how to locate, evaluate, and use the retrieved information effectively? Finally, what skills can we develop to help us cope with information overload?

Identify a Library's Needs

Almost all libraries in North America and Europe are already automated. So, these libraries will not be assessing their needs in terms of moving from a manual-based system to an automated system. Rather, these libraries will be focusing on the issues surrounding the process of migrating from one system to another.

The reasons libraries wish to migrate from one system to another will vary, but, as shown in Figure 10-1, two-thirds of the libraries responding to a survey indicated that the primary reason is the need for increased functionality.[2] About half of the libraries need to move to another hardware platform or are concerned about scalability issues. Problems with support and lack of confidence in the existing vendor are also frequently cited. Surprisingly, cost issues were the least frequently cited reason for wanting to make a change.

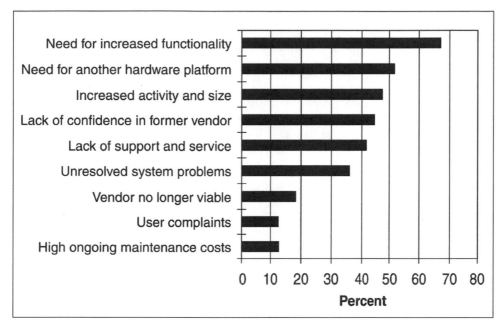

Figure 10-1. Reasons Libraries Choose to Migrate

However, the process of identifying a library's needs is virtually identical in either situation. When a library's current operations are analyzed to identify ways in which improvements might be made, five general areas should be considered: time, costs, control, service, and communications. An analysis of current operations should identify for each broad functional area:

- How much staff time is devoted to it (in smaller libraries, staff members can estimate the time they spend in various activities)?

- What does it cost to provide a particular function, activity, or service?

- Are the records in a system being adequately controlled in terms of quality and security?

- Is there a duplication of effort? Are materials or records handled multiple times and could the workflow be simplified?

- Are the existing LIS set-up parameters—types of patrons, types of materials, location (location codes), statistics, and circulation options—still appropriate?

- Is it possible to involve patrons in maintaining their own patron record and providing self-service that has not been considered previously? For example, can the patron view the list of items overdue or on hold, renew items, or send an e-mail request for service to the librarian?

- How does an activity relate to other areas?

◆ What activities are frequently occurring? What is the volume of transactions?

◆ What are the existing levels of service for each functional area, activity, or service? For example, are there backlogs in cataloging, receiving serials, or placing orders?

> ✎ **Tip!** For an activity that is done frequently (e.g., checking out materials at a public library), it is important to complete the task with a minimum of keystrokes or mouse clicking. This might involve using function keys in some systems or designing the screen so a transaction can be completed in a "hands-free" manner.

Those involved in the analysis process might employ a variety of techniques (e.g., flow charting an activity or activity-based costing). However, it is important to exert a level of effort for the analysis that is proportional to the size of the financial decision. Thus, a library that is able to spend $20,000 would spend considerably less time than a very large library whose investment in a new system might exceed $1 million. In short, the library should not engage in a "paralysis of analysis."

A beneficial activity that a library might want to consider is to identify what systems are installed at peer libraries. More important, one or two staff members might visit multiple libraries to learn what the neighboring library did well, what they wish they could do over, and what lessons were learned the hard way. The idea is to learn how the library "stretched" the automated library system or, as a result of automation, was able to introduce new levels of service.

The result of this analysis might be a report describing the results of the analysis but, typically, the library will produce a document that lists its needs for a new LIS. The document need not be very long, but should clearly identify the most important features and functions that the library needs.

Document the Library's Needs

The list of needs should be organized into similar functional areas, but the document should not attempt to develop an exhaustive list of functions and features that the ideal system should possess. Rather, the library should focus on identifying those 10 or 15 functions or features that will really make a positive productive impact on staff activities as well as significantly improve the level of service offered to the library's users in that particular library. The reality is that there is a significant difference between features that will have a major impact on a library (and should be considered essential) and the system features and functions that are desirable.

Once the list of functions and features has been prepared, some libraries will then assign weights to each specification to indicate its relative importance. Usually an arbitrary scale is chosen, for example, 1–10, with 10 being most important. When assigning weights, make sure that a function with a weight of eight is actually four times as important as a feature with a weight of two.

One approach that libraries frequently use is to review the literature for a list of features and functions that might be considered. Libraries have also been known to collect Requests for Proposals that have been issued by other libraries. When these two techniques are employed, it is not unusual for a fairly lengthy and exhaustive document to emerge. Joan Frye Williams calls these extensive lists of functions and features the equivalent of "recombinant DNA" that take on a life of their own and never seem to die.

Besides features and functions, the library should also establish requirements in other areas. For example, some libraries must comply with company or government IT mandates that certain infrastructure hardware and software be used by the selected system. These mandates might require using a particular brand of hardware, operating system, or relational database management system (e.g., Oracle or MS SQL Server). The library might also wish to state its minimum requirement in terms of system reliability, response times for different types of transactions, and so forth.

Evaluate Alternatives

Once a library clearly understands its needs, it should consider several alternatives for meeting those needs. Three broad categories of options are available:

- ◆ Stand-alone, in-house system
- ◆ Shared system—consortium
- ◆ ASP service.

In-House System

A stand-alone, in-house system means that the library will purchase a system from its preferred LIS vendor. After installation and training, the library will assume responsibility for operating the system, involving the vendor when necessary to troubleshoot problems that will come up from time to time. In broad terms, this approach means that the library will:

- ◆ Select the best system to meet the needs of the library
- ◆ Be able to exercise absolute control about the decisions governing the operation of the system (i.e., set-up parameters)
- ◆ Need to have the necessary budget, as up-front capital costs are involved.

Shared System

The shared-system option means that the library will share a LIS with one or more nearby libraries. The shared system is typically governed by a decision-making board, and it may involve a consortium or cooperative that already exists or a new consortium could be created. The primary reasons why a library joins a consortium is to:

- Improve access to resources
- Share resources
- Work to fulfill a particular need
- Reduce costs.[3]

Obviously, it is much easier for a library to join an existing shared system than it is to organize a new cooperative. Sharing an automated system with other libraries means that:

- The selected system may or may not best meet the needs of your library.
- The library does NOT exercise absolute control over system parameters.
- Up-front capital costs are involved.
- Some kind of formula is usually involved to determine a library's share of costs.
- There are higher administrative costs—meetings!
- It usually saves costs over an in-house system. After the base costs for hardware and software, there are normally small incremental costs for the additional hardware and software that will be needed to support an additional library.

One of the most important issues arising from a shared system is how to equitably allocate a share of the costs to each participating library. While the approaches taken by a number of consortiums are numerous and creative, they all basically boil down to the use of a formula. The question to be answered is: What measures or factors do we include in the formula? Table 10-1 illustrates one formula used by a consortium composed of different types of libraries. This group of libraries selected three factors as the basis for a cost allocation formula. The formula is updated each year. The factors include: number of volumes in a library's collection, the number of patrons, and the number of workstations. The library's percent of the total is calculated for each factor, and then the percentages are averaged to determine the library's share of the costs.

Table 10-1. Sample Factors Used in a Consortium Cost Allocation Formula

	Number of Volumes	%	Number of Patrons	%	Number of Workstations	%	Average Percent
Public A	250,000	30	100,000	51	250	48	42%
Public B	125,000	16	60,000	31	75	15	21%
Academic A	150,000	18	12,000	6	40	8	11%
Academic B	300,000	36	24,000	12	150	29	26%
Totals	825,000	100	196,000	100	515	100	100%

Application Service Provider (ASP) Service

The Application Service Provider (ASP) option is a relatively new alternative in the marketplace. Under the ASP alternative, a library rents access to a service, in this case, access to a LIS. According to the ASP Industry Consortium, "An Application Service Provider manages and delivers application capabilities to multiple entities from a data center across a wide area network." With this option, a library:

- Transfers the *total responsibility of ownership* to a vendor, which is dedicated to designing, implementing, and hosting services tailored to meet its clients needs.
- Reduces the total cost of ownership, sometimes by 25 percent or more.
- Starts to use the ASP service in days rather than months.
- Eliminates the need to recruit, train, and retain "technology smart" staff members.
- Does not need to perform routine system maintenance and data backups.
- Transfers responsibility for installing, upgrading, and maintaining operating system, database, and application software on the central server.
- Eliminates up-front capital expenditures for library automation.
- Retains ownership of its own data.[4]

Process to Evaluate Alternatives

To evaluate each of these options fairly, it is necessary to prepare a cost analysis that compares apples to apples. To that end, a table should be constructed that identifies all of the possible cost components for each of the three major alternatives. It is also important to identify both the initial costs (purchase price) and the ongoing maintenance charges. Determining the total five-year costs is important. Adding the first-year costs plus the ongoing costs over the remaining five years results in the total five-year costs. This is done to clarify actual costs because one vendor may have low initial pricing but high ongoing maintenance charges. Such a cost analysis would usually include the following cost components:

- Consultant, if any
- Client hardware—new and/or upgrade
- Server hardware—new and/or upgrade
- Operating system software
- Library application software
- Transactions (some vendors charge for serials check in and purchase orders, among other things)
- Third party software (e.g., Oracle, MS SQL Server licenses)
- Security software
- ASP service
- Cabling and telecommunications
- Database conversion
- External databases and systems
- Training
- System manager and computer support staff.

Usually a library will prepare a report documenting the results of this analysis to share with funding decision makers and library boards, among others. A summary of the costs for each of the three broad alternatives is shown in Table 10-2.

Table 10-2. Summary of Alternative Library Information System Costs

	In-House	Shared	ASP
Public Library:*			
Hardware	$25,000	$15,000	–
Software	$200,000	$120,000	–
Maintenance	$90,000	$54,000	–
Staff	$300,000	$180,000	–
Telecom	–	$75,000	–
ASP Service	–	–	$51,500/yr
Total 5-Year Cost	$885,000	$660,000	$257,500
Average Cost/Year	$117,000	$132,000	$51,500
Academic Library:**			
Hardware	$19,000	$17,500	–
Software	$105,000	$100,000	–
Maintenance	$189,000	$177,000	–
Staff	$150,000	$70,000	–
Telecom	$40,000	$70,000	$40,000
ASP Service	–	–	$234,000
Total 5-Year Cost	$518,500	$422,000	$234,000
Average Cost/Year	$103,700	$84,400	$46,800

*Public Library has a database with 250,000 titles, 190,000 patrons, and 115 workstations.
**Academic Library has 115,000 titles, 10,000 students, and 100 workstations.

To RFP or . . .

A Request for Quotation (RFQ) or Request for Bid (RFB) is used when the specifications for a particular product can be clearly identified (e.g., paper towels), and several competing suppliers are willing to bid for the business. Using the RFQ process, cost quotes or bids are received by the Purchasing Department, and the selection of the vendor is based *solely* on price. A Request for Proposals (RFP), on the other hand, uses several criteria to make a selection decision; and price is only one of the selection criteria.

The intent of the RFP process is to give all vendors an equal shot at winning the business. The library benefits from an RFP by being able to select the best possible system at an attractive price. An RFP process may be mandated by local purchasing rules and regulations.[5]

Should a RFP be used, the library will want to ensure that the document addresses the following topics:

- Overview of the project
- Required deliverables
- Proposal format
- References
- Submission deadline
- Specifications
- Evaluation process to be followed by the library
- Vendor presentations.

Language is very important. For example, the word "must" versus "should" can mean different things to a vendor.

In some cases, the RFP process does not seem to be objective. Rather, the RFP process can be used to justify a decision that has been made prior to the RFP document actually being issued. It needs to be recognized that a vendor invests considerable time and money responding to a RFP. All of the questions must be answered (often in a very proscribed format), a detailed cost proposal must be prepared, and multiple copies of the proposal must be submitted. And these costs are, in fact, passed on to all customers in the marketplace.

Recognizing the unfairness in the RFP process, many vendors will refuse to respond to an RFP if one of the vendor's salespeople has neither visited the library nor had several candid telephone conversations with one or more library staff members. Contributing to the corruption of the process, most vendors are more than willing to share a copy of their preferred, draft RFP document in word processing format. This preferred RFP document contains specifications that emphasize their product's strong points and most flatter the vendor. If a library uses such a preferred RFP, all vendors are, not surprisingly, able to recognize the source of the RFP document and, thus, the identity of the preferred vendor-of-choice. Consequently, it should not be surprising that most vendors will fail to respond to such an open RFP process.

Once the library has received several vendor proposals, selected staff members are typically involved in evaluating the responses for a particular section. More often than not, a count-the-number-of-boxes-that-have-been-checked approach to evaluation is followed. This approach treats all of the functional specifications equally and ignores the features and functions that are most important to the library. Even if a separate score is calculated for the specifications that have been assigned a high weight, the end result is usually the same. Given this incentive, it is not surprising for some vendors to take as much latitude as possible for interpreting a specification so that the vendor can respond affirmatively (checking the box).

Evaluating Proposals

Should a library decide not to use the RFP process, what are its options? Some libraries have used the list of their requirements or needs and issued a brief Request for Information (RFI) to determine what vendors are most likely to meet their needs. The library then asks the selected vendors to schedule a visit to the library so that the library staff members can see how the vendor accomplishes the most important tasks and activities that the library has previously identified.

Any vendor sales representatives worth their salt will want as much time as possible to demonstrate all of their system's features. While understandable, all the features found within a system are not equally important, so a full system demonstration should be avoided. Rather, the library should control the demonstration by very clearly asking the vendor to perform a particular task or activity—and then asking the vendor representative to keep quiet while the staff members think about what they have just seen and how it might relate to their library. This approach allows the library to understand how a system performs the functions that are most important to the library. Developing a list of questions allows the library to control the sequence of questions asked and prevents a shotgun approach to the demonstration.

After the library clearly understands the strengths and weaknesses of each vendor's system, it should ask for a cost proposal. Waiting until after the functional evaluation of a vendor system means that the costs for a system are not clouding the judgment of library staff members during the evaluation process.

While it is true that most automated systems provide an equivalent level of functionality, these same vendors offer systems that differ in how a task or activity is accomplished. What will be a one- or two-step process with one vendor's product may require four or more steps in another vendor's offering. A system that minimizes those tasks and activities that are performed most frequently is one that will, over time, allow staff to be the most productive.

To evaluate a system, a library might consider any number of factors. Historically, these factors have, in some cases, included:

- Cost—includes both the purchase price, as well as ongoing maintenance charges
- Software functionality
- Software ease of use
- Adaptability/flexibility—system sets up parameters so the software will follow the library's policies
- Documentation—typically includes user manuals for each module
- Hardware manufacturer—the reputation of the company
- Scalability—ability of the system to easily expand
- System reliability—are there system availability (up-time) statistics to demonstrate the server's reliability?
- System response times—what are the response times experienced by other customers? Does the vendor provide any benchmarking data?
- Training services—time spent on-site training staff

- Vendor support services—can a customer visit a Web site to report a problem or track the status of a previously reported problem? How often are new releases of the software distributed to customers?

- Purchase/Maintenance agreement guarantees

- Vendor's past performance

- Vendor's financial stability/profitability

- Overall suitability of the system

- Other

A 1985 survey compared how libraries rated the above evaluation factors before and after a library had implemented an automated library system.[6] After installation, librarians were much less focused on cost and software functionality and were more concerned about system reliability and hardware support. Were this same survey conducted today, system reliability would be much less of an issue—most hardware manufacturers are providing servers with a three-year, on-site maintenance agreement as part of the purchase price. These hardware companies are only able to do this when they know that in the vast majority of cases they will not need to provide the maintenance service.

A more recent survey identified the top 10 reasons for choosing a LIS.[7] The factors include:

- Ease of use by patrons

- Availability of application modules and subsystems

- Completeness of modules and subsystems

- Cost of system

- Cost of hardware

- Need for local programming staff

- Service reputation of vendor

- Ease of use by staff

- Comparable installed site

- Previous experience with vendor.

What Vendors Want to Know

- Is there funding?
- What is the evaluation process?
- Who are the decision makers?
- What is the timeframe?
- Any data conversion needs?
- Any hardware/software constraints?

A library has access to several other information sources about the vendors in the marketplace and their products. Reviewing the literature will often provide systematic product reviews that will prove to be of value. Each year, the April 1 issue of *Library Journal* [8] provides an automated systems marketplace article that discusses each of the vendors and provides statistics about their total revenues, number of new customers, and other relevant information. In addition, each year the *Library Systems Newsletter* publishes the results of a survey on library automation vendors.

Visiting nearby libraries that have a system installed can be quite revealing. It is best if you have a list of questions to ask to ensure that you are collecting the same information at each site. If two or three staff members visit their counterparts in the nearby library, make sure that they get together afterwards to resolve any inconsistencies that may have arisen. It is not unusual for the visiting staff members to feel like they are the "six blind men describing their encounter with an elephant" or find themselves asking, "Are you sure we visited the same library?" In some ways, this is analogous to assembling pieces of a puzzle.

Using Consultants

Consultants can add real value to the process of selecting a new LIS. Their experiences in helping libraries allows the consultant to make sure that a library is not overlooking some information or placing too much emphasis on a particular factor. However, it must be remembered that the library will have to live with the results of the selected LIS so the library should control what the consultant does.

It is also true that any consultant will bring a bias, both positive and negative, about each of the vendors in the marketplace. Determining what systems the consultant's clients have selected over the last year or two will reveal any bias that may exist. Some consultants will explain this bias by stating that they want to ensure that their clients only choose vendors that have a proven track record. Forearmed with this knowledge, a library can then use the consultant more effectively—choosing to use or ignore portions of the advice that is offered.[9]

Consultants are typically compensated on a time and materials basis, or a project will be completed for a fixed price. If the consultant is being involved to help select and implement a new LIS, then it is probably better to use the time and materials approach. The library can manage the costs by controlling the amount of time the consultant is working on the library's project. If there is a specific deliverable, then a fixed price approach is usually followed.

Preparing Written Agreements

Once a vendor has been selected, the library enters the next phase of the selection process. For systems that cost less than $25,000, vendors typically will not enter into a negotiation about the terms and conditions surrounding the purchase of the product. Rather, there is either a "shrink-wrap agreement" or a "click-through agreement" that details the terms under which the library can use the software. In systems that cost more than $25,000, most vendors are willing to negotiate a Purchase Agreement and a Maintenance Agreement, although most vendors will want to use their standard agreements as a starting point. As the cost of the system increases, the more willing vendors will be to make accommodations in the agreements. Remember that any negotiations are a series of compromises, and the objective is to make sure that the interests of both parties are protected and that neither party has an unfair advantage.

Most libraries will usually have an attorney review the terms of the negotiated agreement. Involving a lawyer that has limited or no prior computer contract law experience will mean that the library will be paying for the time it takes the attorney to get up to speed, and the lawyer might not fully understand and appreciate the reasons for some of the language that a vendor may insist upon.

It is really helpful if the library has a clear understanding of what it wants from a system in terms of reliability, response times, scalability, and software functionality. The agreements will spell out the responsibilities for each of the parties, as well as the remedies when the system fails to perform as specified. The agreements must also provide a framework that will be followed should any future conflicts, misunderstandings, or disagreements occur.

Among the more important topics that should be addressed in the System Purchase Agreement and System Maintenance Agreements are:

- **Deliverables**. Exactly what is being delivered to the library is specified. A description of the software modules, hardware (if part of the agreement), training, and so on.

- **Pricing**. The purchase price for each deliverable is specified in the System Purchase Agreement. The ongoing maintenance charges are also detailed.

- **Payment Schedule**. While any number of progress payments can be made, normally three such payments are made: contract signing, installation of the system, and acceptance of the system. Obviously, the vendor will want as much of the monies as soon as possible (vendors incur the majority of their costs in the first few months of a contract), while the library will try and delay a large payment until final acceptance. This is a topic that clearly will involve some negotiation.

- **Delivery and Installation**. The delivery schedule for various components of the system is specified. Note that whenever there are delays to the schedule, in a majority of cases the library is the cause.

- **Training and Documentation**. The amount of training to be provided by the vendor is specified along with any limits on class size. In addition, the provision of training or user manuals is addressed. Most vendors provide such documentation in machine-readable form so a library can modify the users manual as it sees fit.

- **Acceptance Tests**. If acceptance tests are a part of the agreement, generally there are three separate acceptance tests:

    Software Functional Acceptance Test. The purpose of this test is to verify that the software behaves as advertised by the vendor in its written proposal to the library.

System Reliability Acceptance Test. The test requires that the system meet the stated reliability performance standard over a 30- or 60-day test period. Such a reliability performance standard might be a maximum of two percent downtime.

Response Time Acceptance Test. Typically this test is performed over a one-hour period and staff follow a script to perform prescribed transactions at stated intervals of time (e.g., checkout an item every 10 seconds with a maximum response time of three seconds).

♦ **Warranties**. Most vendors will provide a warranty period during which the library does not pay for support. Warranty periods can be as short as 90 days and as long as a year. An important issue that needs to be resolved during negotiations is exactly when the warranty period begins. Does it begin at the time of installation or when the system is accepted by the library?

♦ **Software Escrow**. Some libraries want to have the vendor's source code deposited with a software escrow company. Then, in the event of certain, narrowly defined disasters, the library would receive a copy of the source code. Given the long learning curve that a team of programmers would require to become proficient (and be able to make changes to the source code with confidence), the availability of the source code is really not much insurance.

♦ **Termination**. This section details the conditions under which the library can cancel the System Purchase Agreement with the vendor. Such conditions might include failure to deliver software as scheduled, failure to deliver software that meets minimum acceptable performance levels (may be defined as importing and indexing the library's database within certain time limits, and so forth). Given the experiences some libraries have had with the delivery of the new DRA Taos system, termination provisions are particularly important for a library that will be receiving a new system.

Typically, a separate System Maintenance Agreement is signed at the same time the System Purchase Agreement is signed. Once the library has accepted the system, the terms and conditions of the System Maintenance Agreement then become operative. Important topics that need to be addressed in this agreement include:

♦ **Support**. What are the hours of support and what are the ways in which a library can contact the vendor (e.g., toll-free telephone, fax, e-mail, the Web)? Are reports of software bugs categorized and the more serious problems worked on first? What is the maximum time period that will elapse between the time a bug is reported and it is fixed? (Does this vary by the seriousness of the bug?)

♦ **Enhancements**. How frequently are new releases of the software distributed to customers? What influence do customers have in determining what enhancements are included in future releases of the software?

Begin Implementation Process

Implementing a LIS is an activity that will benefit from thorough planning. The library can take advantage of the experiences of their vendor of choice who has been involved in the implementation process involving a number of libraries. But ultimately, it is important to remember that it is the library staff that will have to live through the experience of implementation on a daily basis, so good planning will pay significant dividends.

Library Policies

Ensuring that library policies are reflected in the LIS software is the responsibility of the library's system manager. The system manager controls the software's operation by using the set-up parameters. These parameters allows the system manager to directly control what data elements are used to build each index, to specify what indexes are made available to the public, to decide what types of patron categories will be created and maintained, to decide whether fines will be charged for overdue materials, and so forth. The available parameters within the software are documented within a set-up manual. Most vendors provide a system overview class that introduces the library to the various set-up parameters and options that control the software's operation.

Managing the Network and Server

The LIS will run on a server, typically either a Windows NT server or UNIX operating system software. The library should plan to send its system manager to a two- or three-day course on managing the operating system software.

The library's parent organization may have an Information Technology department that is responsible for operating the LAN or WAN. If this is the case, then the system manager's responsibilities will be eased somewhat. However, the system manager still needs to have a clear understanding of the current networking environment and the plans for improvement. Sufficient bandwidth must be available to ensure satisfactory response times, even as images and multimedia applications are provided to each end user in the coming years. Managing a LIS is discussed in the following chapter.

Types of Barcodes

Within the library community, there are two types of barcodes that are typically used. The industry standard, originally established by CLSI, uses a 14-digit Codabar barcode label (all numbers). The first digit identifies the type of label (patron or item). The next four digits can be used as a unique library ID number. The next eight digits represent the unique item ID number (leading zeros are used as fill characters). The last digit is a check digit. The second type of barcode label is called the Code 3 of 9 or Code 39. This barcode allows alphanumeric characters (both letters and numbers) in the barcode. Typically these Code 39 labels have eight characters and no check digit.

Coda bar

2 3684 00000104 4

Code 39

2368402587

Data Migration

If your library is migrating from one automated system to another, then the new vendor will work with your library to ensure that all of your "fixed" data is accurately and completely moved from the old system to the new system. Examples of fixed data include bibliographic, authority, patron, and vendor records. In some cases, the vendor of choice can assist in migrating transaction-based files (e.g., items on hold, overdue items, items checked out, and so forth) although a majority of libraries migrating do not attempt moving this type of data.

Libraries have made a significant investment in creating data files that reside in your present automated library system (e.g., bibliographic, authority, patron, vendor, fund, and serial prediction pattern records). The new vendor's implementation team will work with a library to develop a set of mapping tables to ensure that a field of data in the old system is moved to the correct and appropriate place within the new system. In some cases, data stored in coded form in the old system can be updated or corrected (e.g., if a code is no longer valid or useful). It is important to obtain a relatively large sample of records to be moved so the new vendor will have an opportunity to test its conversion programs and identify any data elements that are surprises. An example of such a surprise might be the type of patron codes that have been entered creatively (e.g., all uppercase, upper and lower, various abbreviations, and so forth). The more opportunity there is for testing and refining the data mapping, the happier the library will be with the resulting database.

Another important factor in the migration of MARC records is that there are several MARC variations and so, once again, time to adequately test the bibliographic and authority records that are output from the old system must be provided. A related issue involves how copy and item records are linked to or embedded in the MARC record itself during the export process. *Caveat emptor!* Testing, testing, and more testing is required.

Migrating fixed, non-MARC data, such as patron and vendor records, is complicated by the fact that there is no standard structure to assist in migrating this data. And while the library or vendor might export the data in a "comma delimited format" the data will still need to be manipulated to create an import file that is compatible with the new vendor's system.

Converting transactional data files is more complicated because the transaction files are often stored in a proprietary coded format. However, most vendors will work with the library to determine if migrating this type of data is possible and cost effective.

System Installation

Typically, the new software will be shipped to the library on a CD-ROM. The software installation process will install the database tables and the application software, which will allow the library's bibliographic records to be loaded and indexed. Libraries should pay careful attention to ensure that all directions are faithfully followed. Should questions arise, the library's system manager should contact the vendor for clarification.

Training

The training provided by a vendor is designed to train the library's trainers. Usually there is a limit on the class size, for example, six to eight people per module. Thus, different staff members will be participating in different sessions, depending upon the module being covered. The library staff members being trained become the experts for that particular module and should be carefully selected for their ability to learn quickly and train other staff members.

Each staff member attending the vendor-provided training must have his or her own workstation and sufficient desktop space for taking notes. Vendor experience suggests that training will be more effective if the library can place the students and teacher in a room that is separate from the rest of the library. This will ensure minimal disruption of normal day-to-day events so those attending training can derive maximum benefits. Typically, a day or two of training is provided by the vendor for each module, which covers a seven- to eight-hour period consisting of a combination of lecture and hands-on practice. The vendor representative responsible for providing training at the library will usually provide a copy of the training curriculum and time to be spent on each topic.

The vendors make the assumption that the staff members attending the application training are experienced and knowledgeable about Windows and Web-browser (i.e., they have used other Windows-based applications for several weeks or months). If staff members attempt to participate in a vendor-provided class without this background, they will find they are either not learning much or they are holding back the rest of the class.

Besides on-site training, most vendors offer telephone training and, in some cases, Internet-based training. Such cost-effective offerings should be explored as they can be particularly useful for new staff members.

> ✎ **Tip!** Have every staff member create a list of things he or she doesn't like about the existing system and then save these lists. When people become frustrated with the new system, the lists can be shared to help people find the right perspective.

While the training provided by a vendor is important, ultimately the quality of the training program that will be administered to all other library staff members will have the biggest impact on improving the skills and confidence that staff need to perform their work efficiently.[10] Several things can be done to improve the effectiveness of the training provided to staff members:

- Keep staff informed about the automation project from the outset. Explain why change is necessary so people can begin the process of making adjustments. Let people know about changes to the implementation and training schedules caused by problems that will inevitably arise.
- Start each training session with a review of the big picture.
- The focus on the library-provided training must be on the practical day-to-day activities that staff will actually perform (e.g., checkout, check-in, placing of holds, and so forth). Providing step-by-step instructions has proven to be very helpful in many libraries.
- Schedule training close to the "go live" date and train again if there are implementation delays.
- Each training session should be no longer than two or three hours. Otherwise, people will start to have information overload problems. Allow staff the opportunity to practice what they have learned before moving on to the next scheduled class. Schedule optional review sessions.
- Remember that people have different learning styles and plan accordingly. Some prefer to review manuals, while others will never read a manual and prefer the hands-on approach.
- The key for an effective trainer, aside from being knowledgeable about the system, is to be enthusiastic!
- Make sure that you provide cross-training opportunities to minimize the impact if a key employee leaves.

One of the biggest challenges facing a library and a vendor when the library is moving from one automated system to another is confronting expectations. The old system, despite all of its known flaws, will be familiar to staff. In spite of clear and consistent statements by the library system's staff and the vendor's trainer that the new system will not operate exactly like the old one, it should not be surprising that some staff members will be resistant to change or have longer-than-average learning curves.

Despite the abundance of evidence to the contrary—that change is almost an everyday event in our lives—some people seem to work hard at resisting change. As Spencer Johnson suggests:[11]

- Change Happens
- Anticipate Change
- Monitor Change
- Adapt to Change Quickly
- Change
- Enjoy Change!
- Be Ready To Change Quickly and Enjoy It Again.

Adapting Procedures, Forms, and Workflow

After the new application software has been installed for a few months, staff members should carefully examine their existing procedures, forms, and workflow. Designing forms so they look like the data-input templates found within the application software greatly improves the efficiency of the data-entry process. The library should consider eliminating some of its existing forms, as the data is readily available to all staff members via a workstation. The library's workflow, especially in technical services and at the circulation desk, should also be carefully examined. One objective of examining procedures is to determine how many of them can be eliminated or streamlined. Minimizing the number of times an item is handled before it is placed on a shelf for the patrons should be another objective. Studies have shown that organizations that modify their procedures, forms, and workflow to complement the capabilities of their automated information management system will reap significant benefits. In fact, in most cases, streamlining workflows and re-engineering the various tasks will produce more benefits than automating an activity.[12]

Typical Implementation Schedule

The project plan (see Table 10-3) illustrates the sequence of activities typically associated with implementing the new automated library system.

Table 10-3. Typical System Installation Schedule

Activity	Date	Responsible Party
Agreement signed. Help Desk services for the application software and installation services begins.	0	Vendor/Library
Central site server and related equipment ordered (or server shipped to vendor).	+ 1 week	Vendor
Vendor project manager and library system manager develop a series of data mapping tables to migrate all of the existing files to the new application software (if applicable).	+ 2-4 weeks	Vendor/Library
Loading and indexing library's existing database into the new LIS system.	+ 6 weeks	Vendor
Central site server and related equipment installed.	+ 12 weeks	Vendor
Shipment of application software (cataloging, OPAC, and circulation) and associated documentation.	+ 12 weeks	Vendor
Training for set-up, cataloging, OPAC, & Circulation modules occurs.	+ 14 weeks	Vendor/Library
Use of cataloging, OPAC, and circulation modules begins.	+ 16-20 weeks	Library
Shipment of application software (acquisitions & serials control) and associated documentation.	+ 28 weeks	Vendor
Training for acquisitions and serials control modules occurs.	+ 30 weeks	Vendor/Library
Use of acquisitions and serials control modules begins.	+ 34 weeks	Library

Successful Systems

Despite all of the planning that libraries typically complete in anticipation of installing a new or replacement system, some systems are just not successful. Some mistakes librarians are likely to make include:

- Failure to evaluate a vendor's financial viability or calculate the total five-year cost
- Unrealistic expectations or implementation schedules
- Responsibilities of the library not being met
- Refusal to plan adequately
- Ignoring retrospective conversion or data migration issues
- Decision-making responsibilities not clearly defined
- Buying "too much" system that cannot be afforded on an ongoing basis (buying a Cadillac on a VW budget).[13]

Vendors are not immune from making mistakes either, the most notable of which include:

- Lack of communication at many levels
- Failing to meet promised delivery dates
- Providing inadequate or under-powered systems
- Marginal system support during implementation and after acceptance of the system.[14]

PROFESSIONAL COMPETENCIES

The Special Library Association has developed a list of competencies for librarians that, with little or no modification, would apply to a librarian in any setting—academic, public, or special library. These competencies include:

- Has knowledge of evaluation and filter information resources
- Has specialized subject knowledge
- Provides convenient, accessible, and cost-effective information services
- Provides excellent instruction and support for users
- Markets value-added information services and products
- Uses information technology to acquire, organize, and disseminate information
- Communicates the importance of information services with senior management
- Develops specialized information products

- ◆ Evaluates the outcomes of information use
- ◆ Continually improves information services
- ◆ Is an effective staff member
- ◆ Is committed to service excellence
- ◆ Seeks out challenges and opportunities
- ◆ Sees the big picture
- ◆ Looks for partnerships and alliances
- ◆ Creates an environment of respect and trust
- ◆ Has effective communication skills
- ◆ Works well with others.

PERSONAL COMPETENCIES

Hiring and retaining the right staff is probably the most important factor in determining the quality of service and the kind of experience that a library customer goes through.[15] Among the characteristics that a potential professional librarian should possess are:

- ◆ **Provides leadership**. Is willing and able to assume responsibility for a committee, task force, or team of individuals. The group of people may all be library staff members or some people may come from other departments outside the library.

- ◆ **Plans, prioritizes, and focuses on goals**. A self-motivated staff member thrives in a fast-paced environment and is able to successfully juggle multiple, often conflicting, deadlines.

- ◆ **Is committed to lifelong learning**. A welcome attribute is a staff member who is willing to volunteer for new assignments, especially if he or she affords the individual the opportunity to learn new skills. One of the most effective ways to learn something new is to teach the skill to someone else.

- ◆ **Possesses an understanding of business skills**. Each staff member has a clear understanding of the organization's goals and an appreciation of how the library's goals complement the organization's mission. In addition, the individual is aware of the organization's business processes and value drivers. In other words, it is clear why customers purchase the goods or services provided by the organization.

- ◆ **Recognizes the value of professional networking**. Librarians that spend time reviewing the professional literature, participating in discussion groups, visiting librarian-related Web sites, and attending local, regional, state, and national library conferences are enhancing their value. Building a network of professional peers and mentors in different types of libraries and in different parts of the country is a growth-inducing experience that benefits the librarian both short-term and in the future.

- **Is flexible and positive in a time of continuing change**.

- **Has passion**. Has enthusiasm and is willing to take risks and challenge tradition. Likes to identify and solve problems.

- **Computer literacy is a "given."** Basic technology skills include understanding the operating system fundamentals, as well as being able to use an office suite (e.g., MS Office). Each staff member should know how to navigate the Internet and understand the technology's vocabulary, especially jargon introduced in the last few years.

- **Specific job skills are less important**. All other things being equal, most libraries will hire an individual with specific job skills (i.e., being a cataloging supervisor). However, all things are rarely equal, so most libraries are willing to overlook specific job skills because they can usually be learned in a fairly short time.

- **Has good people skills**. The individual is warm, friendly, and has strong communication skills—verbal, writing, and listening.

- **Thinks outside the box**. Simply because a library traditionally does something in a certain way does not make it the best way to do the job now. Staff members who are willing to consider and embrace outside ideas are attractive job candidates.

Most people respond positively to recognition and rewards. Thus, the library's management should encourage staff members who are exhibiting initiative to develop some of the above characteristics. A combination of formal and informal recognition, as well as public acknowledgment and recognition at staff-only functions, are all ways to recognize employee initiative.

"The hardest lesson to learn is learning is a continual process."

David Gerrald

"In today's world, why would anyone trust a librarian, whose profession is about information and knowledge, who hasn't mastered a computer?"

Eric Lease Morgan

INFORMATION LITERACY

The amount of information is simply staggering to comprehend. A recent study by Peter Lyman and Hal Varian at the University of California at Berkeley found that:

> The world produces between 1 and 2 Exabytes of unique information per year, which is roughly 250 megabytes for every man, woman, and child on earth. An Exabyte is a billion Gigabytes, or 10^{18} bytes. Printed documents of all kinds comprise only .003% of the total. . . . Magnetic storage is rapidly becoming the universal medium for information storage.[16]

Given this super-abundance of information, people need to be able to obtain specific information that will enhance their work and personal lives. These needs are driven by a variety of factors, including personal growth, desire for career advancement, the need to do an excellent job, and the changing social and economic environments. In the end, "information literate people are those that have learned how to learn."[17]

While the term "information literacy" may provoke yawns, the reality is that selling the concept of information literacy really comes down to branding. If you call it "information power," "information competencies," or "information proficiencies," you are more likely to strike a responsive cord, especially in the minds and hearts of people in non-academic settings. For some, helping others become more proficient in information literacy is one way to broaden the scope of the information professional beyond being just a provider of information.[18]

The Association of College and Research Libraries[19] suggests that an information literate individual, whether a college student or not, is able to:

- **Determine the extent of information needed**. Knows the value and potential information resources that are available. Recognizes that information can come from a primary or secondary source.

- **Access the needed information effectively and efficiently**. Is able to develop a research plan and construct an effective search strategy.

- **Evaluate information and its sources critically**. Is able to assess the quantity, quality, and relevance of the information gathered and identify whether any gaps exist.

- **Incorporate selected information into one's knowledge base**. Is able to critically assess whether to incorporate or reject varying viewpoints.

- **Use information effectively to accomplish a specific purpose**. Is able to communicate the results of the retrieved information using a variety of media, such as a written report, oral report, PowerPoint presentation, and so forth.

- **Understand the economic, legal, and social issues surrounding the use of information**. Accesses and uses information ethically and legally. Preserves the integrity of information resources and understands what constitutes plagiarism.

In short, the information-literate individual knows how to find, evaluate, and use information effectively. And while the information-literate person may use information technology skills to acquire and use the required information, these skills complement his or her information literacy expertise. Computer literacy is concerned about learning and retaining specific computer hardware and software skills (e.g., being able to use a specific word processing application). An increasingly necessary skill for library staff members is developing an understanding of how Information Technology can help change their organization and library.

In the academic arena, some accreditation associations are using information literacy as a key outcome for college students.[20] Many universities and colleges have developed information literacy courses—see the suggested Web sites below for more information.

SUGGESTED READINGS

Cohn, John M., Ann L. Kelsey, and Keith Michael Fiels. *Planning for Automation: A How-To-Do-It Manual for Librarians*. 2d edition. New York: Neal-Schuman, 1997.

Cooper, Michael D. *Design of Library Automated Systems: File Structures, Data Structures, and Tools*. New York: Wiley, 1996.

SUGGESTED WEB RESOURCES

CPSU, San Luis Obispo
http://www.lib.calpoly.edu/infocomp
/project/expanded.html

CSU, San Marcus
http://library.csusm.edu/
departments/ilp/

Marylhurst College, OR
www.marylhurst.edu/lib/libinst.htm

Manhattanville College, NY
www.mville.edu/test/library/
instruct/lis1001.htm

Purdue University
thorplus.lib.purdue.edu/
library_info/instruction/gs175/
index.html

SUNY, Plattsburgh
www.plattsburgh.edu/
library/er/lib101sy.htm

York College, PA
www.ycp.edu/library/ifl

NOTES

1. Richard Boss. *The Library Manager's Guide to Automation*. 3d edition. Boston: G.K. Hall, 1990. Richard Boss. "The Procurement of an Automated Library System." *Library Technology Reports*, 30 (3), May-June 1994, pp. 331–440. Edwin M. Cortez and Tom Sorch. *Planning Second Generation Automated Library Systems*. Westport, CT: Greenwood, 1993. Joseph R. Matthews. *Choosing an Automated Library System*. Chicago: IL: American Library Association, 1980. Dennis Reynolds. *Library Automation: Issues and Applications*. New York: Bowker, 1985.

2. Julie Hallmark and C. Rebecca Garcia. "System Migration: Experiences from the Field." *Information Technology and Libraries*, 11 (4), December 1992, pp. 345–58.

3. James J. Kopp. "Library Consortia and Information Technology: The Past, the Present, the Promise." *Library Consortia and Information Technology*, March 1998, pp. 7–12.

4. Joseph R. Matthews. *Internet Outsourcing Using an Application Service Provider: A How-To-Do-It Manual for Librarians*. New York: Neal-Schuman, 2001.

5. Joan Frye Williams. "The RFI, RFP, and the Contract Process." *Integrated Online Library Catalogs*, Jennifer Cargill, ed. Westport, CT: Meckler, 1991, pp. 1–15. Joseph R. Matthews, Stephen R. Salmon, and Joan Frye Williams. "The RFP—Request for Punishment: Or a Tool for Selecting an Automated Library System." *Library HiTech*, 5, Spring 1987, pp. 15–21. M. Stowe. "To RFP or Not to RFP: That is the Question." *Journal of Library Administration*, 26 (3/4), 1999, pp. 53–74.

6. Russell T. Clement. "Cost Is Not Everything: How Experience Changed Some Librarians' Views of the Important Factors in Selecting Automated Systems." *Library Journal*, 110 (16), October 1, 1985, pp. 52–55.

7. Peggy Johnson. *Automation and Organization Change in Libraries*. Boston: G. K. Hall, 1991, p. 113.

8. John Barry. "Automated System Marketplace 2001: Closing in on Content." *Library Journal*, 126 (6), April 1, 2001, pp. 46–58. John Barry. "Automated System Marketplace 2000: Delivering the Personalized Library." *Library Journal*, 125 (6), April 1, 2000, pp. 49–55.

9. Joseph R. Matthews. "The Effective Use of Consultants in Libraries." *Library Technology Reports*, 30 (5), November–December 1994, pp. 745–814.

10. Julie Hallmark and Rebecca Garcia. "Training for Automated Systems in Libraries." *Information Technology and Libraries*, 12, September 1996, pp. 157–63. Kitty Smith. "Toward the New Millennium: The Human Side of Library Automation." *Information Technology and Libraries*, 12, June 1996, pp. 209–16.

11. Spencer Johnson. *Who Moved My Cheese? An Amazing Way to Deal With Change in Your Work and in Your Life*. New York: G. P. Putnam's Sons, 1998.

12. Paul A. Strassmann. *The Squandered Computer: Evaluating the Business Alignment of Information Technologies*. New Canaan, CT: The Information Economics Press, 1997.

13. Jon Drabenstott. "Automating Libraries: The Major Mistakes Librarians Are Likely to Make." *Library HiTech*, 3 (1), 1985, pp. 93–99.

14.   Jon Drabenstott. "Automating Libraries: The Major Mistakes Vendors Are Likely to Make." *Library HiTech*, 3 (2), 1985, pp. 107–13.

15.   The characteristics that managers are looking for in new staff members are drawn from several sources, including: John R. Whitman. *Customer Focus at the Los Alamos National Laboratory Research Library: "Understand 'em and Give It to 'em!"* Available at http://www.surveytools.com.

16.   Peter Lyman and Hal R. Varian. *How Much Information.* 2000. Available at: http://www.sims.berkeley.edu/how-much-info.

17.   Association of College and Research Libraries. *Presidential Committee on Information Literacy.* Chicago: American Library Association, January 10, 1989. Available at: http://www.ala.org/acrl/nili/ilit1st.html.

18.   Julie N. Oman. "Information Literacy in the Workplace." *Information Outlook*, June 2000, pp. 32–43.

19.   Association of College and Research Libraries. *Information Literacy Competency Standards for Higher Education.* Chicago: American Library Association. Available at: http://www.ala.org/acrl/ilintro.html. See also Association of College and Research Libraries. *Information Literacy Competency Standards for Higher Education: Standards, Performance Indicators, and Outcomes.* Chicago: American Library Association, January 18, 2000. Available at: http://www.ala.org/acrl/ilstandardlo .html.

20.   See for example, the Middle States Commission on Higher Education (MSCHE), the Southern Association of Colleges and Schools (SACS), and the Western Association of Schools and Colleges (WASC) accreditation requirements.

Chapter 11

Usability of Systems

First impressions count. Yet, even a good first impression will not keep users coming back time after time. The usability of any system has always been recognized as important but, more often than not, very little attention is paid to this important issue. This is surprising because for most people, the user interface is the experience—whether its application software such as an integrated library system or the Web. It's the user interface the user is immersed in, becomes a part of, and becomes frustrated with if something is not quite right. When the user interface is truly intuitive ("I can't define intuitive, but I know it when I see and interact effortlessly with it"), the user reaches a moment of epiphany and says, "Yes, I get it!"

As libraries have moved from character-based software products, to Windows-based systems, to Web-based products and have developed their own Web pages, it is quite clear that usability normally takes a back seat to other system factors (e.g., features and functions, Web page speed, or software development). Too often, the realities of Mooers's Law, which states, "An information retrieval system will tend not to be used whenever it is more painful and troublesome for a customer to have information than for him not to have it" are ignored.[1]

Yet, there is a significant body of literature suggesting that libraries and LIS vendors should be spending more time and attention on a system's usability. For example, the vast majority of users learn to use (or not use) a library's OPAC on their own rather than attending a bibliographic instruction class or asking a librarian for assistance. In some libraries, the number of people visiting the library and asking reference questions has dropped, often significantly, during the last half of the 1990s. Where are people going to get their information? The Web! No surprise there. When a library's Web page has not undergone any fundamental change for a year or more, it is sending a clear message to those who take the time to visit—the library does not care![2] Web sites that are "sticky" are sites that provide the user with compelling reasons to return again and again. The reasons for the stickiness might have to do with current information resources and an easy-to-use site, among others.

> "The flashiest graphics will never save a poor user interface. Sexy graphics are like lipstick on a bulldog. Lipstick may make the bulldog look better but you still don't want to kiss it."
>
> Norm Cox, designer of the Xerox Star

WEB SITE DESIGN

Web sites are designed to provide access to a plethora of information. Some commercial Web sites, for example, provide a wide range of information about their products and services and will often provide an e-commerce component so visitors can complete a purchase transaction. Yet, because users become frustrated with their inability to complete the purchase process, more than 30 percent of users abandon their shopping carts.[3] Unfortunately, library Web sites don't employee electronic shopping carts, so we are unable to determine how many Web site visitors become frustrated and abandon the site never to return again. However, a library could employ user log software analysis tools to determine at what points users are abandoning the site. Armed with this information, changes can be made to the library's Web site.

The whole experience of using a Web site is tied to a variety of factors, including how the site is organized and what navigation features such as buttons, tabs, menus, links, graphics, site maps, and search engines are provided. When they are visiting a Web site, users have a set of expectations; to be successful, the Web site must either meet or exceed those expectations.

Individuals involved with designing and maintaining a Web site may have a work experience background from one of three professions, as shown in Figure 11-1. This may include a librarian (with a historical focus on text), a graphics designer (with a traditional focus on design and graphics), and finally a computer coding person (whose interest is with the technology itself). If only one or two people are responsible for the Web site, it should not be surprising that the Web site reflects their backgrounds and work experiences. The ideal is to achieve a balance from all three points of view so the end result is a Web site that really works—from the user's perspective.

An ideal Web site will offer access to the library's OPAC and possibly access to other electronic resources accessible through the library. It will provide basic information about the library, including its location, hours, upcoming events, and so forth. It may also provide access to other community-based resources.[4] A library's Web site may be in one of three evolutionary stages. These possible phases include:

- **We are here**. Task-oriented, traditional library message. In a similar vein, early commercial Web sites were often called "brochure ware" sites.

- **User-centered digital library**. Besides having access to the library's online catalog and several online databases, users were able to find information about the status of various activities and communicate with the library to place a hold, change their mailing address, and so forth.

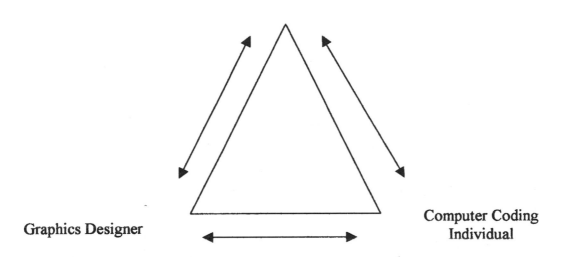

Figure 11-1. Perspectives on Web Site Design

- **Personalization**. Users are able to specify how they want "their" version of the library's Web site, including the OPAC, to look and feel.

However, before visiting some of the fundamental design concepts that should be followed when creating or re designing a Web site, it is important to ask yourself (and know the answers to) the following questions:

- Why are you creating a Web site? What is the purpose of the site? What specific groups of people are expected to use the Web site?

- What do you want to accomplish with this site? Will the site provide more than simple information about the library and access to the library's Web OPAC?

- What do you want your users to accomplish with this site? What can the library patron accomplish directly? Can they customize the site? Can they sign up for an alert service (selective dissemination of information)?

- What will keep a user on your site? Does your site provide access to subject pathfinders with links to recommended Web sites? Can the library patron interact directly with a reference librarian using e-mail, instant messaging, or chat? Is the library adding content-rich information resources on an ongoing basis?

♦ What will encourage a user to return? Is content updated regularly? Does the library provide free e-mail, downloadable wallpaper designs, e-postcards, community message boards, and so forth?

According to a recent survey, people come back to a Web site for the following reasons:[5]

Very entertaining	56%
Grabs my attention	54%
Extremely useful content	53%
Information tailored to my needs	45%
Thought provoking	39%
Visually appealing	39%
Highly interactive	36%
Loads quickly	21%

Jared Spool,[6] a usability author and consultant, suggests that a Web site's design has several characteristics that must be met so visitors will find the Web site compelling and return again and again. After examining numerous Web sites and studying how users are actually exploring and using them, he found that:

1. **Graphic design neither helps nor hurts**. However, larger graphics will slow the Web page's download time and for that reason alone are discouraged.

2. **Text links are vital**. Users don't want to read; they skip explanatory text and move directly to links.

3. **Navigation and content are inseparable**. Users have no patience, so the visitor should have a clear sense of how to accomplish a variety of tasks at the Web site.

4. **Information retrieval is different than surfing**. Thus, a Web site search engine is almost a mandatory requirement. Users don't want to scroll through long lists to find valuable information.

5. **Web sites aren't like software**. People are often forced to use bad software, but another Web site is only a click away. What works well in a Windows environment may not work well using the Web because the underlying technologies and the user interface are different.

Another usability expert, Steve Krug,[7] suggests in his book *Don't Make Me Think* that when people are visiting a Web site, they:

♦ Don't read pages. People scan them.

♦ Don't make optimal choices. People are willing to accept a less-than-perfect solution.

♦ Don't figure out how things work. People muddle through.

Several usability authors (e.g., Steven Krug, Patrick Lynch, Jakob Nielsen, Louis Rosenfeld, and Jared Spool) recommend that high quality Web sites should:

- **Provide locally developed information**. Visitors to a Web site are seeking information that will be of value. This is particularly true when people visit a library's Web site. If the library's Web site supports important tasks or offers useful services that support a user (e.g., e-mail to a librarian, able to check on the status of reserve materials, and so forth), users are more likely to return to the site when confronted with the task of locating information resources.

- **Be easy to find and access**. The use of tabs has become increasingly prevalent in Web sites because tabs indicate to the user what options are available. Thus, tabs provide obvious navigation assistance. They suggest a physical space, and what is behind the tab is obvious (assuming the tab label is clear). However, tabs are only one of several techniques to make navigation within a Web site intuitive.

- **Be well formatted and edited**. Design consistency helps the user navigate the site. The library should consider developing, and then frequently updating, a Style Guide that clearly delineates the look and feel of the library's Web site.[8] Recognize that both novice and experienced individuals will use the Web site, and that both groups should be able to navigate smoothly.

Hypertext links that are no longer up to date or point to resources that no longer exist are an obvious source of frustration for Web site users. Several search engines found that about 25 percent of all links more than a year old will no longer work. This condition is sometimes referred to as "link rot." Web-page developers and designers should use a software tool to check the integrity of all links on a regular basis and repair any broken links as quickly as possible. One of the reasons for link rot is that some Web sites are constantly evolving, which means that the site is pointing to pages that change continuously.[9]

- **Recognize that people are trying to find something of value**. Recent research found that almost 75 percent of users were searching for multiple pieces of information, while another 25 percent were looking for something specific.[10] Users visit a Web site to compare or choose something to make a decision, to acquire a fact or a document, or to gain an understanding of some topic. Thus, the site needs to be well structured and organized. According to Jared Spool, information has a "scent" that people pick up on as they move from page to page (Peter Pirolli at Xerox PARC calls this information scent "information foraging").[11] Marcia Bates has described the approaches that people take to find valuable information, all of which can be supported in the Web environment, as "berrypicking."[12] Strive for efficiency. Make the paths to an information resource as short and productive as possible.

- **Be predictable**. A consistent look and feel, consistent terminology, and an avoidance of jargon (both library and technology buzz words) will improve the overall usability of the Web site. Help users decide where not to go by using clear navigation signposts. Make sure your site uses existing Web conventions (e.g., use blue underline for hyperlinks, no underline for normal text). Make sure the paths from one point to another are as direct as possible (eliminate unnecessary clicks). Should someone become lost, he or she is not likely to return!

♦ **People choose to search or browse**. At some sites, almost half of all users will use the Web site's search engine.[13] The success of searching a specific Web site is not known, but the success rate in searching for a broader set of information available via the Web is truly disappointing—between 60 percent and 80 percent of people fail.[14]

♦ **When browsing, people will use a hierarchy**. Web sites that have many layers (depth) should provide guidance assistance using coordinated colors, graphics, tabs, or a navigation bar. Consistency in designing and rendering navigation bars on each page, regardless of level, is an important concept to consider. Color is particularly effective to differentiate types of information and for setting the tone of a Web site. Design in black and white, and then add one or two colors.

♦ **Each Web page should stand on its own**. Limiting each Web page to one concept or idea allows the user to quickly scan the page and either select something or move on.

♦ **Speed is an important factor.** Most users won't wait more than 10 seconds to download a Web page (or the alternative definition for WWW becomes "World Wide Wait").[15] There are many Web site performance-testing software tools that will indicate where bottlenecks are occurring.[16] Don't use big, slow graphics—no matter how impressive you think they are.

USABILITY GUIDELINES

While several authors, perhaps a majority of authors, who are considered to be usability experts have developed usability guidelines, these seem to be based on observations and personal recommendations rather than the results of careful research.[17] The majority of these guidelines could be placed into three broad groups: navigational characteristics, practical considerations, and visual characteristics. D'Angelo and Little, after thoroughly reviewing the literature, developed a list of 10 factors that could be used to evaluate Web sites.[18] The pair then evaluated 20 Web sites using these evaluation criteria by asking their subjects to perform a series of tasks. They found that, on average, the Web sites incorporated about 6.5 of these evaluation factors. Sites that included more of these factors were more successful, and users spent more time at the Web site.[19] These 10 evaluation factors include:

Visual Characteristics

1. Do not use all capital letters.

2. Put links in prose or definition lists.

3. Break up the content with topic headings, subtopic headings, or horizontal lines, but not images.

4. Do not use more than one font.

5. Use white space effectively.

Practical Considerations

1. Use no more than three (small) images per page.

2. Do not let the background and text clash.

3. Do not let the background and text blend.

4. Use only light blue, gray, or white for the background.

5. Use no more than four colors per screen.

Nielsen suggests that Web designers frequently make several common mistakes. Among his top 10 design mistakes are:

1. **Using Frames**. The use of frames is often confusing to users since a Web page is broken into pieces.

2. **Gratuitous Use of Bleeding-Edge Technology**. Users care about content and customer service, not technology that gets in their way.

3. **Scrolling Text, Marquees, and Animations**. Images that move and other techniques often get in the way of gaining access to information—it's distracting.

4. **Complex URLs**. URLs should reflect directory structures and file names that are understandable and not in code.

5. **Orphan Pages**. All pages should be consistently identified because users may enter a site at any point.

6. **Long Scrolling Pages**. Critical content and navigation options should be at the top of the page.

7. **Lack of Navigation Support**. A good navigation bar, a site search function, and a site map will help users find what they are seeking.

8. **Nonstandard Link Colors**. Links to pages that users haven't seen should be blue, while links that have been seen should be purple or red. Consistency, consistency!

9. **Outdated Information**. Old and outdated information must be deleted from the site.

10. **Overly Long Download Times**. A Web site has 10 seconds to download or the user is gone![20]

"It doesn't matter how many times I have to click, as long as each click is a mindless, unambiguous choice."

Krug's First Law of Usability

Roger Black suggests that good Web sites come from the principles that have informed quality print design for hundreds of years. His 10 rules of good design include:

1. Put content on every page. And make it easy to read since people skim and surf a Web page.

2. The first color is white.

3. The second color is black.

4. The third color is red or . . .

5. Never letter space lowercase.

6. Never set a lot of text type in all caps.

7. A cover should be a poster.

8. Use only one or two typefaces.

9. Make everything as big as possible. Use fonts with larger point sizes.

10. Get lumpy! Break up the consistent look and feel occasionally.[21]

"Design shouldn't be mere decoration; it must convey information. A reader should never have to plow through forests of buttons to get simple news."

Roger Black

Nancy Everhart, of St. Johns University, has developed a framework to evaluate external Web sites that a library could use to determine whether to catalog the Web site or to provide a link to the Web site on the library's own home site. The individual making the evaluation first distributes a total of 100 points to nine evaluation factors. Sites that meet some minimum acceptable score, for example, 60 out of the possible 100, could then be considered a candidate Web site that would be of value to a library and its users. The evaluation factors include:

- **Currency**. The Web site tells visitors when the information was last updated, who is responsible for the accuracy of the information, and whom to contact for a variety of purposes (e.g., reference, circulation, Web master, and so forth).

- **Content/Information**. The content itself should dictate a Web site's design without introducing distracting features or "cool" technologies. Is the information accurate? If a document is provided, is the document's source apparent? Are there any disclaimers or should there be? The value of hypertext is that it is possible to break apart content into smaller pieces. A library may want to provide access to the library's own online catalog, commercial indexes and databases, or Internet resources, as well as local resources.

◆ **Authority**. Users of a library's Web site expect that the same techniques librarians use to select quality resources to add to the physical collection will also be applied to resources that are made available via the Web.

◆ **Navigation**. A uniform look and feel will help the user avoid a chaotic presentation. The library's Web site and OPAC must be visually appealing. Consistent use of color, page layout, and other design elements can be used to present Web pages that are of value to the user. The navigational tools that are selected should be able to accommodate first-time users, as well as the more experienced searcher. Users should always know where they are in a Web site (color-coded pages, graphics, a navigation bar, and a site map have been used effectively at some sites). Multiple navigation styles should be supported including searching, browsing, effective use of links, graphic links, a FAQ list, and so forth. Between 35 percent and 50 percent of site visitors use the search feature for navigation.[22]

◆ **Experience**. The overall experience of using a Web site must be straightforward and intuitive. One of the hallmarks of an intuitive site is that it is organized logically and it supports a wide array of users and technology.

◆ **Multimedia**. If your Web site has links to or uses multimedia tools (e.g., Adobe's PDF files, Shockwave's Flash, RealAudio, Real Video, PowerPoint), the Web site should alert the user of the need to have a plug-in software module installed (and provide a direct link to Web sites that allow the tool to be downloaded without distractions).

◆ **Treatment**. Does the site achieve its purpose of providing access to information about a particular topic? Are there valuable links to Web sites that provide complementary information?

◆ **Access**. The ways in which site visitors are seeking information can be conveniently divided into two groups (similar to online catalog users): those that are *searching* for specific information and those that are browsing a topic. Ensuring that both of these approaches are easy to accomplish means users will be able to locate what they are interested in. If they cannot, then they will become exasperated, leave, and likely never return again.

◆ **Miscellaneous**. Web page download time. Other factors that might be important would be added here. Some Web sites load so slowly that the Web has been called the "World Wide Wait."

The following Web site evaluation scorecard (see Table 11-1) can be used to rate your library's Web site. In addition to rating your site, you can also weight the results of one area over another using Everhart's weighting scheme as noted above. Any Web site that scores less than a 40 (out of a possible 90) needs an immediate trip to the Web site re-design hospital. Also, any factor that scores less than a 6 should be reviewed for ways to make improvements.

Table 11-1. Web Site Evaluation Scorecard

Factor	Rating Criteria	Your Score
Currency	Information last updated: within the last month = 10; last 2–3 months = 7; last 4–5 months = 5; last 6–12 months = 3; more than 1 year = 0	
Content/ Information	If the library Web site provides access to Library Information + the library's OPAC + commercial indexes and full text databases + subject pathfinders + Internet resources + local content, the rating is a 10. Five of this list = 7; four of this list = 5; three of this list = 3; and 2 of this list = 1.	
Authority	Links to selected Web resources + subject pathfinders = 10; links to selected Web resources = 5; No links = 0.	
Navigation	Ease of navigation (ask your users). Easy = 10; Moderate = 5; Hard = 0.	
Experience	Overall experience positive = 10. Do they experience broken hypertext links? = 5. Do your users need to frequently backtrack? = 0.	
Multimedia	Are links to Web browser plug-ins found on your site? = 10. Plug-ins used but no links to download = 0.	
Treatment	Links to other library Web sites with a subject guide to these sites? = 10. Links to other library Web sites (by location or type of library) = 5.	
Access	Possible to conduct a Web site search in addition to a library OPAC search? = 10. No Web site search engine = 0.	
Miscellaneous	Web page download time is less than 5 seconds = 10. Less than 10 seconds = 7; Less than 15 seconds = 5; More than 16 seconds = 0.	

As library Web sites have grown in size and complexity, attempting to maintain an HTML-only site will display the limitations of this primitive tool. A design approach that uses an application server with a database of information resources will allow the library's Web site to scale. While HTML is great for displaying data, a database is a good way to manage data about information resources. A database-driven Web site will combine the best of both worlds and reduce the personnel costs associated with maintaining a Web site.[23]

Libraries should embed keyword attributes in an HTML meta tag in their Web sites and HTML documents because this significantly improves accessibility when a search engine is used.[24]

USABILITY TESTING

A team of librarians have worked long and hard to design and build the library's Web site. A celebration is called for! But then what? Well, some libraries adopt the "Field of Dreams" approach to Web site availability—"if you build it, they will come." But do they? And more important, when people do come to the library Web site, what are their expectations, and are these expectations being met or exceeded?

Sometimes the pride of authorship hides the reality of actual use of the Web site. In fact, some Web site design team members will need to go through a process of grieving to let go and then move forward to a better design.[25] Team members may experience:

- **Denial**. "But this feature is important. Users just don't know how important it is and we should keep things as is."

- **Anger**. "Really, how stupid can users be."

- **Depression**. Some team members may become silent and simply withdraw. "I invested so much in this project and this stinks."

- **Acceptance**. "Well, maybe if we moved . . . " This is where good design begins.

Fortunately, redesigning a Web site does not have to be expensive and time-consuming. Table 11-2 shows a range of methods available to assess the usability of a Web site.

It is possible to develop paper mock-ups of the proposed changes and then ask users to assess the changes by giving them several tasks to perform and observing and recording what they would do using the mockups. Getting the reactions to the proposed changes from five to eight users should be a sufficiently large sample size.[26] Testing typically takes from one to two hours (asking a user to perform several tasks); in some cases, two users are asked to perform the tasks in collaboration with one another. The cost involved in usability testing is normally quite low, while the value of information collected from the test participants is very high.

Table 11-2. Usability Test Methods

Method	Advantages
Automated Data Collection. Software that tracks how users perform a specific task. Can be used anytime.	Automates the data collection process.
Card Sort. An index card is created for each Web page. Users asked to sort cards logically into categories. Typically used early in the design process.	Shows how users organize and name categories of information.
Category Expectation. Tests the understanding of each category including what users think should be in a category and what the category should be named.	Identifies any use of jargon and identifies users' expectations.
Cognitive Walkthrough. Designers try to mimic actual users by performing various tasks themselves.	No need to recruit users for testing.
Field Study. Observe users as they carry out normal tasks.	See what users are actually doing and how they navigate around a Web site.
Focus Groups. A small group of users are asked to discuss their reactions and use of the Web site.	This method leads to more qualitative feedback.
Formal Testing. Asks a sample of users to perform specific tasks and to "think out loud" about their thoughts, feelings, and reactions.	Probably the most thorough method, especially if user reactions are taped, transcribed, and then analyzed. Can be a time-consuming process.
Interview. Provides a semi-structured conversation about the Web site.	Allows an individual to provide extensive feedback about the site.
Opinion Poll. Intended to obtain feedback on a specific topic.	A relatively quick method to gather data but difficult to interpret the data.
Paper Mock-ups. Users are asked to react to the proposed Web pages on paper.	Can be prepared quickly.
Questionnaire. Designed to collect opinions and feedback from a larger sample of users.	Relatively easy to conduct, but wording questionnaires is an art.
Site Usage Logs. The data will reveal how users move about the Web site.	Requires careful analysis.

Rather than a one-time project, a library's Web site should be considered an ongoing, iterative process. This iterative design process means that a new prototype is created, tested, redesigned, released, and then re-evaluated. Relentless adjustment is crucial. The "rap" on Microsoft, for example, is that it hardly ever creates new, great technology. But it does constantly and relentlessly adjust its products so that, over time, they become useful and usable products and, in some cases, become the "usability standard."

The library may wish to administer a questionnaire to obtain a more formal reaction to their Web pages. The System Usability Scale (SUS) is a 10-question survey that uses a Likert scale. SUS scores range from 0 to 100.[27] A longer 50-statement questionnaire, known as the Software Usability Measurement Inventory (SUMI), assesses the usability of a system from five perspectives: efficiency, effect or the emotional reaction, helpfulness, control, and learnability.[28]

As noted above, a library can solicit feedback using a variety of methods, including e-mail links, posting a Web form, conducting surveys, and so on. However, using prototypes is highly recommended by many authors and consultants in the field. While it is possible to use HTML coding or a software package to develop prototypes, these tools should only be used if the total development time can be measured in hours rather than days or weeks. Remember, the purpose of the prototype is to elicit feedback about possible changes and, thus, the software coding used for the prototype will be abandoned.

The library should also make extensive use of Web statistics. Software programs are available that track which Web pages are visited (called "hits"), as well as the paths traveled by people who visit the site. Using this information can provide a clearer picture of what portions of a library's Web site are being used, as well as what navigation paths are actually being used. In addition, Web developers and administrators can identify where users originate, what connections are in use (e.g., dial-up, DSL, high speed), and what sort of technologies are being used by the end user (e.g., type of desktop computer, operating system, brand of browser, and so forth).

In addition to usability, the library should also be concerned about accessibility, especially for those with handicaps.[29] A library can check the accessibility of its Web site by using one or more validation tools (for example, Bobby—http://www.cast.org/bobby/).

There have been several published reports comparing task performance efficiency before and after a redesign. On average, the gain in efficiency was 50 percent.[30] Many libraries have gone through the iterative redesign process, and they all report a significant increase in the amount of traffic to the library's Web site after their sites had been revised.[31] For example, the University of Nevada Las Vegas experienced a nearly 100 percent increase in the number of hits at its site.

INTRANETS AND PERSONALIZED LIBRARY WEB SITES

Librarians are increasingly being asked to participate as team members in developing and maintaining an Intranet for their parent organization, be it a city, county, or federal government agency; corporation; or other information agency. An Intranet is a Web site that is behind a firewall and visible only to employees and select outsiders through login privileges. Besides content from within the organization, many Intranets also provide electronic content from external suppliers. This external content might be news feeds, stock quote information, general business news, or content solely focused on the needs of a particular organization. For example, a hospital might provide access to medical information and related resources to end users.

Even an Intranet with a great look and feel does not address the fundamental underlying reasons for an Intranet. An effective Intranet should address the issues of information overload, effective information access and retrieval, organization of intellectual assets, and the potential for providing a sense of communities built around common interests and practice rather than departmental boundaries.

Yet, given the "invisible" nature of an Intranet, there is usually little incentive to make improvements. Thus, it is not surprising that many usability experts have noted common design mistakes with Intranets. Vincent Flanders,[32] author of the book and Web site *Web Sites That Suck* has his list of the top 10 Intranet mistakes:

1. **Splash pages**. The Intranet's home page is the most important page, and it should have important information and a navigation scheme. Welcome splash pages are distracting and will appear each time an employee visits the Intranet.

2. **Keeping unnecessary design items**. Eliminate the design elements that distract from the site. These design elements might include spinning logos, animations, 3D graphics, music, ugly clip art, and large graphics.

3. **Using the same corporate Web site design for the Intranet**. A corporate Web site has many purposes (e.g., selling products, providing software downloads, providing investor information, and so forth). An Intranet has a single purpose, to dispense information of value that will help employees complete their jobs in a productive manner.

4. **Forgetting the Japanese**. Organizations with an international presence need to remember that users may not have the bandwidth to be able to download large pages quickly. The same applies to U.S. employees that are attempting to dial in using lower speed telephone/modem connections.

5. **Forgetting that the "Top's Gotta Pop."** Screen real estate is valuable, so remember to place site navigation at the top.

6. **Poor navigation**. Users often have difficulty answering the questions: Where am I? How do I get to the parent organization's home page? Ask a member of the Web team to find an item of information buried inside your site.

7. **Flash**. The goal of an Intranet is to provide access to information and Flash is not an appropriate tool to fulfill this mission. Flash is great for entertainment sites but not informational sites.

8. **Forgetting that "Text is text and links are links."** Text is *never* underscored and links *must* be underscored. Never use graphics for text because a site search engine can't index the text within the graphic. If information is buried in a sea of links, it is difficult to find a "sea horse" among all the "sea shells."

9. **Not testing with different browsers**. Many employees have different browsers or older versions of browsers still running on their desktops despite the presence of an organization's standardized browser. Plus, employees might wish to connect from home, a hotel room, or a temporary location.

10. **Too much content**. Get rid of outdated content. A glut of content leads to information overload, and the user will have difficulty finding anything of value.

Fortunately, there are several software tools available that will analyze the log files for your Intranet. The benefits of using such a tool are several, and they include:

◆ **Provide information about who uses your Intranet**. The number of unique users can be identified. This number can then be compared to the number of employees and others who could potentially access the Intranet.

◆ **Estimate the Intranet's return on investment**. Use of the Intranet means that people are saving time. If the Intranet were not available, then people would be visiting the library, spending frustrating time on the Internet, and pursuing other avenues to access the information that could be made available via the Intranet.

◆ **Determine what is important**. Knowing what pages are most frequently accessed means they can be moved closer to the Intranet's home page. This usage information could also mean that there is some unmet need and perhaps additional complimentary information is needed.

◆ **Determine what is not being used**. Analyzing what is not being used may mean re-positioning the pages, embedding metadata tags to improve the indexing, and so forth. It might also point out the need to improve any navigational tools that might be connected to the site.

◆ **Determining the paths followed by users**. Navigation bottlenecks can be identified as well as pages that may need to be re-positioned should they require a large number of clicks to get to that Web page.

"For the past 25 years, OPACs have been at the center of the library world. That era is over. Ask any patron how many times a week he uses an OPAC and how many times a week he uses a Web search engine.

The answer to that question should scare us."

Stuart Weibel[33]

Perhaps the greatest benefit for most Intranets is the improved communication and collaboration that occurs within an organization. Well-run Intranets are changing clerical chores and making it easier to accomplish routine tasks faster, better, and cheaper. To build a transforming Intranet:

- **Eliminate paperwork**. Need to change a benefit? Add a new baby to the health plan? Check on the status of a 401k plan? File an expense report? Besides filing paperwork online, managers can approve requests, and the results can be audited—all online. Such an approach significantly reduces costs and the turn-around time to get something approved.

- **Create a Best Practices forum**. Users connected to the Internet benefit from being connected to so many people, ideas, and information sources at once. An Intranet can capture some of the same excitement and enchantment.

- **Share the limelight**. Reports from the "frontlines" allow employees to share their problems and successes. Seeing their name online makes them feel like they are contributing, as well as receiving some of the credit for their suggestions.

- **Provide relevant news**. Provide access to commercial news sources, especially news sources that allow the organization, as well as the user, to customize the delivery using a filter. Larger organizations have found real value in having a human editor provide an informed insider's judgment about what is likely to be of relevance.

- **Encourage multiple Intranets**. Allowing groups of users to "hang out" together without having to view the information resources and e-mail messages from other groups within the organization will make each group more productive.

- **Provide effective search tools.** An effective search technology is crucial because searching is what most people do to find a specific document. Encourage the use of invisible "metatags" as a part of the document description.

- **Provide an irresistible Intranet**. People need to have compelling reasons to frequently visit your organization's Intranet. A logo, animation, flash page, and other gimmicks will just not be enough of a reason to come back. The bottom line—figure out how to provide real value to your employees.[34]

Increasingly, librarians will have the opportunity to offer their users tools that allow them to customize their online catalog, as well as the library's Web site. These personalization tools provide people, especially knowledgeable and frequent visitors to the library's Web site, with the ability to customize their experience so they are more productive. It will be interesting to observe whether libraries that offer personalization options will also need to develop and recommend style guides or templates so users—even with the best of intentions—don't produce customized versions of a library Web Site/OPAC that renders it virtually unusable.

LIBRARY OPACs

Starting in the mid 1980s, during several invitational conferences sponsored by the Council on Library Resources, and subsequent investigation by others, the issues and complexities associated with the good design of an online catalog screen were addressed.[35] Library automation vendors have generally followed the recommendations of the various individuals who have studied library OPACs. While each of the various data elements have been clearly labeled and the layout is generally clear, a surprisingly large number of libraries continue to use library jargon to identify each data element. For example, main entry, added entries, imprint, physical description, and others are still found in some library OPACs.

FUTURE GRAPHICAL USER INTERFACES (GUI)

The GUI of Windows and the Web browser work well, with some training and experience. However, new technologies such as speech recognition and speech synthesis will fundamentally change the user interface (e.g., eliminate the need for the keyboard). As a part of the Internet II initiative, three research projects are exploring the implications of a new user interface when new technologies are incorporated as part of the design.[36] These projects include:

- **Project Aura** at Carnegie Mellon University is developing a system that's controlled by speech and uses microphones and monitors sprinkled around the user's workplace. The focus of the research is to use existing and recently developed technology.
- **Project Oxygen** at the Massachusetts Institute of Technology is building a system composed of new hardware, software, and network components.
- **The Portolano Project** at the University of Washington is working to build an invisible computing environment.

SUGGESTED WEB RESOURCES

Human Computer Interaction Bibliography
http://www.hcibib.org

IBM's Ease of Use Web Site
http://www.ibm.com/easy

Information and Design
http://www.infodesign.com.au/usability/webcheck.pdf

Jakob Nielsen's Heuristic Evaluation
http://www.useit.com

Really Bad Web Sites
http://www.webpagesthatsuck.com

Usability First
http://www.usabilityfirst.com

Usability Methods Toolbox
http://www.best.com/~jthom/usability/usahome.htm

Usability Professionals Associations: Resources
http://www.upassoc.org/html/resources.html

Usability Testing at Washington State University
http://www.vancouver.wsu.edu/fac/diller/usability/website.htm

Useable Web
http://www.useableweb.com

User Interface Engineering
http://www.world.std.com/~

Web Accessibility Initiative
http://www.w3.org/wai

Web Design/Usability
http://www.webreference.com/design/usability.html

Web Review: Usability Matters Design Studio
http://webreview.com/97/04/25/usability/index.html

SUGGESTED READINGS

Beyer, Hugh, and Karen Holtzblatt. *Context Design: Defining Customer-Centered Systems.* San Francisco: Morgan Kaufmann, 1998.

Black, Roger. *Web Sites That Work.* San Jose, CA: Adobe Press, 1997.

Campbell, Nicole. *Usability Assessment of Library-Related Web Sites: Methods and Case Studies.* LITA Guide #7. Chicago: American Library Association, 2001.

Donnelly, Vanessa. *Designing Easy-to-Use Websites.* London: Addison-Wesley, 2001.

Fleming, Jennifer. *Web Navigation: Designing the User Experience.* Sebastopol, CA: O'Reilly, 1998.

Garlock, Kristen L., and Sherry Piontek. *Designing Web Interfaces to Library Services and Resources.* Chicago: American Library Association, 1999.

Krug, Steve. *Don't Make Me Think: A Common Sense Approach to Web Usability.* Indianapolis, IN: New Riders, 2000.

Lynch, Patrick, and Sarah Horton. *Web Style Guide.* New Haven, CT: Yale University Press, 1999.

Nielsen, Jakob. *Designing Web Usability: The Practice of Simplicity.* Indianapolis, IN: New Riders, 2000.

Pearrow, Mark. *The Web Site Usability Handbook.* Rockland, MA: Charles River Media, 2000.

Powell, Thomas A. *Web Design: The Complete Reference.* Berkeley, CA: Osborne/McGraw-Hill, 2000.

Reiss, Eric L. *Practical Information Architecture.* London: Addison-Wesley, 2000.

Rosenfeld, Louis, and Peter Morville. *Information Architecture for the World Wide Web*. Sebastopol, CA: O'Reilly, 1998.

Rubin, Jeffrey. *Handbook of Usability Testing: How to Plan, Design, and Conduct Effective Tests*. New York: Wiley, 1994.

Spool, Jared M., Tara Scanlon, Will Schroeder, Carolyn Snyder, and Terri DeAngelo. *Web Site Usability: A Designer's Guide*. San Francisco: Morgan Kaufman, 1999.

Veen, Jeffrey. *The Art & Science of Web Design*. Indianapolis, IN: New Riders, 2001.

NOTES

1. C. N. Mooers. "Mooers's Law: Or Why Some Retrieval Systems Are Used and Others Are Not." *American Documentation*, 11 (3), 1990, p. 1.

2. Helge Clausen. "Evaluation of Library Web Sites: The Danish Case." *The Electronic Library*, 17 (2), April 1999, pp. 83–87. L. A. Clyde. "The Library As Information Provider: The Home Page." *The Electronic Library*, 14 (6), 1996, pp. 549–58. Randy Rice. *Randy Rice's Software Testing Page: Web Usability Checklist*. Available at: www.riceconsulting.com/webusability.htm. E. B. Lily and C. Van Fleet. "Measuring the Accessibility of Public Library Home Pages." *Reference and User Services Quarterly*, 40 (2), Winter 2000, pp. 176–80.

3. A. Hill. "Top 5 Reasons Your Customers Abandon Their Shopping Carts." *Smart Business*, 14 (3), 2001, pp. 80–84.

4. K. Diaz. "The Role of the Library Web Site." *Reference and User Services Quarterly*, 38 (1), Fall 1998, pp. 41–48.

5. IntelliQuest Web Evaluation Services. Available at: http://www.intelliquest.com.

6. Jared Spool. "Real Implications from Usability Testing." *Webreview*, September 23, 1998. Available at: http://www.webreview.com/1998/09_25/strategists/09_23_98_2.shtml.

7. Steve Krug. *Don't Make Me Think: A Common Sense Approach to Web Usability*. Indianapolis, IN: New Riders, 2000.

8. Patrick J. Lynch and Sarah Horton. *Web Style Guide: Basic Design Principles for Creating Web Sites*. New Haven, CT: Yale University Press, 1999. Also, examples of Web style guides can be found at http://www.bcr.org/stylemanual, http://www.beadsland.com/weapas/, http://webreference.com/html/, and http://www.sun.com/styleguide/.

9. Link-checking programs include: WWW Link Checker (for Unix systems) http://www.ugrad.cs.ubc.ca/spider/q7f192/branch/checker.html; LVRFY: A HTML Link Verifier http://www.cs.dartmouth.edu/~crow/lvrfy.html; and MOMspider (Multi-Owner Maintenance Spider) http://www.ics.uci.edu/WebSoft/MOMspider/WWW94/paper.html.

10. Jakob Nielsen. "The 3Cs of Critical Web Use: Collect, Compare, Choose." *Alertbox*, April 15, 2001. Available at: http://www.useit.comalertbox/20010415.html.

11. Richard Koman. "The Scent of Information." *Webreview*, May 15, 1998. Available at http://www.webreview.com/1998/05_15/strategists/05_15_98_1.shtml.

12. Marcia J. Bates. "The Design of Browsing and Berrypicking Techniques for the Online Search Interface." *Online Review*, 13 (5), October 1989, pp. 409–24.

13. Jared M. Spool, Tara Scanlon, Will Schroeder, Carolyn Snyder, and Terri DeAngelo. *Web Site Usability: A Designer's Guide.* San Francisco: Morgan Kaufman, 1999.

14. Richard Saul Wurman. "Redesign the Data." *Business2.com*, November 28, 2000, pp. 210–22.

15. A. Clyde. "Ten Things I Hate About . . . Web Pages." *Teacher Librarian*, 27 (2), 1999, pp. 58–59. See also, J. Fairly. "The 6 Mistakes of Highly Ineffective Websites." *Bank Marketing*, 32 (2), 2000, pp. 28–29.

16. Web Site Analysis Tools include: Funnel Web Professional, HitBox Pro, NetTracker, SuperStats Professional, and WebTrends Log Analyzer. For current product reviews and a list of new competing products, check with http://www.zdnet.com.

17. Available at: http://www.useit.com/papers/heuristic/heuristic_list.html.

18. John D'Angelo and Sherry K. Little. "Successful Web Pages: What Are They and Do They Exist?" *Information Technology and Libraries*, 17 (2), June 1998, pp. 71–81.

19. John D'Angelo and Joanne Twining. "Comprehension by Clicks: D'Angelo Standards for Web Page Design, and Time, Comprehension, and Preference." *Information Technology and Libraries*, 19 (3), September 2000, pp. 125–35.

20. Rich Cirillo. "Jakob Nielsen's Top 10 Web-Design Mistakes." *VARBusiness*, February 20, 2001. Available at http://varbusiness.com/components/printArticle.asp?ArticleID=24035.

21. Roger Black. *Web Sites That Work.* San Jose, CA: Adobe Press, 1997.

22. A. Hill. "Top 5 Reasons Your Customers Abandon Their Shopping Carts." *Smart Business*, 14 (3), 2001, pp. 80–84. Jared M. Spool, Tara Scanlon, Will Schroeder, Carolyn Snyder, and Terri DeAngelo. *Web Site Usability: A Designer's Guide.* San Francisco: Morgan Kaufman, 1999.

23. Kristin Antelman. "Getting Out of the HTML Business: The Database-Driven Web Site Solution." *Information Technology and Libraries*, 18 (4), December 1999, pp. 176–81.

24. Thomas P. Truner and Lise Brackbill. "Rising to the Top: Evaluating the Use of the HTML META Tag to Improve Retrieval of World Wide Web Documents Through Internet Search Engines." *LRTS*, 42 (4), October 1998, pp. 258–71.

25. Kelley Schmidt. "Good Grief! The Highs and Lows of Usability Testing." *Webreview*, December 15, 2000. Available at: http://www.WebReview.com/2000/12_15/strategists/index01.shtml.

26. User Interface Engineering. "Eight Is More Than Enough." Available at: http://world.std.com/~uieweb/eight.htm.

27. John Brooke. "SUS: A 'Quick and Dirty' Usability Scale." *Usability Evaluation in Industry*. Patrick W. Jordan, Bruce Thomas, Bernard A. Weerdmeester, and Ian L. McClelland, eds. London: Taylor and Francis, 1996, pp. 189–94.

28.   J. Kirakowski. "The Software Usability Measurement Inventory: Background and Usage." *Usability Evaluation in Industry*. Patrick W. Jordan, Bruce Thomas, Bernard A. Weerdmeester, and Ian L. McClelland, eds. London: Taylor and Francis, 1996, pp. 169–77.

29.   Terry Brainerd Chadwick. "Web Site Accessibility: What, Why and How." *Internet Librarian 2001 Collected Presentations*. Medford, NJ: Information Today, 2001, pp. 36–41.

30.   Thomas K. Landauer. *The Trouble with Computers: Usefulness, Usability and Productivity*. Cambridge, MA: MIT Press, 1995.

31.   Jason Vaughan. "Three Iterations of an Academic Library Web Site." *Information Technology and Libraries*, 20 (2), June 2001, pp. 81–92. Kate McCready. "Designing and Redesigning: Marquette Libraries' Web Site." *Library HiTech*, 15 (3/4), 1997, pp. 83–89. Bruce Harley. "Electronic One-Stop Shopping: The Good, The Bad, The Ugly." *Information Technology and Libraries*, 18 (4), December 1999, pp. 200–209. David King. "Library Home Page Design: A Comparison of Page Layout for Front-Ends to ARL Library Web Sites." *College & Research Libraries*, 59 (5), September 1998, pp. 458–66. Ruth Dickstein and Vicki Mills. "Usability Testing at the University of Arizona Library: How to Let the Users in on the Design." *Information Technology and Libraries*, 19 (3), September 2000, pp. 144–51. David King. "Redesigning the Information Playground: A Usability Study of kclibrary.org." *Internet Librarian 2001 Collected Presentations*. Medford, NJ: Information Today, 2001, pp. 93–102. Anne M. Platoff and Jennifer M. Duvernay. "User Testing Made Easy." *Internet Librarian 2001 Collected Presentations*. Medford, NJ: Information Today, 2001, pp. 155–64.

32.   The list is available at: http://www.fixingyourwebsite.com/top10/intranet .html

33.   Stuart Weibel quoted in Ron Chepesiuk. "Organizing the Internet: The 'Core' of the Challenge." *American Libraries*, 31 (1), January 1999, pp. 59–63.

34.   George Anders. "Inside Job." *Fast Company*, September 2001, pp. 177–85.

35.   See for example, Joseph R. Matthews. "Suggested Guidelines for Screen Layouts and Design of Online Catalogs." *Online Catalog Screen Displays: A Series of Discussions*. Joan Frye Williams, ed. Washington, DC: Council on Library Resources, 1986, pp. 3–26. Walt Crawford with Lennie Stovel and Katherine Bales. *Bibliographic Displays in the Online Catalog*. White Plains, NY: Knowledge Industry Publications, 1986. Walt Crawford. "Testing Bibliographic Displays for Online Catalogs." *Information Technology and Libraries*, March 1987, pp. 20–33. Walt Crawford. *The Online Catalog Book: Essays and Examples*. New York: G. K. Hall, 1992. Nancy Lee Shires and Lydia P. Olszak. "What Our Screens Should Look Like: An Introduction to Effective OPAC Screens." *RQ*, Spring 1992, pp. 357–69.

36.   Niall McKay. "A Failure to Communicate." *Darwin*, 1 (14), November 2001, pp. 34–36.

Chapter 12

Managing
Library Information Systems

Clearly, a LIS has a major impact on the functioning of a library. Not only does staff use it on a daily basis, but the automated system is the library's public face as users visit the library and use the OPAC. In addition, the library has another public face with its Web site/library portal and the Web-based OPAC providing library services remotely. Thus, managing all of these information technology-based services assumes a much more important role within the library than in years past.

Information technology does not exist in a vacuum. The way technology is implemented and managed is as important as the technology itself. Because organizational goals, organizational culture, social mores, and technology are all interconnected, libraries cannot simply implement a new technology without any planning. To exploit the growing potential of information technologies, libraries need the necessary infrastructure of communication networks, application software, internal data, access to external information resources, and knowledgeable employees to manage this technology.

Managing a LIS is an important responsibility. A smooth-functioning system is one that remains invisible until there is a problem with the software or the total system ceases to work because of a hardware failure. Then the telephone calls come! The personality and technical skills of the systems librarian and the computer support staff are crucial in determining in how quickly the problem is identified and solved.

SYSTEM MANAGER CHARACTERISTICS

While it is difficult to generalize about people who are system managers, libraries generally are able to attract talented but inexperienced people or they are willing to train an in-house "technophile" or "nerd." Yet, due to the substantial shortage of trained IT people at all levels, some libraries have found that they are proving to be a training ground. After acquiring a year or two of experience, it is not surprising that systems personnel will move on to higher paying jobs in the private sector.

A successful system manager and computer-related support staff will exhibit the following characteristics:

- **Excellent communicator**. The system manager needs to be able to communicate in non-technical terms, with a wide variety of people, including vendors, library staff members, library managers, and library decision-makers. The system manager must be comfortable dealing with the jargon-rich terminology of the computer hardware and software industries.

- **Thorough and detail-oriented**. Computer systems and networks require retaining a tremendous amount of technical information and understanding how all the hardware and software pieces work together. Often times, it is necessary to install a new software release or anti-virus update. While sometimes the installation is automated and will guide the system manager through the process in a step-by-step manner, other times it will be necessary to follow a detailed set of instructions. Being adventurous and attempting to take short cuts is a sure-fire way to cause system downtime and damage.

- **Patient**. There are times in the life of a systems manager that would try the patience of a saint. Even after following all of the appropriate directions, checking and double-checking the cabling, equipment, and software, something continues to be "not quite right," and so an application doesn't work, a computer workstation can't be connected to the LAN—well, you get the picture. At times like these, it's often necessary to take a break and start the troubleshooting process again to identify and solve the problem. All of this takes patience—lots of patience.

- **Appreciates puzzles**. Time after time, tracking down the root cause of a problem is very much like solving a puzzle or finding your way out of a maze. For some reason, what has worked in the past is not working now. Software that worked fine yesterday will not work today (a new release of another software product may or may not have been installed). A really good systems person will enjoy the thrill of the hunt and have the persistence of a homicide detective.

- **Organized**. The system manager will know the value of being organized. This individual will ensure that the library management team participates in setting priorities for the communications infrastructure and the LIS. Having a clearly defined set of priorities means that the systems office staff is able to proactively handle the inevitable problems and challenges that will arise. Without the proactive approach, staff will simply be in a reactive mode, often rushing to solve the problem for the person who is the loudest "squeaky wheel."[1] While establishing the priorities, the library management team should likely consider: financial benefits, business objectives, intangible benefits, and technical importance.

- **Flexible**. Given the broad range of responsibilities, a system manager needs to remain flexible about a wide variety of things including schedules, changing priorities, and being able to keep multiple balls in the air.

- **Establishes balance**. A good system manager recognizes that things only get accomplished through the collective efforts of many different organizations and individuals. Yet, maintaining an appropriate sense of firmness will ensure that people recognize that there are limits and boundaries that must be adhered to.

- **Has a positive outlook on life**. Typically, the only time a library staff member calls the system manager is to report a network problem or some other system-related problem that needs attention. Over the course of time, this constant bombardment of problems can lead to a negative view of the world—or at least a negative view of the LIS. It's not too often that someone will call the system manager and complement him or her on the fact that the LAN has not suffered any downtime in the last six months!

- **Conservative**. A good system manager is cautious and conservative. Rather than trusting a vendor, system managers become adopted sons and daughters of the great state of Missouri whose nickname is "The Show-Me State." A system manager will test and re-test new software releases using a demo database prior to moving the software into a production environment. Unfortunately, this conservative side has been developed as the result of too many bad experiences.

SPECIFIC JOB SKILLS

The job skills for an effective system manager and his or her staff are quite wide ranging. These skills include:[2]

- **Library skills**. For example, knowledge of the MARC record structure, library services, administrative structure, organization and classification issues, and information retrieval.

- **Library systems skills**. Aside from a good understanding of the typical functions that are automated in most systems, the system manager should be aware of the vendors and products in the marketplace, know hardware and software capabilities, and have a basic understanding of contracts.

- **Computing skills**. The system manager must be aware of desktop operating environments, server operating systems, software programming fundamentals, database design, system design, and troubleshooting skills.

- **Database management skills**. A system manager will often need to learn about a specific database management system to help a vendor expand tables, restore corrupted tables, and produce ad hoc custom reports using a report generation tool.

- **Networking skills**. Understand network design, network services, protocols, network applications, network management, and Internet technologies. Some portion of a system manager's time will be spent on issues such as validating and authenticating users so they can access a wide range of information resources.

◆ **Management skills**. A good system manager will have basic management skills, be able to manage resources and technology, deal with security, and assess risk. The system manager will ensure that the library's database is backed up on a regular basis and that the backups are tested. Most important, the system manager and his or her team must ensure that they have the necessary people skills to maintain and nurture the relationships that will inevitably exist with outside partners.

Because system managers will likely deal with a veritable potpourri of information technologies, the system manager and his or her co-workers will seem like they are consummate jugglers. Among the technologies and tasks being juggled at one academic library are:

◆ Proxy servers

◆ Video editing equipment and software

◆ Filtering software

◆ Network/paid printing

◆ Digital security cameras

◆ Wireless network

◆ E-books

◆ Interlibrary loan software

◆ Web page management

◆ E-mail systems

◆ Supporting classroom instruction

◆ Electronic reserves

◆ Digitizing archival materials

◆ Maintaining "office" applications

◆ Writing local scripts.[3]

MANAGEMENT OF INFRASTRUCTURE

Once the library has installed a LAN, the job is not complete. The LAN, as well as the servers, desktop computers, printers, scanners, fax machines, hubs, routers providing a link to the Internet, and other devices that may be attached to the LAN must all be maintained—a physical security checklist may be found in Table 12-1. Besides the computer equipment, a variety of software must also be sustained. Among this software might be operating systems, desktop operating systems, office suite applications, firewall software, virus scanning software, and other applications.

Table 12-1. Computer System Physical Security Checklist

Location

✓ Above possible flood levels

✓ Away from heavy traffic likely to cause vibrations

Room

✓ One hour fire-rated walls

✓ Adequate drainage

✓ Water pipes routed away from ceiling of the room where the servers will be located

✓ Room locked and keys or code shared with only a few employees

Temperature and Humidity Control

✓ Dedicated air conditioning unit for the room

✓ Air intakes located away from sources of dirt, dust, sand, and steam

✓ Sufficient capacity to provide constant temperature/humidity levels

Electrical Power

✓ Other devices not attached to the computer room circuits

✓ Battery electrical power back-up unit

✓ Wiring, pipes, and ducts should be grounded

Fire Protection

✓ Centrally located emergency power-off switch

✓ Smoke and heat detection units

✓ Hand-held fire extinguishers suitable for electrical fires

Media Protection

✓ A safe with a high fire rating (insulation to withstand heat) of sufficient size to hold copies of all tapes and diskettes considered to be "vital"

Several studies have consistently revealed that the recurring costs of providing access to applications via a LAN could exceed $10,000 per user, per year. Hardware costs comprise less than 15 percent of this total. The majority of costs (85 percent) are for network and communications infrastructure, the cost of personnel required to maintain and update applications and desktop workstations, and on-going technical support.[4]

It is helpful if the individuals who maintain the LAN have more than a working knowledge of the LAN software. LAN managers and others working with LANs can study and become Certified Novell Engineers or certified Microsoft System Engineers. This certification process typically requires the individual to pass several examinations testing their knowledge in a variety of LAN-related areas.

Staff involved with maintaining the LAN will also need to be proficient in installing and maintaining desktop workstations, formatting hard disks, installing accessory cards, and troubleshooting a wide variety of problems.

The system manager or the LAN manager will need to be actively involved with library operations so that as employees are hired and leave they can:

◆ Establish a user account (user name and password)

◆ Authorize the employee for access to specific applications

◆ Configure the employee's workstation

◆ Change access to applications as responsibilities for the individual change over time

◆ Upgrade desktop workstations

◆ Delete the user account.

UPGRADES

LIS vendors will periodically release new versions of their application software (the frequency of new releases will vary from quarterly to once every 18 months). This new release will need to be installed when it will have minimal impact on the library's operation. In general, it is important that the library keep pace with their vendor as new releases of the LIS software become available. Installing the new releases will fix software bugs that the library maybe experiencing, as well as provide access to new features that will improve the library's productivity. From a contractual standpoint, the library may need to keep up with the releases to ensure ready access to the vendor's support infrastructure. Vendors like to keep all their customers on the most current or previous software release; otherwise, their support costs will rise sharply.

Once installed, the software needs to be tested to verify that it has not corrupted any files and that the software is working in a normal manner. The system manager needs to determine, prior to installing the new release, whether the minimum hardware requirements have changed. A new function or feature in the software may require additional RAM memory in the server or on the desktop workstations.

Besides new software releases for the LIS, new releases to the server and desktop workstation operating systems, office suite upgrades, and upgrades for other applications will need to be installed and tested. One troublesome issue is maintaining the most current version of drivers for printers, scanners, and other devices on the network. Perhaps the most time-consuming activity is trying to make sure that the library has received and installed the latest anti-virus updates to minimize threats to the library's servers and desktop workstations.

The key to installing new software releases is a systematic approach, and part of this approach is ensuring that backups are in place, should they be needed.

BACKUPS

The importance of performing backups on all of the library systems on a regular basis cannot be overemphasized. The information contained in a variety of databases found within the library is probably its most important asset. Fortunately, system backups can be scheduled to run unattended (without a computer operator standing by) in the early hours of the morning.

Typically, a daily system backup will record each file that has changed in the last 24 hours (this is also called an incremental backup). A full backup will record every file, whether it has recently changed or not (normally it is recommended that a full backup be performed weekly). Each backup should have some accompanying documentation that lists all of the directories and subdirectories to be found on the backup.

However, it is crucial for the library system's staff to periodically verify that not only were the backups made, but that the data contained in the backups can be restored (used again). Given the busy schedules in some libraries, it is not surprising that some will skip the verification of the restore option. Once this step is skipped, Murphy's Law will rear its ugly head when the library discovers that it is unable to read and restore the data from a backup. This may mean that the library will lose a day's, a week's or several weeks' worth of data. Imagine losing your library's circulation data, cataloging records added to the library, or material orders placed for several days or weeks! Not a pretty picture. Thus, the final word regarding backups—have a schedule to check and double-check your ability to restore the data from a partial or full backup.

The other component of backups is that some copies of the backups should be stored off-site at a relatively secure location. These off-site backups should be done on a regularly scheduled basis.

Staff members should be encouraged to backup the work files that exist on their desktop workstations to a network drive so their data is protected and available for use should they experience a hardware failure or have their disk drives become infected with a virus.

Both desktop backups and virus control can be managed at the system level for some software systems, with system-wide scans and periodic backups of all workstations.

MANAGING APPLICATIONS AND LICENSES

The system manager may also manage several software licenses. Depending upon the LIS that is installed at the library, licenses for different types of software may need to be purchased. Among the software licenses that may need to be maintained are LIS application software, other application software, search engine software, database management system software (e.g., Oracle, MS SQL Server), utilities, and operating system software. These software licenses will be needed for all the servers connected to the library's LAN and all of the desktop workstations.

Besides purchasing the initial license to use the software, the library must also budget and pay for the annual software maintenance licenses. Unfortunately, there is a bewildering variety of ways to license software and, in some cases, the library needs to count the total number of desktop workstations, the number of simultaneous users, the size of the database, and so on. Some applications can only have designated or named users. Other applications restrict the number of simultaneous users that can access the software. Usually, the LAN software (or the application software itself) will provide a set of tools for setting and monitoring an application's use.

Any software vendor can request the opportunity to visit the library and verify that the library is paying for the requisite number of licenses. Should the library not have the required number of licenses, it can look forward to not only paying for the additional licenses that are needed, but it can also expect to pay a fine (and the size of the fine is often significant!).

EMERGENCY/RECOVERY SUPPORT (DISASTER PLAN)

A Disaster Recovery Plan anticipates the consequences of being without some or all of a library's information systems and determining what could be done to mitigate the disaster. The cause of the disaster might arise from several sources:

- **Power brownout or blackout**. If the library has installed battery backup capabilities, then staff will have the time for an orderly shutdown of some or all of the applications.

- **Physical disaster**. This includes fires, floods, and earthquakes, among other things. If the equipment or software is seriously damaged, then the library should have an action plan for quickly replacing the necessary components so it can become operational again.

- **Security disaster**. The library's LAN or LIS has been infected with a computer virus or has been hacked and the various databases have become corrupted. This portion of the Emergency Disaster Plan may well be identical to a Computer Security Plan.

The Disaster Recovery Plan should provide a step-by-step blueprint of the actions to be taken and the people to be notified in the event of a major emergency. Besides notifying library staff members, it may be necessary to inform personnel from the parent organization (e.g., IT staff members), as well as contacting selected vendors about the emergency and actions that might be required by them.

Depending on the seriousness of the situation, it may be necessary to order—on an emergency basis—replacement equipment and software so the library can become operational as soon as possible.

SECURITY

Security issues are a serious concern for any organization, including a library. Because of the proliferation of security incidents, including viruses and denial of service attacks, any computer system that is accessible via the Internet must have the appropriate security hardware and software in place to protect the library and its valuable databases. A security breech is a silent venom that can infect and seriously damage the library's ability to provide service.

Threats to a computer system's security fall into three possible categories: natural (e.g., fire, lightning strikes, electrical surges, flood, earthquakes), unintentional (carelessness, poor training, and bad habits [e.g., leaving passwords and log-in commands on visible sheets near a desktop workstation]), and intentional. Obviously, the most dangerous threat comes from a disgruntled employee who wants revenge against a supervisor or the institution.

Vulnerability in a computer system is a weakness that could be exploited. The vulnerability might be physical (providing easy access to the computer equipment), hardware-related, or software-related. A countermeasure is an action, device, or procedure that reduces the vulnerability of an information system.

Libraries, similar to any other organization connected to the Internet, have experienced hacking of their computer systems, hacking of library Web sites as well as receiving countless e-mail viruses. In addition, libraries that provide public access to the Internet must also be aware that one or more of their users may be downloading pirated software, visiting pornographic Web sites, obtaining dangerous information (about bombs or drugs), or engaging in illegal activities. For example, a patron of the Brooklyn Public Library, using the Internet from the library, was able to discover personal information about a number of wealthy individuals and then was able to transfer funds to his own account by impersonating these individuals.

The Computer Security Institute, in conjunction with of the Federal Bureau of Investigation, conducts an annual "Computer Crime and Security Survey."[5] A total of 538 organizations—primarily large companies and federal government agencies—responded to the 2001 survey and they indicated:

- Eighty-five percent detected computer security breaches within the last year.

- Sixty-four percent suffered financial losses as a result of the computer breaches.

- The value of their financial losses totaled some $377 million. Each type of breach experienced a different average value of loss.

- The primary loss was the result of the theft of proprietary information.

- The Internet connection was the most frequent point of attack.

- More than half indicated they had experienced 10 or more incidents.

- More than three quarters of these organizations experienced denial of service attacks.

The National Computer Security Act of 1987 requires federal government agencies to develop a security plan and provide periodic security-related training. There are a host of publications devoted to the topic of computer security and security planning that would be of assistance should a library wish to create a computer security plan.[6] In all probability, a majority of libraries that are responsible for maintaining their own LIS and IT infrastructure have not developed a security plan. Unfortunately, the need for such a plan will not become obvious until the library experiences a major disaster from an unauthorized user. Security requires constant monitoring and is a continual process rather than a one-time event, such as installing firewall software.

Those within the library or IT department responsible for computer system security must be constantly monitoring and auditing all security points for threats. A recent survey suggests that organizations learn about security threats in a variety of ways, including:

- Analyzing server and firewall logs
- Being alerted by colleagues
- Using an intrusion detection system
- Noticing damaged data
- Receiving a heads-up from a supplier or partner.[7]

An intrusion detection system attempts to identify suspicious patterns from someone trying to compromise or hack into a system by examining all network activity. An intrusion-detection system could use one of three methods:

- **Passive system vs. reactive system**. A passive system identifies and logs the potential security breach and issues an alert. Even though an alert has been issued by a passive detection system, the intruder is still active within the computer system and may do serious damage. A reactive system will, however, detect the security breach, and either log off the user or reprogram the firewall to block network traffic from the suspected hacker. A reactive system is sometimes called an Intrusion Prevention System.

- **Misuse detection vs. anomaly detection**. A misuse detection system will analyze the suspected threat and compare it to a large database of known attack signatures and characteristics. This approach is particularly effective when a specific attack has already been recognized, for example an e-mail virus. An anomaly intrusion detection system monitors the network looking for irregularities.

- **Network-based vs. host-based systems**. A network-based intrusion detection system looks for packets that may have been overlooked by the firewall. A host-based intrusion detection system analyzes the activity on each individual computer or server that is attached to the LAN, looking for problems.

Once a threat has been identified and a patch has been developed to fill the security hole that exists within the operating system or other software, it is incumbent on the system manager to download the patch and then install the patch on the appropriate machines. This would be a relatively simple task if there were only one or two software products to track regarding security alerts. Typically, though, the number of software products that need to be tracked can be quite large.

Furthermore, applying a patch is not necessarily a trivial task. Applying a patch to one product may well cause a problem, even a serious problem, in another software product. It gets worse when a software vendor warns a customer that if one or more patches are applied to another software product, then the vendor will cease supporting its own product.

The ISO 17799 security standard, which is gaining acceptance within both private industry and government agencies, was framed using the British Standard 7799 as a foundation.[8] The standard is composed of 10 major sections:

1. **Business Continuity Planning**. What are the plans to prevent interruptions to business activities and critical business processes from the effects of a major failure or disaster?

2. **System Access Control**. How is access to information controlled? How is unauthorized access to computer systems prevented? How are networked services protected?

   Access control is the classification of resources, the separation of duties, and the implementation of a system that defines and enforces a relationship between resources, duties, and the user. The application-specific security level is sometimes called "sandbox security," because the user is restricted to a specific sandbox to play in.

   Discretionary access controls. Access is granted based on authorizations granted to a user.

   Mandatory access controls. Access is granted based on classifications of data and an overall access policy determined by those classifications. Mandatory access controls are normally preferred over discretionary ones, because systems administrators control access, not users.

   Location. Access to data or programs may need to be restricted based on physical or logical location.

3. **System Development and Maintenance**. Are procedures in place to ensure that security is built into operational systems to protect the confidentiality and integrity of information, prevent loss and misuse of user data, and maintain the security of application system software and data?

4. **Physical and Environmental Security**. Are procedures in place to prevent unauthorized access to business premises, prevent the loss or damage of assets, and ensure no interruption to business activities?

   Site location and construction. Data center sites should be selected after considering items such as whether the location is prone to flooding, earthquakes, and other natural disasters.

   Physical access. Access to computer facilities should be restricted to a small number of employees.

   Tape and media storage. Data storage media should be protected from unauthorized access. Both on-site and off-site backups should be protected from unauthorized access. Sensitive documentation should be located in a physically secure area.

5. **Compliance**. Does the library or organization comply with the provisions of any criminal or civil law, statute, regulatory or contractual obligation as they pertain to security and to maximize the effectiveness of the system audit process?

6. **Personnel Security**. Are procedures in place to minimize risks of human error, theft, fraud, or misuse of facilities and to minimize the damage from security incidents and malfunctions?

7. **Security Organization**. Does the organization manage information security to maintain the security of information assets accessed by third parties and maintain responsibility when information processing has been outsourced?

8. **Computer and Network Management**. Are procedures in place to ensure the correct and secure operation of the information processing facilities, minimize the risk of system failures, protect the integrity of software and information, ensure the safeguarding of information in networks, and prevent the loss or misuse of information exchanged between organizations?

9. **Asset Classification and Control**. Do the organization's physical and information assets receive an appropriate level of protection?

10. **Security Policy**. Is management involved to set the direction and support of information security?

There are other security standards that the library may wish to explore as it reviews the current status of its security measures.[9]

Ideally, the library will have developed a written plan to cope with a security breach, should one occur, rather than reacting to an emergency situation. The plan should identify the members of the incident response team, as well as the vendors (hardware and software) that may have to be contacted to cope with the situation. The plan should outline the escalation of procedures that will be followed should the attack turn out to be protracted or especially damaging. At some point, it may be appropriate to contact the suitable government agencies to get them involved in providing technical assistance, as well as gathering information for possible prosecution.[10]

Firewalls are designed to keep unwanted (e.g., SPAM) and unauthorized traffic from an unprotected network out of a LAN, yet still allow users to access network services. The firewall, which is similar to a security gate for a gated community, provides security to those components inside the gate and controls who can get in and go out.[11] The firewall can be a separate device, or it can be integrated into a router.

Good security requires ongoing staff training and expenditure of capital to ensure that the appropriate set of tools are in place. Because of the complexity of security technology, this may be an area that the library might wish to consider outsourcing to a security service provider.

ERGONOMICS

Despite the fact the furniture manufactures have known for decades that people come in a wide variety of shapes and sizes, office furniture typically comes in one standard size. Despite their traditional response to the marketplace, some improvements have been made in the last decade with the introduction of adjustable (sometimes called ergonomic) furniture. Ergonomics is the process that seeks to adapt work and working conditions to suit the worker. An adjustable surface for a desktop workstation's keyboard is crucial because carpal tunnel syndrome may result if an individual must reach up to use it.

Working for extended periods at a desktop workstation causes an individual to repeatedly use the same muscles in the arms, hands, and eyes while, at the same time, the rest of the body is held in an immobile position. This combination of factors leads to repetitive stress syndrome injuries. Thus, it is important for the library to pay particular attention to the furniture provided to its employees, as well as ensuring that the working conditions are optimized to minimize injuries. This is best accomplished by providing employees with adjustable everything—chairs, work surfaces, keyboards, monitors, task lighting, and so forth.[12]

WORKFLOW

A LIS has the *potential* to significantly boost productivity within the library. However, the productivity gains will not occur unless the library re-designs the workflows within the separate departments. Every LIS has a unique set of strengths or weaknesses. The challenge for each manager within the library is to redesign the workflows to take advantage of the system's strengths and institute work procedures to overcome the system's limitations.

First, the library should examine all of the forms used by library staff members to gather and input data into the LIS. Whether this be a Consider for Acquisitions Form, a Materials Order Form for acquisitions, a Bibliographic/Authority Original Cataloging Record Form for review, or a Patron Registration Form for circulation, library staff should revise any existing forms or create new forms so that they have the same look and feel as the data input screens of the LIS (i.e., the sequence of data fields for the input form should match the data input screens). The less eye movement that needs to occur during the data entry process, the more productive the staff will be. Also, fewer errors will occur during the data input process if the staff member is not searching for a particular field of data.

Some libraries may wish to use a systems analysis tool called flow-charting to document the steps involved in a particular activity. Besides recording the steps involved in a process (e.g., adding a bibliographic record to the library's database), the flow chart should also reflect the time spent completing a task. Once documented, library staff members can examine whether all tasks still need to be done or whether the sequence of tasks can be changed or combined to reduce the number of steps involved.

One of the easiest ways to gather information about the workflows, especially within technical services, is to gather a sample of contact information. A slip of paper is placed in each book or item ordered as it is received at the library for some period of time. An appropriate sample size would be approximately 250 items. Each time staff members handle the item, they record their initials, the time a task was started, the time the task was completed, and select a code for the task, as well as a code for the location within technical services. The slips are collected just prior to the items being placed on the library shelves.

The data found on the slips can then be used to prepare an activity flow chart, as well as a workflow diagram, as illustrated in Figure 12-1. The results of the workflow diagram will, in some cases, suggest that chaos is alive and well in technical services. Using this information, it is possible to redesign the workflow. One of the design caveats for technical services should be to "minimize the number of times an item is handled." If the library routinely receives multiple copies of an

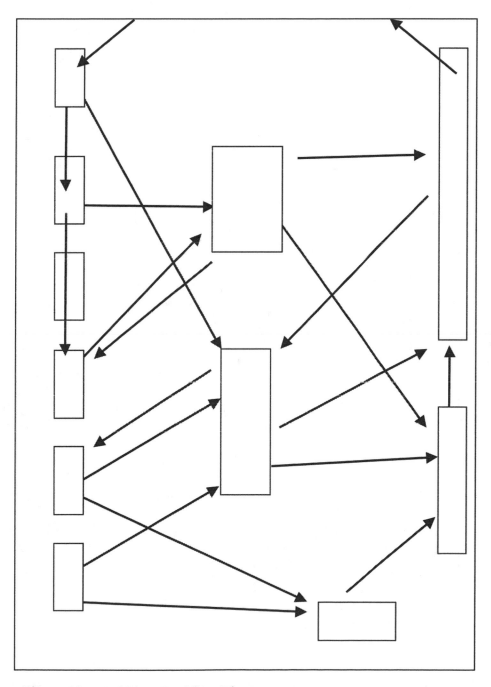

Figure 12-1. Existing Workflow Diagram

item, perhaps one copy is routed for cataloging purposes while the remaining copies are moved directly to physical processing. A redesigned workflow diagram is shown in Figure 12-2.

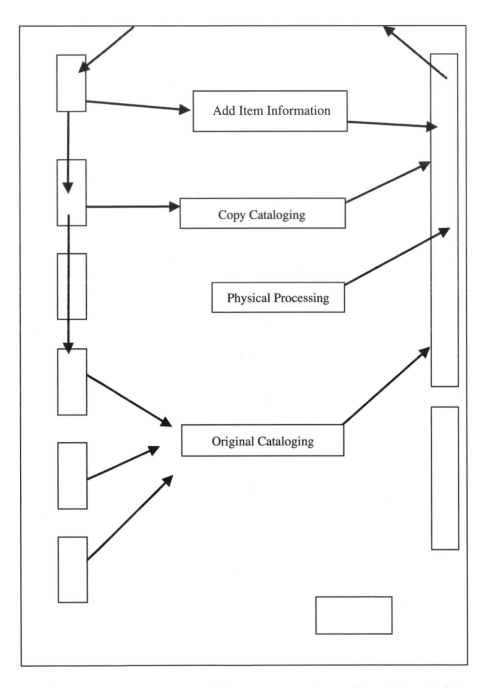

Figure 12-2. Revised Workflow Diagram

ASSISTIVE TECHNOLOGY

Computer technology is available that will assist individuals who have a variety of handicaps. Public and academic libraries will, in general, provide computer hardware and software that is primarily intended for the vision-impaired/blind users and people with physical handicaps that restrict typing. Libraries that are providing assistive technology are using the technology as part of the library's response to ensure compliance with the Americans with Disabilities Act. There is a wide variety of computer hardware and software that will assist individuals who:

- are blind or visually impaired
- are deaf or hard of hearing
- have learning disabilities
- have cognitive disabilities
- require mouse alternatives
- require keyboard alternatives
- require text-to-speech converters or
- can benefit from speech recognition software.

The systems librarian is usually responsible for ensuring that this assistive technology can be used in conjunction with the Internet and the library's local information system, as well as in a stand-alone mode. For additional information about assistive technology, see "Suggested Web Resources" at the end of this chapter.

Should a library decide to provide assistive technologies, then it will need the obvious: space to place the equipment (typically a separate room to containing voices coming from machines) and staff to manage and provide assistance and training in how to use the equipment. Usually the systems manager will not need to be concerned about the communication protocols required by the assistive technologies because these devices are designed to interface and interact with most systems.

SYSTEM INTEGRATION

One of the latest challenges for a system manager is dealing with the possibility of automatically moving data from one application to another. The data movement is accomplished using APIs. An API is an agreed-upon communication format that will facilitate moving data or providing inquiry access to another system. An example of an API in the library community is the Z39.50 standard.

The first set of APIs was developed using the MARC format as a model. Two of the more popular fixed record lengths, MARC-based APIs were developed by the Book Industry Standards Advisory Committee (BISAC) and the Serials Industry Standards Advisory Committee (SISAC). A few library automation vendors and only a couple of book and serial vendors actually implemented these API standards (each implementation was actually unique rather than complying with the proposed standard).

The next attempt to develop a set of useful APIs was based on EDI technology. Again, both BISAC and SISAC committees worked to develop useful message sets so a library could place an order, receive an acknowledgment of the order, receive an update on the status of an order, and so forth. An EDI-based message provides a fair amount of flexibility, yet it is limited primarily to using codes. The intent of the proposed standards was to mask the complexity of the codes from the user with a helpful and informative front-end interface. In most cases, EDI-based transactions had to be moved from one location to another using a value-added network (VAN). Typically VANs charged a premium price to a customer with an anticipated low level of transactions—as would be the case with a library. Yet, just as these EDI standards were about ready to be adopted, work stopped as XML appeared on the scene. XML is a markup specification language, and XML files are just data. The data file will simply sit there until a program is run that can display the data (like a Web browser), does some work with the data (imports and verifies the data as a part of an application), or modifies the data (using an editor).

XML transactions have two appealing characteristics. First, it is relatively easy to identify each data element and the value of each data element that is included in a message. Second, the messages can quickly and easily be moved from one location to another using the Internet, bypassing the VANs (and their associated normally high transaction charges). As of early 2002, the BISAC and SISAC committees were finalizing the proposed standards for EDI XML-based book and serial transactions.

SUMMARY

Managing a LIS is crucial because it determines what services are provided to its patrons, wherever they may be located. The personality characteristics of the systems manager determine the kind of response that will be provided when the inevitable problems arise. Effectively managing the library's network infrastructure, system backups, system upgrades, and applications and their associated licenses are all important tasks. The library should also prepare a disaster plan, acknowledge and address security issues, assess the ergonomic factors for employee work areas, and modify workflows. More recently, the fundamental issue of system integration has arisen and must be addressed by the library.

SUGGESTED WEB RESOURCES

Adaptive Technology for the Internet: Making Electronic Resources Accessible to All
http://www.ala.org/editions/samplers/mates/

Adaptive Technology Resource Center
http://www.utoronto.ca/atrc/

The Alliance for Technology Access
http://www.ataccess.org/

Cast Bobby (a site that checks your HTML code)
http://www.cast.org/Bobby

Equal Access to Software and Information
http://www.rit.edu/~easi/itd.htm

Enablemart
http://www.enablemart.com/

IBM Accessibility Center
http://www-3.ibm.com/able/disability.html

Mary Minow's Map to Library Law
http://www.librarylaw.com/

W3C Web Accessibility Initiative (WAI)
http://www.w3c.org/WAI/

WebABLE
http://www.webable.com

NOTES

1. Scott P. Muir. "Setting Priorities for the Library's Systems Office." *Library HiTech*, 19 (3), 2001, pp. 264–73.

2. Thomas C. Wilson. *The Systems Librarian: Designing Roles, Defining Skills*. Chicago: American Library Association, 1998.

3. Dan Pfohl and Sherman Hayes. "Today's Systems Librarians Have a Lot to Juggle." *Computers in Libraries*, 21 (10), November/December 2001, pp. 30–33.

4. Atul Kapoor. *Total Cost of Application Ownership (TCA)*. A White Paper, No. 199503. Manasquan, NJ: The Tolly Group, 1999. Available at: http://www.tolly.com

5. A copy of the "2001 Computer Crime and Security Survey" is available at http://www.gocsi.com.

6. The "INFOSEC Rainbow Series" of publications available from the National Computer Security Center. See also, Federal Information Processing Standards (FIPS) publications.

7. George V. Hulme. "Management Takes Notice." *Information Week*, Issue 853, September 3, 2001, pp. 28–34.

8. For information about ISO 17799, including the ability to download a copy of the standard itself, a directory of software that will assist in preparing an ISO 17799 audit, and other helpful resources go to http://www.iso17799software.com.

9.   CIS develops standards for operating systems, firewalls, routers, and VPNs. Available at: http://www.cisecurity.org. Common Criteria is a set of broad guidelines for evaluating IT security products. Available at: http://www.commoncriteria.org. DITSCAP (Department of Defense Information Technology Security Certification and Accreditation Process) is a process that documents, assesses and certifies the security of computer systems. Available at: http://iase.disa.mil/ditscap. Federal Information Technology Security Assessment Framework is a tool for assessing IT security programs and developing goals for improvement. Federal Information Systems Controls Audit Manual (FISCAM). Available at: http://www.gao.gov/policy/12_9_6.pdf. Generally Accepted System Security Principles (GASSP) developed by the International Information Security Foundation. Available at: http://www.auerbach-publications.com /white-papers/gassp.pdf. Internet Engineering Task Force (IETF) Site Security Handbook. Available at: http://www.ietf.org/rfc/rfc2196.txt?number=2196. Information Systems Audit and Control Association (ISACA). Available at: http://www.isaca.org /cobit.htm. National Institute of Standards and Technology (NIST) Principles and Practices for Securing IT Systems. Available at: http://www.csra.nist.gov/publications/nistpubs/800-14/800-14.pdf. OCTAVE (Operationally Critical Threat, Asset, and Vulnerability Evaluation) is a process to conduct an IT security risk assessment. Available at: http://www.cert.org/octave. SysTrust Principles and Criteria for Systems Reliability. Available at: http://www.aicpa.org/assurance/systrust/edannoun .htm.

10.   Possible government agencies that could be contacted include: the Electronic Crimes Branch of the Secret Service (www.ustreas.gov); The FBI's Internet Fraud Complaint Center (www.ifccfbi.gov); U.S. Department of Justice (www.cybercrime .gov); and CERT Coordination Center (www.cert.org).

11.   William Cheswick and Steven Bellovin. *Firewalls and Internet Security: Repelling the Wily Hacker*. Reading, MA: Addison-Wesley, 1994.

12.   Keith C. Wright. *Computer-Related Technologies in Library Operations*. Brookfield, CT: Gower, 1995.

Part IV
Future Considerations

Part IV offers a review of technology trends affecting LIS development and implementation and closes with a chapter on digital libraries.

Chapter 13

Technology Trends

One of the undeniable facts associated with computer and communications technologies is that emerging technologies are being adopted with increasing speed by the marketplace. Thus, librarians need to be aware of some of the more significant technologies trends likely to impact libraries in the future. These technologies will challenge libraries to address issues such as service delivery, how a library can add value for its patrons, and how to support new ways to deliver information to the library customer, wherever that customer is located. As current emerging technologies are adopted, they will be replaced by even newer emerging technologies. Thus, any list of technology trends will be constantly evolving and changing over time. This chapter discusses trends that are likely to impact libraries in the next three to five years.

The Internet is not included as a trend, since it is a reality, but it should also not be ignored. The Internet is impacting libraries directly as more students and other individuals visit Web sites to find bibliographic citations and full text of journal articles to complete projects and other homework assignments, rather than visiting a library.[1] Some academic libraries report declining use of reference services, and annual circulation figures are also falling.

Given the pervasive adoption of computer workstations and the ready availability of accessing the Internet, the following technologies are presented so librarians will be aware of some of the emerging technologies that are likely to have an impact directly or indirectly on a library's ability to provide quality services. The technologies presented below are in no particular order—all deserve to be watched and considered by library managers, library decision-makers, systems personnel, and interested professional librarians. After all, it is likely that these technologies will have a major impact on the library in the not-too-distant future.

Among the technologies that should be monitored are:

- TCP/IP Everywhere
- Peer-to-Peer Networking
- XML

- ◆ Wireless Connections
- ◆ Voice and Translation Capabilities
- ◆ Web Services

TCP/IP EVERYWHERE

The number of people connecting to the Internet will continue to grow for the foreseeable future, but there will come a time when the pace will decline. But this will not mean that the Internet will see a decline in usage. Rather, an increasing number of non-computer workstation devices will be connected to the Internet. With increasing frequency, computer chips are being installed in a wide variety of devices, ranging from automobiles to vending machines to clothing, and these devices are being connected to the Internet. Feedback loops are incorporated so existing products and services are improved. Kevin Kelly calls these feedback loops virtuous circles.[2] These virtuous circles feed upon themselves so prices decline and quality improves significantly over time. In computer chip technology, this phenomenon is referred to as "Moore's Law."

The implications of Moore's Law is that not only does the price/performance of computer systems continue to improve each year, but the computer chips are being embedded in a host of other products. These products range from handheld personal digital assistants, cellular phones that interact with the Internet, pagers, and other "net appliances" to the chips being embedded in automobiles, vending machines, household appliances, and clothing.

The glue that connects all of these devices to the Internet is TCP/IP software. TCP/IP provides telephone services via the Internet (called telephony), desktop videoconferencing, audio and video broadcasting, and, soon, on-demand movies. The reason for all of this activity is that using TCP/IP significantly decreases the complexity and, therefore, the cost of providing the service. Having one network communication protocol means that *from* anything, you can talk *to* anything.

Metcalfe's Law, which indicates that the value of a network increases exponentially as more participants are included, results in what is sometimes called the Network Effect—value rises exponentially with market share. Today, because everybody is linked, more goods and services gain their value from this widespread Network Effect.

One of the implications of making connections to all of these devices is that a wide range of services is now available without regard to distance. No longer is it necessary to visit a bank branch, be physically present to attend a university, call a broker to execute a stock transaction, or obtain a cost quote for insurance, a product, or a service. All of this, and much, much more, is now being accomplished using the Internet. Consequently, a library must consider and identify ways that it can provide some or all of its services without requiring the customer to physically visit the library. Whether it is document delivery, online 24/7 reference services, borrowing of materials, or providing access to online databases, libraries must change the way they provide services.

"In the networked age, in the digital era, power and value lies in the connections. It's exactly the process of thesis, antithesis, and synthesis—the search for new and different connections—where exponential power and value can be found."

Carly Fiorina, Hewlett-Packard

PEER-TO-PEER NETWORKING

The fundamental idea behind peer-to-peer (P2P) networking is simplicity itself: you share files, programs, and computer processing cycles, and communicate directly with other people over the Internet without having to rely on a centralized server. The end result is the prospect of distributed file systems, distributed search engines, virtual supercomputers, and so much more.[3] This idea has been applied in several interesting ways, ranging from sharing music files (yes, Napster did have a central index of songs available for sharing—but other file-sharing options do not use a central index), using collaborative software with a shared workspace, sharing "idle" computer processing cycles, and so forth. If you have used instant messaging, then you have used a P2P program. The whole idea of P2P software is to eliminate the middleman (the server on the network).

P2P computing differs from client/server in three fundamental ways:

- In P2P processing, the exchange of services is symmetric (i.e., it is happening between peers running identical software and having roughly the same processing power), and each computer has equivalent responsibility.

- In client/server, there is a one-to-many relationship—one server supports many clients. In P2P processing, there are many cooperating peers, and any of them can initiate an interaction or transaction with another peer.

- The client/server interaction has a fixed capacity, while P2P provides transparent access to services of any kind with an almost unlimited capacity.

P2P collaborative software allows groups to share information and documents among themselves, across an entire organization, or with outside groups. This approach has the potential for significantly improving the productivity among all employees within an organization. One company attracting considerable attention with P2P collaborative software is Groove Networks. Such software allows people to route documents, electronically annotate each other's work, view ideas on a white board, have online discussions, and so forth. Any work done offline is immediately shared and updated as soon as you connect to the network.

Besides improving personal productivity, P2P computing offers the opportunity to reduce centralized computer resources and eliminate redundant computer storage. Such an approach takes advantage of the unused processing power and disk storage space on each desktop workstation. Imagine the number of e-mails, often with attachments, and their associated storage space that have been forwarded, saved, and then forwarded again. Not only do P2P software solutions keep track of files across an organization's entire network, they offer interesting possibilities for searching and indexing documents and other files that exist on the desktop workstations of individuals within an organization.

P2P search engines offer the prospect of using metadata (e.g., the XML-based Dublin Core) to describe and classify information found at a Web site. The Dublin Core, combined with the RDF, a data model, and XML serialization syntax for describing resources, means that new approaches can be used to overcome the serious limitations of the existing Web search engines.

P2P systems will likely raise some interesting issues. Among these are:

♦ Who owns a document or other work that has been created and enhanced through the collaborative process? It is an interesting intellectual property issue.

♦ How do you exert leadership in a peer-to-peer world?

♦ How will values within an organization change in a peer-to-peer world? Currently, some people within an organization retain their value by being an expert in a subject area. In some cases, this same individual also exercises control by being a gatekeeper and controlling when and with whom he or she is willing to share information.

♦ The peer-to-peer world seems to blur the distinction between the workspace and personal space.

XML

XML is a simpler version of the original and more complex SGML, but designed specifically for the Web. Using the XML organizations can define, transmit, validate, and interpret data between applications and databases. XML provides structure rather than being a presentation system. XML separates the underlying data from how the data is displayed; thus, the data itself can be more easily organized, programmed, edited, and exchanged between Web sites and applications. XML and its associated DTD plays an important role in the exchange of information. Besides the rules for establishing XML entities, there are nine other key XML-related standards.

XML Schema Definition (XSD) defines a standard way of describing XML document structures and adding data types to XML data fields. The intent is to facilitate cross-organizational document exchange and verification. Tools are available for converting XML DTDs to XSD that will assist in the exchange of information.

Simple Object Access Protocol (SOAP) is one of the more popular XML Schema Definitions that allows applications to pass data and instructions to one another. SOAP was originally developed for distributed applications to communicate over HTTP and through corporate firewalls. SOAP defines the use of XML and HTTP to access services, objects, and servers in a platform-independent manner.

SOAP itself does not define any application semantics such as a programming model or implementation-specific semantics; rather, it defines a simple mechanism for expressing application semantics by providing a modular packaging model and encoding mechanisms for encoding data within modules. This allows SOAP to be used in a large variety of systems ranging from messaging systems to a remote procedure call.

BISAC and SISAC are developing XSDs to facilitate ordering, acknowledging receipt of an order, claiming, and other transaction sets. Once adopted as standards by NISO, these XSDs will be incorporated into applications by both the LIS vendors and the book and serials jobbers.

Resource Description Framework (RFD) is an XML-based infrastructure that enables structured metadata to be encoded, exchanged, and reused. RFD allows for more than one data type to be included in the same metadata package. A group of interested parties is working on representing the Dublin Core in RFD.

WIRELESS CONNECTIONS

The growth of the wireless industry has been truly amazing. In 1999, there were approximately 469 million wireless subscribers worldwide, and by 2003, it is anticipated that this number will grow to 1.26 billion. Some industry experts expect that wireless Internet access will exceed wired access by the end of 2003.

The first- and second-generation wireless protocols were for voice only, while the third-generation protocol is designed for both voice and data. Because of the high implementation costs, it is expected that third-generation services will be slow to arrive. Existing wireless technologies will be used to deliver services for the foreseeable future. A popular second-generation service in Japan, called I-mode or DoCoMo, offers low-cost instant messaging and limited Internet services from I-mode-enabled cellular phones. This service is particularly attractive to students, parents, and businessmen.

Increasingly, libraries are being asked to provide wireless service within the library so that library customers may use their laptops and PDAs to access library services.

Basic Truths About Wireless

◆ Wireless data is slower than wired and is likely to remain so for the next several years.

◆ Wireless access to the Internet is more about retrieving specific information to meet a particular need. Because of the slow data transmission speeds, users do NOT surf the Internet.

◆ Users can use wireless to receive e-mails and other alerts, sometimes called "push" technology, as well as "pulling" information from the network.

- ◆ The focus is on easy-to-read information. Most wireless applications do not use graphics given the slow data transfer rates.

- ◆ The true value proposition of wireless for any organization is where information and transaction bottlenecks frequently occur.

- ◆ As wireless data transmission speeds increase, most existing data modems will be replaced every two to three years.

VOICE AND TRANSLATION CAPABILITIES

Speech recognition is actually a combination of computer hardware and software that recognizes spoken words. Some systems require that the speaker speak slowly and distinctly; these are called discrete speech systems. However, major improvements have been made in continuous speech systems—voice recognition systems that allow the individual to speak naturally and usually do not require users to teach the system how to recognize their voice. Such systems are useful in instances when the user is unable to use a keyboard to enter data or the individual has a low typing speed.

Even though speech recognition software is now about 95 percent effective—that is, the system correctly recognizes and displays the spoken words in text form on the screen—that still means that five words in a 100 or five words in 10 lines of text would need to have the "typos" corrected by the individual. Fortunately, the spell-checking feature of most word processing applications will assist in this process. Over time, speech recognition systems will improve so the individual can speak at a faster rate with fewer associated typos.

Voice-based browser technology is promising full-fledged access to Internet services from any telephone. VoiceXML 2.0, a draft standard being worked on by W3C, is a standard markup language for voice data, and it will provide a common means for integrating touch pad signals, synthesized speech, and speech recognition within a Web-based application. VoiceXML is a server-driven technology.

One of the by-products of computer-telephony integration is that TCP/IP will be used to place phone calls or deliver a fax. There already are Web sites that will translate a Web page from one language to another.

WEB SERVICES

As more and more business is conducted over the Internet, organizations face the problem of making their applications work with those of their suppliers and customers. This process of having applications communicate with one another is called integration or systems integration. There are several approaches to integration, but they can be grouped into three categories: custom integration, middleware products, and Web services.

Custom Integration

In custom integration, the two parties agree on a communications standard or protocol, write any needed data conversions, and the two applications are linked. The obvious problem with this approach is that, as the number of applications or partners increase, the number of possible data protocols and custom data conversions begins to increase—seemingly at an exponential rate. Clearly this is an expensive process.

Middleware Product

The organization could purchase a "middleware product," which establishes a common communications standard. The organization simply writes a data conversion routine (software program) for each application it wishes to integrate. The problems with this approach are three-fold: first, the middleware software is expensive; second, the organization must have, or contract to an outside third party, the necessary computer programming resources to create and maintain these data conversion programs; and third, the organization must convince each of its customers or suppliers that they should adopt the same middleware software product.

Web Services

Web services are applications that have been enabled to use a standard universal language to send data and instructions to one another, with no data translation or conversion required. Because the Internet is being used, the connection problems are minimized or eliminated. To date, most data and information that is accessible via the Internet is viewed by people using a browser; thus, the Internet can be thought of as "people-centric." To be used by an application within an organization, the information must either be "scraped" from the screen or sent by the information supplier (the variety of non-standard formats depends upon the number of information suppliers).

Rather than relying on brute-force, custom approach, or using proprietary middleware software, Web services rely on an open, standards-based approach that, at least in theory, obviates the disadvantages of the first two options. Some examples of a Web service include:

- A credit checking service that returns credit information when given a person's social security number.

- A purchasing service that allows a computer system to buy office supplies when given an item code and a quantity.

- A stock quote service that returns the latest stock price associated with a particular ticker symbol.

Let's look at a library-based example to better understand some of the possibilities that could be achieved by effectively using Web services. Consider a library that wishes to place an order for several books. The library may enter the information into an Acquisitions module that is a part of its LIS. The LIS will then send the order electronically using an EDI protocol to the vendor of choice. Alternatively, the library can connect to several vendor sites to discover the pricing and availability of the items they wish to order—a fairly time-consuming process.

> *N* **Tip!** The majority of EDI implementations between commercial-based LIS and book and serial vendors are a one-off, custom implementation using an EDI-based standard as a starting point. Thus, a minimal amount of benefits accrue to either party.

Using Web services, a different approach would be taken. The LIS vendors, or the library itself, if it has the programming resources to develop and maintain its own systems, could set up a price/availability comparison shopping option within the Acquisitions module. This optional comparison-shopping feature would then automatically check with several vendors about price and availability for the items of interest. The results would then be displayed so the library could make a decision about where to place the order.

Each book and serial vendor or other suppliers could set up a Web service that provides pricing and availability information. The address of the Web service would be published in a directory—the Universal Description, Discovery, and Integration (UDDI) Directory—which locates each Web service that is available on the Internet. Vendors would include in their Web service UDDI registration what data fields and their associated format was required as input and what information would be given out in return. For example, the vendor might want a unique library ID number, customer account number, and password (if a customer). The format for this description would be defined in the XML-based Web Services Description Language.

Web services are likely to be at the heart of the next generation of distributed services. Here's why:

- **The Internet**. The Internet is a way in which various applications and services are linked—and almost every library and organization is linked to the Internet.

- **Interoperability**. Any Web service can interact with any other Web service. Web services can run on any platform and can be written in any programming language.

- **Low barrier to entry**. The concepts behind Web services are easy to understand. They offer a more flexible or loosely coupled way of linking applications. In addition, free toolkits are being provided by a host of vendors that allow developers to more quickly develop and deploy Web services. Web services are a way to link existing applications rather than a platform for new development.

- **Ubiquity**. Because Web services rely on HTTP and XML, any device that supports these technologies can both host and access Web services. Even wireless services can be provided using Web services.

- **Industry support**. All major vendors support and are involved with extending the standards around which Web services are built.

The book or serial vendor would verify the accuracy of the information using authentication procedures through passwords, public keys, or some other mechanism. The vendor may extend to the library a higher than normal discount because of the amount of prior spending or the presence of a contractual agreement between the vendor and the library.

One of the interesting side effects of Web services is that the range of services can be extended beyond the simple sending and receiving of EDI-based messages. After the order has been placed, the Acquisitions module could automatically search for and download a cataloging record (MARC or XML or . . .). Once the library has received the order and invoice, the module could automatically alert the library's parent organization's accounting system that funds have been expended and that the book or serial vendor should be paid. What new, unforeseen applications will emerge when applications can interact with other applications—regardless of machine, operating system, programming language, or middleware? Obviously, in such an environment, the number of transaction messages moving about the Internet will increase the amount of network traffic.

There are, however, some issues that must be addressed before Web services become more popular. These issues include:

- **Reliability**. Some Web services will, inevitably, be more reliable than others. What happens when a Web service is unavailable for some period of time?

- **Security**. Will the Web service use encryption plus authentication to improve the level of security? Will the authentication process identify the required level of security for a transaction to occur?

- **Transactions**. In a closed, client/server-based system, a transaction is performed once the appropriate records have been locked so that another transaction does not alter the record or data field until the original transaction is completed. Such an approach will not work using Web services since transactions may span minutes, hours, or even days.

- **Scalability**. Supporting distributed Web services will require system monitoring tools to make sure the system can support the volume of transactions, recognizing that there will peaks and valleys of demand.

- **Accountability**. How are Web service users charged? How long can a user use a Web service for a specific charge?

- **Testing**. When a system is comprised of many Web services whose location is distributed, potentially, across thousands of miles, testing and debugging become even more challenging. Will Web services be quality assured and certified?

SUMMARY

Attempting to keep up with technology can be a daunting task. While it is important to systematically review the library literature, it is equally important to spend some time reviewing the technology literature as well. Reading current awareness publications and periodically visiting some of the technology-oriented

Web sites can assist in the process of trying to see the big picture.[4] Connect with people, whether it's participating electronically with a discussion group, personally with colleagues via e-mail, or attending professional conferences. Observe yourself in terms of what you are personally paying attention to and how your life is changing as a result of a new technology. And never forget to challenge your assumptions. Why do you think something is or is not going to change?

The fundamental evaluation criteria for any new technology is to make sure that it is going to provide value to the library's customers (as opposed to being some "really cool or 'sexy' new technology").

SUGGESTED WEB RESOURCES

World Wide Web Consortium has information about Web-based standard activities at: http://www.w3c.org.

The Organization for the Advancement of Structured Information Standards (OASIS) has cataloged more than 100 standard vocabulary definition projects at their Web site: http://www.xml.org.

NOTES

1.   Philip M. Davis and Suzanne A. Cohen. "The Effect of the Web on Undergraduate Citation Behavior 1996–1999." *The Journal of the American Society for Information Science and Technology*, 52 (4), April 2001, pp. 309–14.

2.   Kevin Kelly. *New Rules for the New Economy: 10 Radical Strategies for a Connected World*. New York: Viking, 1998.

3.   Andy Oram, ed. *Peer-to-Peer: Harnessing the Benefits of a Disruptive Technology*. Cambridge, MA: O'Reilly, 2001.

4.   Roy Tenant. "Technology Decision-Making: A Guide for the Perplexed." *Library Journal*, April 15, 2000, p. 30.

Chapter 14

Digital Libraries

WHAT IS A DIGITAL LIBRARY?

Perceptions of the term "digital library" are a bit like perceptions of the elephant in the poem by John Godfrey Saxe "The Six Blind Men and the Elephant." Based on an old Indian fable, the storyteller presents an array of descriptions from each of six blind men when in the presence of an actual elephant. If we were to ask several people today to define digital library, we would undoubtedly get several different definitions. The digital library has been variously called the electronic library, the virtual library, the library without walls, the cybrary, the digital spatial library, digitized collections, and the library of the future.

While these are not necessarily synonyms for digital library, they do have some aspects in common. For example, the notion of a virtual library, a term that preceded the words digital library, is often used to describe the extension of existing library services into the digital realm. For example, an online catalog was considered to be a virtual library by some library professionals. The term electronic library became popular in the United Kingdom to represent the same concept—that of modernizing existing library services to include digital resources. Others used some of the various terms mentioned above to describe the "elephant." So, what is meant by the term digital library, as opposed to these other phrases?

Edward Fox, who has edited several special issues on the subject for the *Journal of ASIS* and *Communications of the ACM* states:

> A digital library is an assemblage of digital computers, storage, and communication machinery together with the context and software needed to produce, emulate, and extend those services provided by conventional libraries based on paper and other material means of collecting, cataloging, finding and disseminating information. . . . A full-service digital library must accomplish all essential services of traditional libraries and also exploit the well known advantages of digital storage, searching and communication.[1]

Paul Kantor postulates that "while we are accustomed to thinking of the bibliographic database as an access tool," library catalogs can be considered as a "prototype digital library." He specifies that a digital library "is that set of global inter networked libraries" that includes the following criteria:[2]

- ♦ A collection of texts, images, or data in digitized form
- ♦ A set of systems for indexing and navigating or retrieving in that collection
- ♦ One or more defined community of users.

Christine Borgman states:

> We find that the term 'digital library' is used in two distinct senses. In general, researchers view digital libraries as content collected on behalf of user communities, while practicing librarians view digital libraries as institutions or services.[3]

Similarly, Levy points out:

> For some groups, most notably librarians, the phrase refers most directly to *institutions that oversee digital collections*, while for other professions, primarily computer and information scientists, it refers to *digital collections*, without regard to institutional settings (if any) in which they might be managed.[4]

However defined, these perceptions are likely to evolve as activities move from research and development endeavors to full-scale practice. It is equally likely that multiple perspectives regarding the definition of the term digital library will always exist.

FOUNDATIONS FOR THE DIGITAL LIBRARY

Going back to the earlier part of last century, when the world was primarily analog, we find a few classic thought pieces by some exceptional thinkers. H.G. Wells wrote a piece that proposed the idea of what some came to call a "world brain."[5] Wells actually had this notion of a world-mind prior to publishing his monograph, but had not yet recorded the idea.

Just after World War II, Dr. Vannevar Bush, scientific advisor to both Presidents Roosevelt and Truman, published a classic thought piece titled "As We May Think," in which he postulated the notion of the Memex (short for "Memory Extender"), which would hold the entire collection of works pertinent to a scientist in pursuit of his research in a single desktop device.[6] This was a remarkable suggestion, since the digital computer had just been built! Bush himself was an analog thinker, and his suggestion for a desktop memory extender was based on an analog technology involving microforms.

These two thinkers planted ideas in the minds of others, ideas that would later evolve into real applications. Another, less-mentioned but well-known, contributor was J. C. R. Licklider, an MIT professor who was commissioned in the early 1960s to write a thoughtful summary of the impact digital technologies would have on the future library.[7] In this monograph, Licklider, an engineer, advocated incorporating digital technologies into library work, and postulated what might be loosely interpreted as the first digital library. He described plans for developing what he called "procognitive systems," the over-all aim of which was "to get the user the fund of knowledge into something more nearly like an executive's or commander's position."[8] Licklider goes on to mention the idea of a desktop console, and what he considered to be the most vital part: "the telecommunication-telecomputation system and the cable" that connects the console "into the procognitive utility net."

Many credit Licklider, who conducted his study between November 1961 and November 1963, as being the first to fully recognize the possibility of creating what we now refer to as a digital library. Interestingly, the book is dedicated to Dr. Bush, although at the time of its writing, Licklider had not read that 1945 article. Still, prior to that, the words digital library had not been recorded as being adjacent to one another in print or, as far as we know, in recorded speech.

Bush laid the groundwork with his suggestion that some desktop device could store all the information the end user would like to know, and that associative trails would relate this information in a fashion that would make it retrievable from that desktop. This metaphor was advanced and given a more appealing name in the 1960s: hypertext. In 1965, Ted Nelson renamed Memex as hypertext, defined it as "non-sequential writing" and explained that the structures of ideas are not sequential. Nelson states, "They tie together every which-way. And when we write, we are always trying to tie things together in non-sequential ways."[9] Hypertext became a reality in the 1980s with the introduction of large amounts of memory and storage in the development of personal desktop computing. Earlier experimental versions by Nelson (Project Xanadu) and Douglas Englebart (NLS/Augment) were based on large-scale computing systems.

In 1980, Tim Berners-Lee began to code the pieces of an application that, when coupled with the Internet 10 years later, would change the way individuals perceived access to digital information. That initial work on the Enquire project would lead to what some refer to as the Internet's killer application: the World Wide Web. What distinguished this client-server applications software was that it not only displayed text and graphics using graphical software that clients found on server-side data archives marked up in HTML, but it incorporated a feature that both Bush and Nelson had proposed: the capability to "hypertext" to another document within that data archive. This linking function would turn end users into browsers instead of searchers. As browsers, end users found the nature of computing had changed by making large amounts of information accessible in a convenient and flexible fashion. These types of projects provided the groundwork for the highly interactive and highly interconnected systems that we see today, most of which are based on using the Internet as a connection backbone. It is this groundwork that laid the path for digital libraries to follow.

The Seeds of Digital Libraries

Vannevar Bush may have created the metaphor that sparked the imagination of those who followed his ideas, but few had actually developed a prototype Digital Library system. Project INTREX at MIT (1965 through 1973) was one of the first storage and retrieval systems designed to experiment with online, interactive, computer-assisted retrieval of library-type information.[10] This experimental project involved a hybrid combination of digital computing and analog microforms. The project conducted a series of information transfer experiments (hence the name INTREX), involving approximately 20,000 scientific and technical articles, all stored on microfiche. Retrieval was supported by an online catalog and an index, along with abstracts.

In the late 1960s, Mead Data developed the Ohio Bar Automated Research (OBAR). This was the precursor to the now-familiar and popular full-text LEXIS search service (a legal database available online). OBAR provided online access to full-text legal statutes. It was one of the first online full-text databases, a precursor of things to come.

In 1971, Michael Hart began Project Gutenburg (http://www.gutenberg.net/) with the goal of producing full-text versions of classic monographs that had been cleared by copyright compliance. His original goal was to produce 10,000 such artifacts by 2000. One of the Project's goals was to distribute one trillion e-text files by December 31, 2001. This is 10,000 titles, each accessed by 100 million readers [10,000 x 100,000,000 = one trillion].

A Project Gutenberg e-text is a public domain work distributed through the Project Gutenberg Association (also known as the "Project"). Among other things, this means that no one owns a United States copyright on this work, so the Project can copy and distribute it in the United States without permission and without paying royalties. Special rules apply if you wish to copy and distribute this e-text under the Project's trademark. Project Gutenberg presently contributes approximately one e-text each day of production.

In 1982, the Library of Congress announced the Optical Disk Pilot Project, an electronic digital imaging system containing images of books, journals, and other research materials held by the library. In this program, a variety of visual media had been recorded on analog laser videodisks to test the ability of this technology to help preserve pictorial materials and to improve researchers' access to pictorial collections. This linked the still images selected from the LC Prints and Photographs Division to a microcomputer database for retrieval purposes. The project focused on preservation and access, but also examined collections management and security issues.

In 1989, the American Memory Project began with a survey of ARL membership. To help launch the project, a consultant surveyed 101 members of the ARL and the 51 state library agencies. The survey disclosed a genuine appetite for on-line collections, especially in university research libraries. The project (1990–1995) identified multiple audiences for digital collections in a special survey; an end user evaluation; and thousands of conversations, letters, and encounters with visitors.[11]

The most thorough audience appraisal carried out by the LC consisted of an end user evaluation conducted in 1992–1993. Forty-four school, college and university, and state and public libraries were provided with a dozen American Memory collections on CD-ROMs and videodisks (videodisks are no longer being supported). Participating library staff, teachers, students, and the public were polled about which digitized materials they had used and how well the delivery systems worked. The evaluation indicated continued interest by university libraries, as well as public libraries. The most surprising finding, however, was the strong enthusiasm in schools, especially at the secondary level.

These initial explorations proved that digitizing images and various media was, in fact, feasible, but that a continued research initiative needed to be implemented to create a solid base for production purposes.

Research in Digital Libraries

In 1991, a workshop funded by the National Science Foundation (NSF) and co-sponsored by the University of Nebraska Center for Communication and Information Sciences brought together leading scientists involved in analyzing and retrieving textual information stored in digital formats. This invitational workshop, titled "Future Directions in Text Analysis, Retrieval and Understanding," resulted in a report on current research in the area of text retrieval and a white paper calling for the establishment of a "National Electronic Library," the ideas for which were originated during the workshop. The report was published in two volumes, one summarizing the workshop and some follow-up activities, and the other a collection of position papers presented at the workshop.[12] In the first volume, M. Lesk, E. Fox, and M. McGill called for the funding of a "National Electronic Science, Engineering, and Technology Library." This "White Paper on Digital Libraries" challenged U.S. funding agencies with a call for "international information competitiveness" and for an improvement of the U.S. educational system. Its recommendation was that "NSF should solicit proposals from groups of researchers to create on-line libraries in key scientific areas . . . " in accordance with a set of guidelines pointed towards developing "reasonable coverage of basic science and engineering," to be made available using distributed networked technologies. The report specifically identified NSF, Defense Advanced Research Projects Agency (DARPA), and NASA as potential collaborative funding sources, and called for as much as $50 million in funding for research and development. It was this white paper that lead directly to the call for research into digital libraries first made in 1993.

In 1994, the Digital Library Phase One Initiative was launched, providing up to $24 million to support six large-scale research projects over a four-year period. This multi-agency research initiative was jointly sponsored by the NSF, DARPA, and NASA. It demonstrates the U.S. government's efforts to build the National Information Infrastructure and remain competitive on the global information environment. The shared vision is best illustrated in the mission statement of Digital Library Initiative:

> The Initiative's focus is to dramatically advance the means to collect, store, and organize information in digital forms, and make it available for searching, retrieval, and processing via communication networks.[13]

The six research institutions receiving support from this initial Digital Library Initiative were:

1. The University of Michigan Digital Library Research Project. The core of the Digital Library at the University of Michigan has been the "agent architecture that supports the teaming of agents to provide complex services by combining limited individual capabilities." The content focuses on earth and space sciences.

2. The University of Illinois at Urbana-Champaign Digital Library Research Project. This research effort concentrated on building an experimental test bed with tens of thousands of full-text journal articles from physics, engineering, and computer science.

3. The University of California at Berkeley Digital Library Research Project. The project's goal is to develop the technologies for intelligent access to massive, distributed collections of photographs, satellite images, maps, full-text documents, and "multivalent" documents on environmental information.

4. Carnegie Mellon University Digital Library Research Project. The Infomedia Digital Video Library at Carnegie Mellon University studies how multimedia digital libraries with digital video, audio, images, and text information can be established and used.

5. The Stanford University Digital Libraries Project. This project focuses on interoperability. It aims to develop a single, integrated virtual library that will provide uniform access to a variety of services and information sources.

6. The Alexandria Project at the University of California at Santa Barbara. The project focuses on geographically referenced information. It aims to provide easy access to collections of maps, images, pictorial materials and other spatially referenced information.

Phase I of the Digital Libraries Initiative ran from 1994 until 1998. New funding was secured from some of the original agencies, and several new agencies joined in to form the 1998 Digital Libraries-Phase II Initiative. This funding period runs through 2004 for several of the projects identified within this initiative.

In 1994, the Library of Congress's National Digital Library Program (NDLP), supported by Ameritech, addressed the details of electronic document imaging, text storage, and retrieval of selected print and non-print materials held by LC. The NDLP was focused on assembling a digital library of primary source materials reproductions to support the study of U.S. history and culture. Begun in 1995, after a five-year pilot project, the program began digitizing selected collections of LC archival materials that chronicle the nation's rich cultural heritage.

To reproduce collections of books, pamphlets, motion pictures, manuscripts, and sound recordings, the library has created a wide array of digital entities: bitonal document images, grayscale and color pictorial images, digital video and audio, and searchable texts. To provide access to the reproductions, the project developed a range of descriptive elements: bibliographic records, finding aids, and introductory texts and programs, as well as indexing the full texts for certain types of content. The reproductions were produced using a variety of tools: scanners, digital cameras, devices that digitize audio and video, and human labor for re-keying and encoding texts.

American Memory employs national-standard and well-established industry-standard formats for many digital reproductions (e.g., texts encoded with SGML and images stored in Tagged Image File Format (TIFF) files or compressed with the Joint Photographic Experts Group (JPEG) algorithm). In other cases, the lack of well-established standards has led to the use of emerging formats (e.g., RealAudio [for audio], Quicktime [for moving images], and MrSid [for maps]). The Library of Congress leads the NDLP with financial support from the U.S. Congress, which provided $3 million per year from 1995 for five years, provided each dollar was matched with three dollars from other sources. The LC has successfully raised an additional $45 million to create a $60 million five-year program.

Digital Libraries Initiative Phase II, mentioned previously, is a multi-agency initiative that seeks to provide leadership in research fundamental to developing the next generation of digital libraries; to advance the use and usability of globally distributed, networked information resources; and to encourage existing and new communities to focus on innovative applications areas.[14] It seeks to address the digital library's life cycle from information creation, access, and use, to archiving and preservation. Research to gain a better understanding of the long-term social, behavioral, and economic implications of and the effects of new digital library capabilities in such areas of human activity as research, education, commerce, defense, health services and recreation is an important part of this initiative.

Besides research support from multiple agencies, specific projects have been identified for funding by the LC and various private foundations. Many of these are oriented towards building actual digital libraries, but research plays an active role in each. Building on the efforts in basic research and development and in identifying functional requirements for digital libraries, we now see a move by many developers to create practical digital library applications. This leads us to consider some of the basics in digitization, design, and computing architectures required to support practical digital libraries' development.

PRACTICAL DIGITAL LIBRARIES

The rapid rise and development of digital libraries has resulted in the need to develop tools and skill sets relating to encoding information objects in this new digital format. The following list presents considerations that developers must face when developing digital library applications:

- How will the content be captured?
- What quality controls will be used?
- What standards will be adhered to for capture purposes?
- What is the organizational basis for the "collection"?
- What are some design considerations for digital libraries?
- What are the searching and access capabilities?
- How might the contents be best disseminated?
- What are the long-term preservation issues for digital libraries?

While many new resources are being created in digital format, these formats are neither standardized nor do they address the wealth of content that exists in analog or print form. The costs associated with scanning existing materials can be quite high. Still images can be captured and stored as JPEGs, GIFs, BMPs, or one of the many other common formats, including some that are proprietary (e.g., Qtake files from Apple digital cameras). Most of these storage formats are "lossy" in the sense that they must leave some information out to meet the requirements for that format. TIFF formats, which are less lossy, are preferred for quality storage, but these formats must be converted to JPEG or GIF to use them in Web-based delivery systems, resulting in dual database storage requirements and a linking routine. Howard Besser is a good source of information regarding digitization basics that ensure more standardized approaches to capturing information content as binary files.[15]

Cataloging digital materials has taken on a life of its own. There are those who attempt to use standard library practices involving MARC structures for conventional cataloging purposes. Others advocate the use and continued development of the Dublin Core as a solution for improved organization and identification of digital artifacts. Regardless of the choice, it appears that XML or some similar markup convention is the direction to take.

Design considerations take into account the hardware/software decisions that are made to support such systems. With the continued development of low-cost, PC-based servers and the adoption of free systems software such as Linux, we are beginning to see an explosion in the numbers of very powerful hardware/software environments that cost less than $15,000. Of course, it is possible for an individual user to build a personal desktop server for a fraction of that cost. The diversity of options leads to a need for a common dissemination protocol, and that delivery option is more often than not the Web. As costs associated with the computing and telecommunications industries continue to drop, we will begin to see a corresponding increase in the development of services aimed directly at the end user.

Developers are moving beyond text to include streaming audio, video, and videoconferencing. In some instances, these transmission formats are proprietary in nature, but as developments occur, look for standards to emerge, possibly based on XML.

Preserving digital materials presents real challenges, especially as we encounter changing formats and new standards for encoding, representing, and archiving digital artifacts. Combine that with the relatively quick degradation of digital bits on magnetic media and the obsolescence of equipment and software to read digital information, and one begins to fathom the challenges posed by long-term preservation.

DIGITAL LIBRARIES WITHIN LIBRARY INFORMATION SYSTEMS

The applications of digital technologies within libraries began with the development of turnkey software solutions. In the 1990s, libraries extended their collections by promoting access to licensed databases, often connecting end users to these resources via the Internet using a Web-based interface. The next logical step being taken by many libraries is to augment their physical collections and licensed resources with links to special collections selected from among the growing base of digital library development projects. The Web-based interfaces developed by specific library institutions connect all these resources in a potentially seamless fashion (as seen by the end user). This is the role of practical digital library development—to augment the collections of existing libraries, and to extend the range of resources available to end users.

DIGITAL LIBRARY ISSUES AND CHALLENGES

Listed below are some issues and challenges related to the continued development and deployment of digital libraries:

- Dealing with the enormous archive of previously published works now in print
- Continually deploying a global information technology infrastructure
- Developing tools to support networked information retrieval
- Dealing with copyright issues
- Adhering to and developing standards for interoperability
- Including user-centered design principles
- Acquiring administrative commitment
- Continually seeking funding sources for research and development, prototype designs, testing, implementation, and evaluation of digital library projects

There exists a wealth of information, originally created in print, now stored in libraries distributed around the world that has yet to be digitized. Whether to go back and identify valuable information content that needs to be disseminated more widely, or to move forward with existing content being created in digital format presents an interesting set of problems. One is associated with cost. Another lies in the realization that not all content needs to be converted and made available. What we are seeing in the early stages of digital library development is the identification of pockets of content that are seen as most important by those who hold the keys to digitization: money, talent, and infrastructure. This is a natural step in the progression of building large-scale information systems proffering content in digital format. In a sense, these are special digital libraries, created because someone or some group put the resources together to accomplish this.

The fact that much digital library research and development has occurred within the United States is no accident. The U.S. has made a huge investment in its information infrastructure, based on policy from its executive branch, as well as corporate investment of resources to support Internet activities. Other nations have invested as well, but the key to wide distribution is the continued growth and deployment of not just national infrastructures, but worldwide alliances in building a global information infrastructure.

Correspondingly, there has been a renewed interest in developing tools to support networked information retrieval. The rise of Dialog in the 1980s paved the way for Yahoo and AltaVista in the mid-1990s. While Dialog and the other database aggregators focused on commercial database building and the associated indexing of those controlled literatures, Internet search engines focused on providing access to Web resources and gave this access away. While that was an odd approach for the likes of Dialog (to give information access away), it identified new sources of revenue that, at least for a while, fed the Web search engine and the "dot com" industry. That source was investment capital (from the pockets of venture capitalists and the public fervor over Internet-based IPOs), and the stream was advertising. Once this frenzy was revealed, it did result in some collapse of the dot coms, but overall the investments continued. It would be safe to say that the current time is one of more investment in information retrieval (IR), specifically networked information retrieval, than any other time since the 1960s.

One sticky issue in the digital world revolves around ownership and access. Copyright has been the traditional means for protecting information owners (often primary publishers, not authors) and their control over dissemination of content and the resulting charges associated with such access. This is what had lead to the growth of the publishing industry (both print and electronic) as we know it today. Then along comes the Web with its seemingly "anti-business" attitude of providing what users perceive to be free and unlimited access to content. Copyright in a digital world is a more challenging environment in that the primary objects are not bound by conventional containers (books, journal issues, CDs, and so forth). There is much to be resolved and rethought in this new digital millennium.

Standards for capturing and disseminating digital content are emerging. Developers and decision makers seem to agree that if it doesn't conform to TCP/IP standards, then chances are the product or service will not survive long. Challenges still exist in standardizing newer richer media such as streaming audio and video. Interactions supported by higher bandwidth, such as video conferencing, are pushing these standards developments even further. Add to that the continued developments in wireless technologies, and you have a mix of options that will need to be sorted out over time. Nevertheless, standards across all levels are the keys to continued growth, and it is in the best interests of all partners to continue collaborating and developing standards to support distributed network information access.

Earlier we pointed out that information technologies appear to move through several stages of development. Pioneering stages are focused on the technology itself, and subsequent developments often focus on providing certain functionality. After these attainments, the user comes into play, or at least should be a factor. We are at that point in the development of networked information access that, while there are new and better ways for technology to provide increased functionality, the user plays a heightened role in those developments. Developers have learned that users drive success. As such, users have the prime pole position in future developments surrounding access to networked information. This trend should continue.

For any organization to play a role in either developing or providing access to digital library content, there needs to be a commitment that support will continue regardless of success or of slow adoption or development. Most organizations struggle at some point in this process (development and deployment), and there needs to be the understanding that, despite short-term failures, commitment will be forthcoming and progress will occur. This is a key element in the long-term picture of digital libraries. There will be successes and there will be failures. Administrative buy in can help smooth out these rough spots as they arise.

Continued funding sources for research and development, investing in and developing prototype designs, testing, and implementing and subsequently evaluating digital library projects must exist. We began with much support from our government agencies. Then private foundations found reasons to invest. In the future, it will be up to individual organizations to make the investments necessary to sustain the drive and direction of digital library development.

PROFESSIONAL INVOLVEMENT
IN DIGITAL LIBRARY DEVELOPMENT

What are some areas that professionals can begin to explore and contribute to relating to digital libraries? The following is a brief list of some areas for professional commitment:

- Collection development
- Organizing principles and techniques
- Research and retrieval
- User studies
- end user training
- Standards participation.

This list is essentially a portrait of what professional librarians contribute to their existing print environments. Professional librarians are steeped in the principles of developing library collections, and digital libraries are no exceptions. The quality of materials, their source, and external professional reviews are all part of the process for selecting materials to develop a digital library collection. Developers may know the hardware and software intricacies (and well they should!), but librarians are needed to make good decisions regarding content inclusion.

Professional librarians are also experienced in the principles associated with and techniques used in making that collection accessible to the end user. There is much intellectual thought that needs to go into properly organizing digital renderings of content. This includes not only the behind-the-scenes organizational schemes employed, but also the design of the user interface.

Networked information retrieval offers new challenges for the developer. Professional searchers who work with end users are in a position to better understand this process and make suggestions for developers to consider implementing. Much collaboration is needed between practitioners and developers to build the next generation of digital libraries.

Hand-in-hand is that knowledge the professional has gained in working side-by-side with end users. In the past 10 years, librarianship has shown a renewed interest in user studies, especially those linked to networked access of digitally encoded content. This also translates to training opportunities for end users. Borgman has noted that most end users are amateur searchers at best, and librarians with these skills are needed to help end users become even better at locating materials relevant to their needs.

Last, but not least, information professionals must not only be aware and require that vendors adhere to important standards, but they themselves must get involved in developing those standards. This will ensure that end users are part of the important equation that guides successful search and retrieve functions, connecting content with end users.

SUMMARY

Digital libraries and DL development are new avenues of exploration for professionals seeking to deliver content directly to end users. Libraries and librarians are constantly seeking to develop new resources that serve their users, especially if they are convenient and flexible in nature. The marketplace for digital library development is nascent and, with time, will grow to be a worthy contributor to the overall marketplace for information services. Combined with existing resources, these new developments may be able to better satisfy the end users' information needs.

NOTES

1.   Edward Fox. "Perspectives on Digital Libraries." *Journal of the American Society of Information Science*, 44 (8), 1993, pp. 440–91.

2.   Paul Kantor. "Information Retrieval Techniques." *Annual Review of Information Science and Technology*, 1994, pp. 53–90.

3.   Christine L. Borgman. "Where Are Digital Libraries? Competing Visions." *Information Processing and Management*, 35, 1999, p. 254.

4.   David Levy. *Scrolling Forward: Making Sense of Documents in a Digital World.* New York: Arcade Publishing, 2001.

5.   H. G. Wells. "World-Mind." *Science and the World-Mind.* London: New-Europe, 1942.

6.   Vannevar Bush. "As We May Think." *Atlantic Monthly*, 176 (1), July 1945, pp. 101–8.

7.   J. C. R. Licklider. *The Libraries of the Future.* Cambridge, MA: MIT Press, 1965.

8.   Ibid. p. 32.

9.   Theodore Nelson. *Dream Machines* (published by the author), 1974.

10.   Carl F. Overhage and J. Francis Reintjes. "Project INTREX: A General Review." *Information Storage and Retrieval,* 10, 1974, pp. 157–88.

11.   Elisabeth Betz Parker. "The Library of Congress Non-Print Optical Disk Pilot Program." *Information Technology and Libraries*, 4 (4), December 1985, pp. 289–99.

12.   *Methodologies for Intelligent Text Processing and Information Resources Management: Achievements and Opportunities.* A report of the NSF Invitation Workshop on Future Directions in Text Analysis, Retrieval and Understanding. Funded by the NSF grant IRI-9114210 and co-sponsored by the University of Nebraska Center for Communication and Information Sciences. Jitender S. Deogun, Edward Fox, and Vijay Raghavan, eds., 1991.

13.   NSF/DARPA/NASA Digital Libraries Initiative—Phase I. 1994–1998.

14.   Digital Libraries Initiative—Phase II information can be found at: http://www.dli2.nsf.gov/.

15.   Howard Besser's writings on a variety of digitization efforts can be found at: http://www.gseis.ucla.edu/~howard/Papers/publicationslist.html.

Conclusions

This text has attempted to lay out a sequence of topics that are grounded in the broad domain of Library Information Systems. Beginning with the historical context of applying computing systems to libraries, the book considered the marketplaces that underlie the LIS domain, including the active and now mature markets for integrated library systems solutions and online databases.

Part II of the text addressed the technologies behind these applications, including some design considerations and standards that impact the recording, storage, retrieval, and dissemination of information content proferred by LIS solutions.

Part III of the text covered an array of topics related to the management of such projects, starting with planning and concluding with overall management principles. Chapters also addressed circumstances surrounding most applications of technology to libraries (basic axioms), the attempt to ascertain the impact of technology, basics on systems decision making, and a brief tour of the state of activity regarding the usability of the resulting solutions. The book closed with a review of technology trends and coverage of a topic that may have the most impact on libraries to date—digital libraries.

The authors hope that this tour has been beneficial and that the knowledge gained will support even greater design, development, implementation, and evaluation of future solutions involving libraries and their end users.

Glossary

abstract. A non-evaluative summary of a book, journal article, or other information resource.

Acceptable Use Policy (AUP). A written policy specifying how an employee should use and not abuse network resources.

access control. The ability to selectively control who can access a software application or manipulate information in a computer-based system.

Active Server Pages. A specification developed by Microsoft for a dynamically created Web page with a .ASP extension that utilizes ActiveX scripting. Active Server Pages run under Microsoft's Internet Information Server on a Microsoft Web server; although referred to with the acronym "ASP," it should not be confused with "Application Service Provider."

ActiveX. A Microsoft component standard, designed to allow interoperability between common desktop and Web-based applications; ActiveX's strength lies in its ability to allow development in a wide variety of programming languages, such as Visual Basic, Java, or C++.

agent. Software applications that carry out pre-programmed functions on behalf of a user, operating within specific, tailored boundaries (e.g., an "intelligent" e-mail filter used to eliminate spam or scan for viruses or a shopping device that can search the Web and transact a purchase under predetermined price parameters).

American National Standards Institute (ANSI). ANSI, pronounced "antsy," is the U.S.-based organization dedicated to developing industry-wide standards for technology. ANSI is a member of the International Organization for Standardization (ISO). ANSI has assigned responsibility for library-related standards to the National Information Standards Organization (NISO).

analog. The distinguishing feature of analog representations is that they are continuous (e.g., the human voice). In contrast, digital representations consist of values measured at discrete intervals.

antivirus. Software used to detect viruses and stop them from infecting a computer or network.

applet. A program designed to be executed from within another program. Because applets have small file sizes, are cross-platform compatible, and can't be used to gain access to a user's hard drive, they are ideal for small Internet applications accessible from a browser. Applets are often embedded in Web pages.

253

AppleTalk. A local area network architecture built into all Macintosh computers and Apple laser printers.

application. Also seen as "application program," and sometimes abbreviated to "app," an application is a software program that performs a specific task such as word processing, spreadsheets, accounting, and so forth.

application logic. The computational aspects or business rules that tell a software application how to operate.

Application Programming Interface (API). A set of routines, protocols, and tools for building software applications. A good API makes it easier to develop a program by providing all the building blocks and links. A programmer puts these blocks together.

Most operating environments, such as Microsoft Windows, provide a set of APIs so programmers can write applications consistent with the operating environment. Although APIs are designed for programmers, they are ultimately good for users because they guarantee that all programs using a common API will have similar interfaces. This makes it easier for users to learn new programs.

Application Service Provider (ASP). An ASP deploys, hosts, and manages access to a packaged software application by multiple parties from a centrally managed facility. The applications are delivered over networks on a subscription basis.

Ariel. Ariel software (available from the Research Libraries Group) allows a library to scan articles, photos, and other documents; transmit the electronic images to other Ariel workstations anywhere in the world using either FTP or e-mail; and convert them to PDF for easy patron delivery. Ariel provides superior document transmission faster and clearer than a fax, and there are no long-distance phone charges.

assembler. A computer software program that translates programs from assembly language to machine language.

Asymmetrical Digital Subscriber Line (ADSL). The most common form of DSL. "Asymmetrical" indicates that the service is faster for downloads than uploads.

Asynchronous. Asynchronous communication is sometimes called "start-stop transmission" because start and stop bits are used with each message. Data can be transmitted intermittently rather than in a steady stream.

Asynchronous Transmission Mode (ATM). An information transfer standard for routing high-speed, high-bandwidth traffic such as real-time voice and video, as well as data bits.

authentication. The process for identifying an individual, usually based on a user name and password. Authentication is distinct from authorization, which is the process of giving individuals access to system components based on their identity.

authority control. The process for ensuring that the headings in surrogate records are consistent with the headings established in an authority file.

authority file. A collection of authority records.

authority record. A record that contains all of the decisions made about an authority work. Typically an authority record will contain the "authorized" heading along with cross references.

availability. The portion of time that a system can be used for productive work, expressed as a percentage. Sometimes call up-time.

backbone. A backbone is a network that only has other networks attached to it, instead of user devices like PCs and servers. This allows backbones to operate at much faster speeds than local networks.

bandwidth. The transmission speed or the number of information bits that can move through a communications medium in a given amount of time; the capacity of a telecommunications circuit/network to carry voice, data, and video information. Typically measured in Kbps and Mbps.

bibliographic record. A description of a book, journal, or other materials located in the library. It may include author, title, publication information, collation, and subject headings.

bit error rate. The number of transmitted bits expected to be corrupted when two computers have been communicating for a given period of time.

bits per second (bps). A measure of data transfer rates. Faster is better and the bigger the number, the faster the rate.

bloatware. Software programs that require large amounts of disk space and RAM (random access memory), effectively consuming valuable computer resources.

Boolean logic. Connecting terms that enable the user to conduct a more specific search of an online catalog or database. The Boolean connector "and" narrows, "or" broadens, and "not" eliminates items from a search.

Boolean searching. The process of searching using keywords that are linked by Boolean operators (some systems require the user to select a Boolean operator and other systems use an implied operator if none are specified).

bots. Bots, from robots, are smart software programs that run in the background of a computer, performing specific repetitive tasks. A bot can search the Internet, comparison shop, clip news articles, and so forth. Hotbots, search bots, shopping bots, and spiders are among the species of bots. They are sometimes called intelligent agents.

browser. Software that is used to view various Internet resources and is capable of viewing text, images, and various other file formats, as well as playing sound and showing videos.

C. A popular programming language that has been supplanted by C++ and Java.

C++. A high-level programming language that adds object-oriented functions to its predecessor language, C. C++ is a popular language for GUI-based applications that run on Windows or the Macintosh.

cache. Information saved in computer memory for later use. For example, Web browsers save recently viewed pages in a cache so the exact pages are not downloaded again should the user request them. This feature saves the Internet resources and time.

call number. A combination of letters and numbers assigned to each book and other materials in a library's collection. The purpose of a call number is to group materials on the same subject together plus provide a unique shelf location or address to the item. Most academic libraries use the Library of Congress system, while public libraries rely on the Dewey system.

capacity. The ability of a network to provide sufficient transmitting capabilities among its available transmission media, and respond to customer demand for communications transport, especially at peak times.

CAT-5 wiring. CAT is short for "category," and there are five categories of twisted-pair wiring specified by the American National Standards Institute/Electronic Industries Association (ANSI/EIA).

catalog. A file of library materials, which describes and indexes the resources of a collection or library. A catalog may be an online catalog, a card catalog, a microform catalog, or a book catalog.

Cathode Ray Tube (CRT). The technology used in televisions and computer display screens.

Challenge-Handshake Authentication Protocol (CHAP). A secure procedure for validating a network connection request. The server sends a challenge request message to the requestor, who responds with encrypted authentication information—the user name and password.

Channel. A broad term referring to the pathway between two locations on a voice or data network.

Channel Server Unit/Digital Server Unit (CSU/DSU). A device used to terminate telephone company equipment and prepare data for router interface.

chat. A real-time conversation, typically using text, among multiple online users. Chat rooms have discussions focused on a particular topic.

circuit. A line that connects devices.

citation. The basic information needed to find specific information. Citation information might include author name, title of book or article, journal name, page numbers, and publication information.

click-stream. Information collected about where a Web user has been on the Web.

client/device. Hardware that retrieves information from a server.

client/server. Client/Server replaced mainframe computing as the dominant system for business information architecture in the late 80's; clients (see "client side") are typically less powerful, graphically enabled software platforms that request computation from a server. The server is typically a more powerful processing platform that serves requested data or tasks back to the requesting clients. Web browsers have emerged in the 1990s as a universal client able to access multiple applications, fueling the movement away from the client-server to the ASP business.

client side. The side of an application that resides on the user end of a network; the PC or terminal where the end user works would be the client side of client-server model; the client side of an ASP application would be the browser.

clustering. Group of independent systems working together as a single system. Clustering technology allows groups of servers to access a single disk array containing applications and data.

Codabar barcode label. A barcode label that uses 14 numeric-only digits.

Code 39 barcode label. A barcode label that can use both alpha and numeric characters.

collaboration. A set of software applications designed to assist groups of people communicate and share information in order to complete a task or activity.

collocation. The placement of one company's computer/network equipment on the premises of another company.

comma-delimited. A data format in which each piece of data is separated by a comma. This is a popular format for transferring data from one application to another, because most database systems are able to import and export comma-delimited data.

Common Gateway Interface (CGI). A specification for transferring information between a World Wide Web server and a CGI program. A CGI program is any program designed to accept and return data that conforms to the CGI specification. The program could be written in any programming language, including C, Perl, Java or Visual Basic. One problem with CGI is that each time a CGI script is executed, a new process is started. For busy Web sites, this can slow down the server noticeably.

Common Object Request Broker Architecture (CORBA). An architecture that enables a software program, called objects, to communicate with one another regardless of the programming language the object is written in. Two competing models are Microsoft's COM and Sun's RMI.

Component Object Model (COM). A binary code developed by Microsoft. Both OLE (Object Linking and Embedding) and ActiveX are based on COM.

cookie. While browsing certain Web pages, small files are downloaded to your computer that hold information that can be retrieved by other Web pages on that site. Cookies contain information that identifies each user: login or registration information, specified preferences, passwords, shopping cart information, and so on. When the user revisits the Web site, his or her computer will automatically distribute the cookie, establishing the user's identity.

Cooperative Online Resource Catalog (CORC). An OCLC Web-based system that helps libraries provide guided access to Web resources using automated tools and library cooperation.

cracker. Someone who intentionally breaches the security of a computer system, usually with the intent of stealing information or disabling the system.

cross references. Instructions, which lead to related information, listed under other subject headings or terms. A "see" reference leads to the "correct" headings while a "see also" leads to a related heading.

cross talk. Interference on analog lines created by cables that are too close together. Cross talk may produce static, buzzing, or multiple conversations on one line.

Customer Relationship Management (CRM). An application that manages crucial customer relationships by automating customer-related services (e.g., order processing, sales, marketing, and help desk assistance).

cyber fraud. The most common crime using the Internet is online credit card theft. Typically someone will order goods over the Internet using stolen credit cards. Another form of cyber fraud is non-delivery of merchandise or software bought online.

data center. A centralized computer facility for remote access by customer end users.

Data Communications Equipment (DCE). A term used for a modem-to-modem connection.

database. A group of records in machine-readable form, which is accessible by computer.

database management system (DBMS). Sophisticated software system that controls a database.

datagram. A packet of information sent to the receiving computer. It is conceptually similar to a telegram in that the message can arrive any time, without notice.

data mining. An analytic process that examines large sets of information for hidden patterns and relationships.

data warehouse. A database containing copious amounts of information, organized to help organizations make decisions. Data warehouses receive batch updates, and are configured for fast online queries to produce succinct data summaries.

dedicated line. A point-to-point, hard wire connection between two service locations.

denial of service (DOS) attack. An attack by a hacker who generates so many messages to a Web site that regular users cannot get through or the site shuts down.

digital. Data is represented by 0 (off or low) and 1 (on or high). Computers must use an analog modem to convert digital data into analog form for transmission over ordinary telephone lines. Alternatively, no conversion is necessary if a digital modem and digital data communications option is chosen.

Digital Subscriber Line (DSL). A technology designed for the Internet that brings high-speed, digital data to a home or office over ordinary copper telephone lines. It comes in various bandwidth and simplicity for installers and users. Asymmetric Digital Subscriber Line or ADSL supports data rates from 1.5 to 9 Mbps when receiving data. Symmetric Digital Subscriber Line or SDSL supports data rates up to 3 Mbps.

DoCoMo. DoCoMo means "anywhere" in Japanese. It is the name of a NTT subsidiary and Japan's biggest mobile service provider, with over 31 million subscribers as of June 2000. It has overtaken traditional Japanese Internet service providers to become Japan's biggest Internet access platform. DoCoMo's i-mode is the only network in the world that now allows subscribers continuous access to the Internet via mobile telephone. The service lets users send and receive e-mail, exchange photographs, do online shopping and banking, download personalized ringing melodies for their phones, and navigate among more than 7,000 specially formatted Web sites. The current i-mode data transmission speed is just 9.6 Kbps; its next-generation mobile system, based on Wideband CDMA (W-CDMA), will support speeds of 384 Kbps or faster, making mobile multimedia possible.

document type definition (DTD). Defines how the markup tags in SGML and XML documents should be interpreted by the application presenting the document.

domain name. The name of a service, Web site, or computer in a hierarchical system of delegated authority—the Domain Name System.

Domain Name System (or Service) (DNS). An Internet service that translates domain names into IP addresses. Since domain names are alphabetic, they're easier to remember. Every time a domain name is used, a DNS service must translate the name into the corresponding IP address. For example, the domain name www.example.com might translate to 128.105.732.14.

download. To receive data from a remote computer.

downstream. The direction data flows from a remote computer to your computer.

downtime. When your computer, computer network, access to the Internet, or an Internet-based service provider isn't working. The opposite of uptime.

DS-1. Data communications circuit capable of transmitting data at 1.5 Mbps. Currently, DS-1 or T-1 lines are widely used by organizations for video, voice, and data applications.

DS-3. A data communications circuit capable of transmitting data at 45 Mbps. A DS-3 or T-3 line has the equivalent data capacity of 28 T-1's. Currently used only by organizations and carriers for high-end applications.

Dublin Core. A set of 15 fields that can be filled in by the creator or an electronic document to create a metadata record for the document.

dumb terminal. A display monitor that has no processing capabilities and does not support some display features. A dumb terminal will typically only display alphanumeric characters.

Dynamic Host Configuration Protocol (DHCP). Allows computers using the TCP/IP protocol to be assigned an IP address automatically rather than requiring that a fixed IP address be assigned to the computer.

dynamic HTML. New HTML extensions that enable a Web page to react to user input without sending requests to the Web server. Both Microsoft and Netscape have submitted proposals to the W3C, which is developing a final specification.

dynamic IP address. An IP address that is assigned by a device acting as a HDCP server. A dynamic IP can be different each time you turn on your computer.

eBook. The contents of a book that may be downloaded for viewing and/or printed locally.

electronic data interchange (EDI). The electronic communication of business transactions (e.g., orders, confirmations, invoices) of organizations with differing platforms. Third parties provide EDI services that enable organizations to connect with incompatible equipment.

eJournal. A magazine or scholarly journal that is available online. The online version may stand alone or it may be published in conjunction with a print version.

Encoded Archival Description (EAD). An XML-based description of archival materials. The EAD header consists of four sub elements: EAD Identifier, File Description, Profile Description, and Revision Description.

encryption. The translation of data into a secret code. To read an encrypted file, you must have access to a secret key or password that enables you to decrypt it. Encrypted data is sometimes called cipher text.

entry. A citation or record in an index or catalog.

Ethernet. A local area network used to connect computers, printers, workstations, and other devices within the same building. Ethernet operates over twisted wire and coaxial cable.

Extensible Markup Language (XML). A version of the Standardized General Markup Language (SGML) designed especially for the Web.

Extranet. An Intranet that is partially accessible to authorized outsiders using a username and password. Typically, suppliers and important customers are able to access an Extranet.

fast Ethernet. A LAN transmission standard that supports data transmission rates up to 100 Mbps. Fast Ethernet is 10 times faster than standard Ethernet and is sometimes called 100 Base-T.

fat client. A computer that includes an operating system, RAM, ROM, a powerful processor, and a wide range of installed software applications that can execute either on the desktop or on the server to which it is connected. Fat clients can operate in a server-based computing environment or in a stand-alone fashion.

fault tolerance. A design method that incorporates redundant system elements to ensure continued systems operation in the event any individual element fails.

Fiber Distributed Data Interface (FDDI). A standard for transmitting data on optical-fiber cables at a rate of about 100 Mbps.

fiber optic. Fiber-optic technology—again, made possible by photonic science—uses glass, plastic, or fused silica threads to transmit data. A fiber-optic cable consists of a bundle of super-thin glass threads that are capable of transmitting data via pulses of light. Key advantages of these laser-powered cables include vastly higher-speed data transmission over longer distances and with less data loss.

field. A category of information, typically found in a record. A record is composed of several fields.

File Transfer Protocol (FTP). The protocol used on the Internet for transferring or sending files.

firewall. A system designed to prevent unauthorized access to or from a private network. All messages entering or leaving the Intranet pass through the firewall, which examines each message and blocks those that do not meet the specified security criteria.

frame. The basic logical unit in which bit-oriented data is transmitted. The frame consists of the data bits surrounded by a flag at each end that indicates the beginning and end of the frame. A primary rate can be thought of as an endless sequence of frames.

frame relay. A high-speed packet-switching protocol popular in networks, including WANs, LANs, and LAN to LAN connections across vast distances.

frames. A feature support by most Web browsers that divides the browser display area into two or more sections (frames). While frames provide great flexibility and data can be drawn from two or more sources, many designers avoid using frames because they are supported unevenly by Web browsers.

Gigabits per second (Gbps). A measurement of data transmission speed expressed in billions of bits per second.

Graphical User Interface (GUI, pronounced "goo-ee"). Microsoft Windows and the Macintosh are examples of computers with a GUI.

groupware. A class of software that helps groups of colleagues, sometimes called workgroups, organize their activities. Groupware supports meeting scheduling, e-mail, preparation of documents, file distribution, and electronic newsletters.

handheld computer. This is a portable computer that is small enough to be held in one's hand. Although extremely convenient to carry, handheld computers have not replaced notebook computers because of their small keyboards and screens. The most popular hand-held computers are those that are specifically designed to provide PIM (personal information manager) functions, such as a calendar and address book. Some manufacturers are trying to solve the small keyboard problem by replacing the keyboard with an electronic pen. However, these pen-based devices rely on handwriting recognition technologies, which are still in their infancy.

handheld device markup language (HDML). Used to format content for Web-enabled mobile phones. HDML is phone.com's (formerly known as Unwired Planet) proprietary language, which can only be viewed on mobile phones that use phone.com browsers. HDML came before the WAP standard was created.

heading. A word or phrase used to indicate some aspect of an item. For example, an author or subject.

high-bit-rate digital subscriber line (HDSL). Also called G. S. HDSL. A DSL that delivers up to 1.544 Mbps of data symmetrically over two copper twisted-pair lines. The range of HDSL is limited to 12,000 feet; signal repeaters extend the service farther from the local telephone company office.

holdings. Materials owned by a library. Frequently used to denote the number of volumes and journals owned by the library.

hop. An intermediate connection in a string of connections linking two network devices. The more hops, the longer it takes for data to go from source to destination.

host. Any computer on a network that is a repository for services available to other computers on the network.

host name. The name given to an individual computer or a server attached to a network or the Internet.

hyperlink. Text that contains a word or phrase that can be clicked on to cause another document, record, or Web site to be retrieved and displayed.

hypertext. Documents that contain links to other documents. When a user selects a link, the second document is automatically displayed.

hypertext markup language (HTML). The authoring language used to create documents on the World Wide Web. HTML defines the structure and layout of a Web document by using a variety of tags and attributes.

hypertext transfer protocol (HTTP). The underlying protocol used by the World Wide Web. HTTP defines how messages are formatted and transmitted, and what action Web servers and browsers should take in response to various commands.

independent software vendor (ISV). Generally a firm that develops software applications not associated with a computer systems manufacturer.

instant messaging. Provides the ability to identify someone who is online and send and receive messages with them in near real-time.

Integrated Services Digital Network (ISDN). An information transfer standard for transmitting digital voice and data over telephone lines at speeds up to 128 Kbps.

interface. The part of the system that controls the interaction between the computer system and the user.

International Federation of Library Associations (IFLA). An organization that promotes library standards and the sharing of ideas and research.

Internet. A global network connecting hundreds of thousands of networks, with compatible communication standards, that connect millions of computers. Each Internet computer, called a host, is independent.

Internet Message Access Protocol (IMAP). A standard format for retrieving e-mail messages. IMAP uses simple mail transfer protocol (SMTP) for communication between the e-mail recipient and the server.

internet protocol (IP). The protocol that governs how computers send packets of data across the Internet. It allows a packet to traverse multiple networks on the way to its final destination.

internet service provider (ISP). A company that provides access for users and businesses to the Internet.

internetworking. Sharing data and resources from one network to another.

Internetwork Packet Exchange (IPX). A Novell NetWare networking protocol. IPX is used for connectionless communications.

interoperability. The ability of systems or products that adhere to standards to work together automatically. Examples of such standards include HTTP and TCP/IP.

Intranet. A network belonging to an organization, accessible only by the organization's members, employees, or others with appropriate authorization.

IP address. A numerical identifier for a device on a TCP/IP network. The IP address format is a string of four numbers, each from 0 to 255, separated by periods.

ISDN digital subscriber line (IDSL). A form of DSL providing a symmetrical speed of 144 Kbps over the copper wire provisioned for ISDN. Repeaters enable service up to 35,000 feet from the local telephone company office.

Java. A high-level programming language developed by Sun Microsystems. Java is an object-oriented language similar to C++, but simplified to eliminate language features that cause common programming errors.

Java 2 Enterprise Edition (J2EE). A Java platform designed for mainframe-scale computing that provides an environment for developing and deploying enterprise applications. J2EE simplifies development and decreases programming by utilizing modular components and allowing the middle tier to handle much of the programming automatically.

JavaBeans. A Sun specification that defines how Java objects interact. JavaBeans are similar to Microsoft's ActiveX controls, except they can run on any platform.

Jini. Based on Java, this is a Sun system for easily connecting any type of devices, including a Net device, to a network.

Joint Photographic Exports Group (JPEG). Pronounced jay-peg, this is an image compression technique that reduces file sizes to about 5 percent of their normal size.

Journal Storage Project (JSTOR). A not-for-profit organization that provides electronic access to scholarly journals. JSTOR began as an effort to ease the increasing problems faced by libraries seeking to provide adequate stack space for the long runs of back files of scholarly journals. The basic idea was to convert the back issues of paper jounals into electronic formats to save space while simultaneously improving access to the journal content. Linking a searchable text file to the page images of the entire published record of a journal offers a level of access previously unimaginable.

kernel. The core components of an operating system.

key. In security systems, a password needed to decipher encoded data.

kilobits per second (Kbps). A data transmission rate of 1,000 bits per second.

latency. In networking, the amount of time it takes a packet to travel from source to destination. Together, latency and bandwidth define the speed and capacity of a network.

leased line. A telecommunications line dedicated to a particular customer along predetermined routers.

legacy application or system. Computer systems that remain in use after more modern technology has been installed. Organizations are often reluctant to cease using legacy applications because they represent a significant investment in time and money.

Library of Congress Subject Heading (LCSH). A word or phrase, which indicates a book's subject, created and maintained by the Library of Congress.

Lightweight Directory Access Protocol (LDAP). A set of protocols for accessing information directories. LDAP should eventually make it possible for almost any application running on virtually any network to obtain directory information, such as e-mail addresses and public keys.

Linux. An open-source, multitasking operating system written in the C programming language that is a variant of Unix and named after its developer of the kernel, Linus Torvalds of Finland.

local area network (LAN). A network of workstations that are linked together. Each node (individual computer) in a LAN has its own CPU with which it executes programs, but it is also able to access data and devices anywhere on the LAN. This means that many users can share expensive devices, such as printers, as well as data. Users can also use the LAN to communicate with each other, by sending e-mail or engaging in chat sessions.

local loop. The wires that connect an individual subscriber's telephone or data connection to the telephone company central office or other local terminating point.

lossy compression. A data compression technique in which some amount of data is lost.

Machine Readable Cataloging (MARC). MARC is a standard method for encoding surrogate records so that they can be read and processed by a computer.

mainframe computer. A very large and expensive computer capable of supporting hundreds or even thousands of users simultaneously. IBM is the dominant manufacturer of mainframe computers.

MARC 21. An international MARC standard agreed upon by Canada, the United States, and England that represents the consolidation of USMARC, CAN/MARC, and UK/MARC.

megabits per second (Mbps). A transmission rate where one megabit equals 1,024 kilobits.

metadata. An encoded description of an information package.

middleware. Software that connects two otherwise separate applications. Middleware is the "plumbing" that passes data from one application to another.

minicomputer. A minicomputer is a mid-sized computer that lies between mainframes and workstations that typically can support several hundred users simultaneously.

modem. A device for converting digital (data) signals to analog and vice versa, for data transmission over an analog telephone line.

Moving Picture Exports Group (MPEG). A family of digital video compression standards and file formats developed by the group. MPEG (pronounced *em-peg*) generally produces higher-quality video than competing formats, such as QuickTime. MPEG files can be decoded by special hardware or by software. MPEG achieves high compression rate by storing only the changes from one frame to another, instead of each entire frame.

MS-DOS. A disk operating system developed by Microsoft for the IBM personal computer or PC.

Multimedia Internet Mail Extensions (MIME). A protocol that defines several content types, which allow programs like Web browsers, to recognize different kinds of files and deal with them appropriately.

multiplexing. Combining multiple data channels onto a single transmission medium. Sharing a circuit—normally dedicated to a single user—between multiple users.

multi-user. The ability for multiple concurrent users to log on and run applications from a single server.

name server. A computer that matches Web site names to IP addresses. Also sometimes called a DNS server.

National Information Standards Organization (NISO). An organization that oversees the creation and maintenance of standards used in information processing.

net-centric software. Ready-to-use software solutions that can be downloaded or delivered via the Internet rather than out-of-the-box from a retailer (or e-tailer).

network access point (NAP). A location where ISPs exchange each other's traffic.

network computer (NC). A "thin" client hardware device that executes applications locally by downloading them from the network. NCs adhere to a specification jointly developed by Sun, IBM, Oracle, Apple, and Netscape. They typically run Java applets within a Java browser, or Java applications within the Java Virtual Machine.

network computing architecture. A computing architecture in which components are dynamically downloaded from the network onto the client device for execution by the client. The Java programming language is at the core of network computing.

network file systems (NFS). A set of protocols that allows files located on other computers to be used as if they were located locally.

network interface card. Often abbreviated NIC, a network interface card connects devices to a network.

network packets. Data transmitted over a network is subdivided into packets.

offsite storage. A Web-based service that rents computer disk space for storing documents and files to individuals and companies. Access is available 24 hours a day/7 days a week.

online. Direct communication between a user and a computer that allows a request to be processed and the results displayed immediately on the monitor.

online profiling. Using cookies and personal information obtained from other sources, a Web site will create a profile of customers' buying and browsing habits.

open source. Source code or "source" is the instructions created by programmers to develop software. Most source code is proprietary for obvious reasons, for example Microsoft's Windows. Advocates of open source projects, such as Linux and the Mozilla browser, claim that others can quickly and easily enhance a product that then can be shared by others. Opponents point to the incompatible product versions that are available.

outsourcing. The transfer of components or large segments of an organization's internal IT infrastructure, staff, processes, or applications to an external resource such as an Application Service Provider.

packaged software application. A computer program developed for sale to consumers or businesses generally designed to appeal to more than a single customer. While some tailoring of the program may be possible, it is not intended to be custom-designed for each user or organization.

packet. A bundle of data organized for transmission, containing control information (e.g., destination, length, origin), the data itself, and error detection and correction bits. In IP networks, packets are often called "datagrams."

packet switching. A network in which messages are transmitted as packets over any available route rather than as sequential messages over switched or dedicated facilities.

password. A secret series of characters that enables a user to access a file, computer, or program. The password helps ensure that unauthorized individuals do not access the computer.

Password Authentication Procedure. A procedure for validating a network connection request. The requestor sends the network server a user name and password. The server can validate and acknowledge the request.

Personal Digital Assistant (PDA). A handheld device that combines computing, telephone/fax, and networking features. Most PDAs use a stylus rather than a keyboard for input. John Sculley, former CEO of Apple, first used the term PDA in 1992.

peer-to-peer. A type of network in which each computer has equivalent capabilities and responsibilities.

performance. A major factor in determining the overall productivity of a system, performance is primarily tied to availability, throughput, and response time.

Permanent Virtual Circuit (PVC). A PVC connects the customer's port connections, nodes, locations, and branches to each other. All customer ports can be connected to each other, resembling a mesh, but PVCs usually run between the host and branch locations.

personal computer. A small, relatively inexpensive computer designed for individual use and often called a PC. The IBM PC was first introduced in 1981.

plain old telephone service (POTS). Standard telephony for placing and receiving calls.

point of presence (POP). A dial-in location so you can connect to the Internet. To the user, a POP is a local telephone number.

point-to-point protocol (PPP). This protocol allows a computer to use the TCP/IP protocols with a standard telephone line and a high speed modem.

point-to-point protocol over Ethernet (PPPOE). A protocol that allows DSL providers to meter connection time and to acquire a smaller, cheaper block of IP addresses. PPPOE changes DSL from an always-on to an on-demand service and lets providers reduce the size and cost of their Internet connection infrastructures.

Portable Document Format (PDF). A file format developed by Adobe Systems that captures formatting information to preserve the look-and-feel of a document viewed online or sent to a printer.

portal. A Web site or service that offers a broad array of resources and services.

post office protocol (POP). A mail protocol that allows a remote mail client to read mail from a server.

practical extraction and report language (Perl). Perl is a programming language designed for processing text.

privacy. The right to freedom from unauthorized intrusion. The proliferating use of several technologies has made it easier to gather volumes of information about individuals and companies. Some concerned citizens are calling for legislative protection.

protocol. A definition of how a computer will act when talking to other computers. Standard protocols allow computers from different manufacturers to communicate.

proxy server. A server that sits between a client application, such as a Web browser, and a real server. It intercepts all requests to the real server to see if it can fulfill the request itself. If not, it forwards the request to the real server. Proxy servers are designed to improve performance and filter requests.

public-key encryption. A cryptographic system that uses two keys—a public key known to everyone and a private or secret key known only to the recipient of the message. Only the public key can be used to encrypt the message and only the private key can be used to decrypt the message. What's needed is a global registry of public keys, which is one of the promises of LDAP technology.

quality of service (QoS). A collective measure of the level of service a provider delivers to its customers. QoS can be characterized by several basic performance criteria, including availability (low downtime), error performance, response time and throughput, lost calls or transmissions due to network congestion, and connection set-up time.

random access memory (RAM). A type of computer memory that can be accessed randomly. Dynamic RAM must have its contents constantly refreshed, while static RAM does not need to be refreshed.

redundant array of inexpensive disks (RAID). A category of disk drives that employ two or more drives in combination for fault tolerance and improved performance. There are several different RAID levels. The three most common are 0, 3, and 5:

Level 0: Provides data striping (spreading out blocks of each file across multiple disks) but no redundancy. This improves performance but does not deliver fault tolerance.

Level 1: Provides disk mirroring (two sets of disks to store two copies of the data).

Level 3: Same as Level 0, but also reserves one dedicated disk for error correction data. It provides good performance and some level of fault tolerance.

Level 5: Provides data striping at the byte level and also stripe error correction information. This results in excellent performance and good fault tolerance.

relational database management system (RDBMS). A system that stores data in the form of related tables. Oracle and MS SQL Server are examples of RDBMS systems.

Regional Bell Operating Company (RBOC). Pronounced R-bock, the seven Baby Bells were created with the 1983 breakup of AT&T or Ma Bell. The seven include Ameritech, Bell Atlantic, Bell South, NYEX, Pacific Bell, Southwestern Bell, and U.S. West.

remote access. The hookup of a remote-computing device via communications lines such as ordinary phone lines or wide area networks to access distant network applications and information.

Remote Presentation Services Protocol. A set of rules and procedures for exchanging data between computers on a network, enabling the user interface, keystrokes, and mouse movements to be transferred between a server and client.

resources description framework (RDF). A general framework, developed by the World Wide Web Consortium, for describing a Web site's metadata. For example, RDF will identify the Web site's map, keywords for search engines to use in indexing, and the Web page's intellectual property rights.

router. A communications device between networks that determines the best path between them for optimal performance. Routers are used in complex networks of networks such as enterprise-wide networks and the Internet.

scalability. Ability to expand the number of users or increase the capabilities of a computing solution without making major changes to the systems or application software.

search engine. A retrieval tool on the Web that matches keywords input by a user to words found at a Web site.

secure electronic transaction (SET). A security standard that ensures privacy and protection for conducting credit card transactions over the Internet. Rather than a credit card number, a digital signature is employed.

Secure Sockets Layer (SSL). A protocol for transmitting private documents via the Internet. SSL works by using a private key to encrypt data that transferred over the SSL connection. Most Web browsers support SSL.

security software. Computer software installed on a computer network or individual workstation that protects it from a hacker attack. Typically, the software includes firewall and antivirus software.

"see" or "see also" reference. Directions in an index or catalog to look under another term or a related term, respectively.

Serial Line IP (SLIP). Allows a computer to connect to the Internet using a telephone line and a high-speed modem. SLIP is being superseded by the PPP protocol.

server. The computer on a local area network that often acts as a data and application repository and controls an application's access to workstations, printers, and other parts of the network.

server-based computing. A server-based approach to delivering business-critical applications to end user devices, whereby an application's logic executes on the server and only the user interface is transmitted across a network to the client. Its benefits include single-point management, universal application access, bandwidth-independent performance, and improved security for business applications.

Service Level Agreement (SLA). A binding contract or agreement between an end user organization and an ASP. It details the specifics of your partnership, including customer service and data security.

servlet. An applet that runs on a Web server. A servlet is persistent—it stays in memory and can fulfill multiple requests.

shelflist. A record of materials in a library arranged in Call Number order, the order in which they stand on the shelves.

short message service (SMS). A service for sending text messages of up to 160 characters to mobile phones that use global system for mobile (GSM). The cell phone can receive the message even if the phone is being used.

Simple Mail Transfer Protocol (SMTP). A TCP/IP-based standard for sending e-mail messages between servers on the Internet. Once received, the messages are stored using either Internet message access protocol (IMAP) or point of presence (POP).

Simple Object Access Protocol (SOAP). A common format for exchanging data stored in diverse formats and databases. Approved by the World Wide Web Consortium, SOAP uses XML and HTTP to define a component interoperability standard on the Web. Microsoft's implementation of SOAP is called BizTalk and IBM's is WebSphere.

source code. Program instructions in their original form using a specific programming language.

spider. A simple software program used by a search engine to scan the Web. Spiders are bots that crawl from link to link searching for new sites.

Standard Generalized Markup Language (SGML). SGML is an international standard for organizing and tagging elements of a document. SGML is the basis for HTML and a precursor to XML.

static IP address. An IP address that never changes and is typically used in businesses rather than with consumers.

streaming. The end user sees video or hears an audio file as a continuous stream as it arrives rather than waiting for the entire file to be received.

Structured Query Language (SQL). SQL (pronounced "SEE-kwell") is a standardized query language for requesting information from a database.

symmetric digital subscriber line (SDSL). A form of DSL that transfers data upstream and downstream at the same speed (up to 2.3 Mbps) over a single copper twisted-pair line.

T-1. Data communications circuit capable of transmitting data at 1.5 Mbps.

T-3. A digital carrier facility used for transmitting data through the telephone system at 44.7 Mbps (its like 30 T-1s put together).

Tagged Image File Format (TIFF). Format for storing bit-mapped images. Files typically end in a .tif extension.

telephony. The technology associated with the electronic transmission of voice, fax, or other information between two parties, historically associated with the telephone. A telephony application is a programming interface that helps provide these services. Using the Internet, three new services are now available:

>   Ability to make a normal telephone call

>   Ability to send fax transmissions

>   Ability to send voice messages along with text e-mail.

thin client. A low-cost computing device that accesses applications and/or data from a central server over a network. Categories of thin clients include Windows-Based Terminals (which comprise the largest segment), X-Terminals, and Network Computers (NC).

topologies. A network topology refers to the architecture of how network nodes are connected.

total cost of ownership (TCO). A model that helps IT professionals understand and manage the budgeted (direct) and unbudgeted (indirect) costs incurred for acquiring, maintaining, and using an application or a computing system. TCO normally includes training, upgrades, and administration, as well as the purchase price. Lowering TCO through single-point control is a key benefit of server-based computing.

Transmission Control Protocol (TCP). The transport layer protocol built on top of the Internet Protocol (IP) in a TCP/IP network. The IP deals only with moving packets of information, TCP enables servers to establish a connection and exchange data streams. It guarantees the data packets will be delivered in the same order in which they were sent.

Transmission Control Protocol/Internet Protocol (TCP/IP). A suite of network protocols that allow computers with different architectures and operating system software to communicate with other computers on the Internet. It is the *de facto* standard for communicating data over the Internet.

tunneling. A technology that enables one network to send its data via another network's connections. Sometimes called IP tunneling.

Unicode. A standard for representing characters as integers. Two integers or bytes are used to represent each character.

universal description, discovery, and integration (UDDI). A DNS-like distributed Web directory that would enable services to discover each other and define how they can interact and share information. The end result is expected to be a standards-based Internet directory of business information.

universal resource identifier (URI). The string (often starting with http://) that is used to identify anything on the Web.

uniform resource locator (URL). A term used sometimes for certain URI's to indicate that they might change. The URL appears in the address line in the Web browser window, for example, http://www.wiley.com.

uptime. The amount of time your system is working; the ideal is 100 percent of the time.

user interface. The part of an application that the end user sees on the screen and works with to operate the application, such as menus, forms, and "buttons."

user name. A name used to gain access to a computer system. In most systems, users can choose their own usernames and passwords.

value-added network (VAN). A private network provider that facilitates electronic data interchange (EDI) or provides other network services. Before the arrival of the World Wide Web, some organizations hired value-added networks to move data from their location to other locations. With the arrival of the World Wide Web, many companies found it more cost-efficient to move their data over the Internet instead of paying the minimum monthly fees and per-character charges found in typical VAN contracts.

very high data rate digital subscriber line (VDSL). An evolving form of DSL that can deliver data at a rate of 13 to 52 Mbps downstream and 1.5 to 2.3 Mbps upstream over a single copper twisted-pair line. The operating range of VDSL is up to 4,500 feet from the local telephone company office.

virtual private network (VPN). A secure, encrypted private Internet connection. Data is encrypted before being sent and decrypted at the receiving end to maintain privacy and security. A set of communication rules has been created called point-to-point tunneling protocol (PPTP) to create VPNs.

virus. A software program that is loaded onto your computer without your knowledge and runs against your wishes. Most viruses can also replicate themselves. A simple virus that can make a copy of itself over and over again is dangerous because it will quickly use all available memory and bring the system to a halt. An even more dangerous type of virus is one capable of transmitting itself across networks and bypassing security systems. Antivirus programs periodically check your computer for the best-known viruses.

Voice Extensible Markup Language (VXML). VXML or VoiceXML allows a user to interact with the Internet using voice-recognition technology.

Voice Over Internet Protocol (VOIP). The delivery of voice information in the language of the Internet (i.e., as digital packets instead of the current circuit protocols of the copper-based phone networks). In VOIP systems, analog voice messages are digitized and transmitted as a stream of data (not sound) packets that are reassembled and converted back into a voice signal at their destination. The killer idea is that VOIP allows telephony users to bypass long-distance carrier charges by transporting those data packets just like other Internet information. With VOIP, your PC becomes your phone and you can call anywhere in the world for the cost of a local call.

Web. Refers to the World Wide Web (WWW) and is what the Internet became with the introduction of HTML.

Web browser. A software application used to locate and display Web pages. The two most popular browsers are Netscape Navigator and Microsoft Internet Explorer.

Web hosting. Placing an organization's Web page or Web site on a server that can be accessed via the Internet.

wide area network (WAN). Local area networks linked together across a large geographic area.

Windows-based terminal. Thin clients with the lowest cost of ownership, as there are no local applications running on the device.

Wireless Applications Protocol (WAP). WAP is a specification that allows wireless devices to access interactive information services and applications from screens of mobile phones.

wireless local loop (WLL). A broadband connection system that uses high-frequency radio links to deliver voice and data without the problems of gaining right-of-way for a fiber-optic cable installation or finding adequate copper connections for DSL. Also known as fixed-point wireless.

Wireless Markup Language (WML). WML is an XML language used to specify content and user interface for WAP devices; the WAP forum provides a DTD for WML. Almost every mobile phone browser around the world supports WML. WML pages are requested and served in the same way as HDML pages.

World Wide Web Consortium (W3C). An entity composed of many organizations that work on developing common standards for the evolution of the Web.

XDSL. This term refers to the assorted flavors of the DSL connections including, but not limited to, ADSL (Asymmetric Digital Subscriber Line), HDSL (High bit-rate DSL) and RADSL (Rate adaptive Asymmetric Digital Subscriber Line).

Z39.2. A standard for encoding information in machine-readable form. Often referred to as a MARC record.

Z39.50. A standard protocol that allows one computer to query another computer and transfer search results without the user needing to know the search commands or the remote computer.

N Excellent online resources for keeping abreast of technical terms and acronyms include: http://www.whatis.com and http://www.webopedia.com.

Index